Business Analytics

An Introduction

Business Analytics

An Introduction

Edited by Jay Liebowitz

CRC Press
Taylor & Francis Group
Boca Raton   London   New York

CRC Press is an imprint of the
Taylor & Francis Group, an **informa** business
AN AUERBACH BOOK

CRC Press
Taylor & Francis Group
6000 Broken Sound Parkway NW, Suite 300
Boca Raton, FL 33487-2742

Version Date: 20131021

International Standard Book Number-13: 978-1-4665-9609-2 (Hardback)

Visit the Taylor & Francis Web site at
http://www.taylorandfrancis.com

and the CRC Press Web site at
http://www.crcpress.com

Contents

Preface

It is plain and simple: Big Data and business analytics are hot! Whether the cover of the October 2012 *Harvard Business Review*, the December 2012 MIT conference on "Big Data: The Management Revolution," or the January 2013 issue of *KMWorld*, these emerging areas will continue to gain ground with great momentum in the coming years. According to a Cisco study, as mentioned in the January 2013 *KMWorld* issue, Kapil Baskhi (Chief Architect, Cisco Public Sector) states that global IP traffic will reach 1.3 zettabytes annually by 2016, which is a fourfold increase from 2011. By 2016, there will be 19 billion global network connections, the equivalent of two-and-a-half connections for every person on earth. According to Dan Vesset, Program VP for Business Analytics Solutions at IDC (in the same *KMWorld* issue), the Big Data market is expected to reach $16.9 billion by 2015, up from $3.2 billion in 2010.

Steve Lohr's December 30, 2012 *New York Times* article headline indicates, "Sure, Big Data Is Great—But So Is Intuition." The point here is that with all this data coming in at various volumes, velocities, and varieties, how can we make sense of it all, especially for improving decision-making capabilities in organizations? This is where the field of business analytics can add value.

Think about cybersecurity, finance, marketing, healthcare, education, energy, and many other sectors—all of these fields could benefit from applying and improving their analytics. Better detection of fraud through visual analytics and better prediction of the likelihood of someone getting an infection while in the hospital are interesting examples where analytics play a role. The field of business analytics is multidisciplinary, borrowing expertise from applied mathematics, statistics, management science, marketing, information technology, and finance. According to the McKinsey Global Institute report in 2011, the United States needs 140,000 to 190,000 more workers with "deep analytical" expertise and 1.5 million more data-literate managers, whether retrained or hired.

To address this need, companies like IBM teamed with the College of Business at Ohio State University in November 2012 to educate future "data scientists." Other universities, like the University of Maryland University College and Stevens Institute of Technology, are offering graduate programs in analytics and business intelligence. Other universities and companies are collaborating to address this vacuum.

This is where this new book fits in. As the field of business analytics continues to emerge, there is a dearth of textbooks geared for this market. This book presents the important areas of business analytics with concepts, techniques, applications, and trends that those in business, information systems/information technology, or even some computer science programs may find it useful. The book is geared for the graduate level, but may be helpful for undergraduate seniors as well. It could easily have been 500 printed pages, but we focused on some of the key areas where the material could be adequately covered in a one-semester, or even a one-quarter, course.

To the contributors to this book, I am especially grateful that we have some of the leading educators and practitioners who have either taught courses in these areas or have extensive professional experience working in this field. As we had a quick turnaround time to develop and publish the book, we hope we are able to present some of the key issues facing management today.

I would like to thank my publishing editor John Wyzalek and his Taylor & Francis colleagues for encouraging me to move forward with this book. In May 2013, we published *Big Data and Business Analytics* with Taylor & Francis, which primarily deals with how organizations are applying these techniques. That book could be a nice companion piece to accompany this business analytics textbook.

Finally, a debt of gratitude goes to my students, colleagues, and family who encourage me to keep looking ahead and be on the "bleeding edge." Enjoy!

Jay Liebowitz, D.Sc.
Orkand Endowed Chair in Management and Technology
University of Maryland University College
Adelphi, Maryland

About the Editor

Jay Liebowitz, D.Sc. is the Orkand Endowed Chair in Management and Technology in the Graduate School at the University of Maryland University College (UMUC). He previously served as a professor in the Carey Business School at Johns Hopkins University. He was ranked one of the top 10 knowledge management researchers/practitioners out of 11,000 worldwide, and was ranked #2 in KM Strategy worldwide according to the January 2010 *Journal of Knowledge Management*. At Johns Hopkins University, he was the founding program director for the Graduate Certificate in Competitive Intelligence and the capstone director of the MS-Information and Telecommunications Systems for Business Program, where he engaged over 30 organizations in industry, government, and not-for-profits in capstone projects.

Prior to joining Hopkins, Dr. Liebowitz was the first knowledge management officer at NASA Goddard Space Flight Center. Before NASA, he was the Robert W. Deutsch Distinguished Professor of Information Systems at the University of Maryland–Baltimore County, Professor of Management Science at George Washington University, and chair of Artificial Intelligence at the U.S. Army War College.

Dr. Liebowitz is the founder and editor-in-chief of *Expert Systems With Applications: An International Journal* (published by Elsevier), a top-tier journal worldwide for OR/MS-related journals, according to the most recent Thomson impact factors. The *ESWA Journal* had 1.8 million articles downloaded worldwide in 2011. Liebowitz is a Fulbright Scholar, IEEE-USA Federal Communications Commission Executive Fellow, and Computer Educator of the Year (International Association for Computer Information Systems). He has published over 40 books and a myriad of journal articles on knowledge management, intelligent systems, and IT management. Dr. Liebowitz's most recent books are *Knowledge Retention: Strategies and Solutions* (Taylor & Francis, 2009), *Knowledge Management in Public Health* (Taylor & Francis, 2010), *Knowledge Management and E-Learning* (Taylor & Francis, 2011), *Beyond Knowledge Management: What Every Leader Should Know* (Taylor & Francis, 2012), and *Knowledge Management Handbook: Collaboration and Social Networking*, 2nd ed. (Taylor & Francis, 2012). His newest book is *Big Data and Business Analytics*

(Taylor & Francis). In October 2011, the International Association for Computer Information Systems named the "Jay Liebowitz Outstanding Student Research Award" for the best student research paper at the IACIS Annual Conference. He has lectured and consulted worldwide. Dr. Liebowitz can be reached at jay.liebowitz@umuc.edu.

Contributors

Angelos Barmpoutis
Professor
University of Florida
Gainesville, Florida

Julia Deng
Principal Scientist
Intelligent Automation, Inc.
Rockville, Maryland

Jeremy P. Floyd
President
Bluegill Creative
Adjunct Professor
University of
    Tennessee–Chattanooga
Knoxville, Tennessee

Arnold Greenland
IBM Distinguished Engineer
Business Analytics
IBM
Bethesda, Maryland

Barry Keating
Professor
Mendoza College of Business
University of Notre Dame
Notre Dame, Indiana

Tung Thanh Nguyen
Research Scientist
Intelligent Automation, Inc.
Rockville, Maryland

Onur Savas
Senior Research Scientist
Intelligent Automation, Inc.
Rockville, Maryland

Frank Stein
Director
Analytics Solution Center
IBM
Bethesda, Maryland

Evan Stubbs
Chief Analytics Officer
SAS Australia/New Zealand
Lane Cove, New South Wales
Australia

Luca Toldo
Associate Director
Merck KGaA
Darmstadt, Germany

Patrick Yurgosky
CEO
Yurgosky Consulting
Adjunct Faculty
New York University
New York, New York

Elana Zeide
Law Offices of Elana Zeide
New York, New York
Privacy Fellow
New York University School of Law
New York, New York

1

The Value of Business Analytics

Evan Stubbs

CONTENTS

Learning Objectives

By the end of this chapter, you should understand:

- The importance of business analytics.
- The difference between business analytics and analytics.
- How value creates a reason to act and support change.
- The importance of value definition and quantification in business analytics.
- How to take communication preferences into account when communicating value.

CONCEPTS

Why Business Analytics?

Knowing more than one's competitors creates advantage. The intelligence generated by Bletchley Park arguably shortened World War II by as much as two to four years.[*] Gosset's research gave Guinness market advantage through clarifying the relationship between crop yields and beer production.[†] Firms that are able to generate information asymmetries through data-sourced insight have the opportunity to build competitive differentiation.[‡]

While not always easy to empirically test, there are many examples of how information asymmetries create advantage in various forms. Whether it is in selling cars,[§] the service industry,[ˢ] research

---

[*] "The Influence of ULTRA in the Second World War." Interview by Harry Hinsley. 26 November 1996. *The Influence of ULTRA in the Second World War.* TMA Lomas and Computer Security Group, Computer Laboratory, University of Cambridge. Web. 21 April 2013. http://www.cl.cam.ac.u k/research/security/ Historical/hinsley.html.

[†] Box, Joan Fisher. "Guinness, Gosset, Fisher, and Small Samples." *Statistical Science* 2.1 (1987): 45–52. Print.

[‡] Stubbs, Evan. *The Value of Business Analytics: Identifying the Path to Profitability.* Hoboken, NJ: John Wiley, 2011. Print.

[§] Genesove, David. "Adverse Selection in the Wholesale Used Car Market." *Journal of Political Economy* 101.4 (1993): 644. Print.

[ˢ] Nayyar, Praveen R. "Information Asymmetries: A Source of Competitive Advantage for Diversified Service Firms." *Strategic Management Journal* 11.7 (1990): 513–19. Print.

and development,* or even real estate,† unique insight that is acted on improves results. In the private sector, this has the potential to fuel competitive differentiation. In the public sector, it enables better social outcomes. In intelligence and defense, it reduces risk and improves national security.

The Changing Role of Insight

The idea that insight leads to competitive differentiation is not new.‡ Three things, however, happened in the late 20th century that drastically changed the potential influence that insight has on organizational advantage. These are:

- Large-scale digitization of information, also known as *Big Data*.
- Exponential increases in processing power, also known as *high-performance computing*.
- Technological automation, also known as *decision management*.

The Rise of Big Data

The data we have access to today dwarfs that which we had even a decade ago. Thanks to the personal computer and constantly falling storage costs, data volumes have grown geometrically over the last few decades.§ There is more to the rise of "Big Data" than just data volumes: by common definition, it also includes a significant increase in data variety and the velocity at which data is being generated.

While there is no strict litmus test that distinguishes a "large data" repository from a "Big Data" repository, Big Data repositories tend to be characterized by orders of magnitude more information than a "typical" data warehouse. They also tend to include large amounts of unstructured and semi-structured data in addition to the usual structured data. They

* Aboody, David and Baruch Lev. "Information Asymmetry, R&D, and Insider Gains." *The Journal of Finance* 55.6 (2000): 2747–766. Print.
† Garmaise, M. J. "Confronting Information Asymmetries: Evidence from Real Estate Markets." *Review of Financial Studies* 17.2 (2003): 405–37. Print.
‡ Davenport, Thomas H. and Jeanne G. Harris. *Competing on Analytics: The New Science of Winning.* Boston, MA: Harvard Business School, 2007. Print.
§ Manyika, James, Michael Chui, Brad Brown, Jacques Bughin, Richard Dobbs, Charles Roxburgh, and Angela Hung Byers. "Big Data: The Next Frontier for Innovation, Competition, and Productivity." *Insights & Publications.* McKinsey Global Institute, May 2011. Web. 21 April 2013.

are often designed to accommodate extremely frequent data updates, sometimes in the order of microseconds.

This massive increase in data has been driven in no small part by:

- Increasing consumer demand for intangible goods such as digital music and online entertainment.
- The pervasiveness of the Internet across OECD nations leading to greater online communication.
- The shift toward online and electric banking and commerce.

In an online world, every interaction leaves a trail. Every purchase, every click, and every message creates a data footprint. This data, if analyzed, has the potential to generate historically unimaginable insight.

The Advent of High-Performance Computing

In isolation, Big Data itself does not create advantage; data is useless without the ability to effectively analyze it. The key to creating advantage from Big Data has been parallel exponential increases in processing power, sometimes referred to as *high-performance computing*. Without the ability to cost-effectively analyze data in a timely way, it becomes nothing more than noise. Moore's law[*] and its storage-focused counterpart, Kryder's law,[†] are well known but their impact cannot be underestimated. Current smartphones that fit in a pocket are now thousands of times faster than the Apple II, a revolutionary personal computer by any measure.

What once might have needed thousands of people in a room performing calculations in parallel[‡] or even a supercomputer the size of a building can now be completed in real time by a piece of commodity hardware. Together, Big Data and sheer computational horsepower create an unprecedented ability to generate insight. And this insight,

---

[*] Schaller, R. R. "Moore's Law: Past, Present, and Future." *Spectrum, IEEE* 34.6 (1997): 52–59. Print. The trend for the number of transistors on an integrated circuit to double roughly every two years, leading to significant ongoing increases in computing power. It was defined by Gordon E. Moore, co-founder of Intel.

[†] Walter, Chip. "Kryder's Law." *Scientific American* 293.2 (2005): 32–33. Print. The trend for magnetic disk storage to double annually, leading to significant ongoing increases in storage capacity. It was defined by Mark Kryder while at Seagate.

[‡] As recently as the 19th century "computer" was simply a job title referring to a person who performed computations in some manner.

when held disproportionately to the market, has the potential to create a significant advantage.

The Role of Decision Management

Data and processing power create insight. Insight alone, however, does little to improve outcomes; realizing value requires action. *Insight without action is the same as doing nothing.* If Big Data and high-performance computing are, respectively, the fuel and the engine, the driver is the move from manual to automated systems. Together, these are changing the landscape of modern business and social engagement.

Insights are the building blocks to making a decision. Workflow is the glue that links insight to action. The progressive adoption of digital workflow support tools such as email and Enterprise Resource Planning (ERP) systems have allowed organizations to coordinate their activities, automate decision making, and embed "smarts" into operational business processes.[*]

Section Summary

The ongoing impact of insight cannot be understated—automated processes make performance and outcomes less dependent on the individual and more on the system. Automated systems allow organizations to scale their decision-making abilities by orders of magnitude. By leveraging more and more information in operational decision making, operational analytics[†] significantly improves the accuracy and return of not one but millions of decisions made on a daily basis.

Together, Big Data, high-performance computing, and decision management have made business analytics the cornerstone of any data-driven organization.

---

[*] Operational processes are activities, usually conducted repeatedly, that drive an organization's core business and create primary revenue streams. Common examples include customer management, purchasing, marketing, logistics, and sales. These can be contrasted against supporting processes that, while they do not usually generate direct revenue streams, enable the business to deliver their operational processes. Common examples include accounting, recruitment, and technical support/IT operations.

[†] The process by which advanced analytics is embedded in automated operational processes with the intention of driving better outcomes. This can range from entirely automated processes that occur with no human interaction, driven entirely by advanced analytics, through to decision-support systems that simply present a recommended action to an operational decision-maker. Common examples include automated inventory re-ordering systems that leverage forecasting and operations research right through to real-time recommended next-best-activities presented to contact center operators while they talk on the phone.

Questions

- What has changed that has increased the importance of business analytics?
- What has not?
- Why does having disproportionate insight create competitive advantage?

What Is Business Analytics?

The long-term impact of Big Data, high-performance computing, and the ability to automate decision making will not be known for decades. Together they have already changed the way organizations operate. And yet we are only at the beginning of the journey. It is possible that in another century these will be seen as significant as the invention of the combustion engine. Even at this early stage, one thing is clear: together, they mark the advent of *business analytics* as a point of competitive differentiation and social opportunity.[*]

There are many points of view on how to define business analytics. Within this chapter, business analytics is about more than just analysis; while analytics and business analytics are sometimes used interchangeably, they have different foci. While essential, analytics is only a part of business analytics.[†]

The relationships between these are shown below.

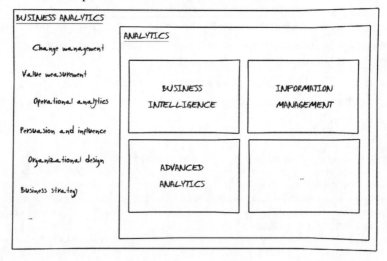

---

[*] Stubbs, Evan. *Delivering Business Analytics: Practical Guidelines for Best Practice*. Hoboken, NJ: John Wiley, 2013. Print.

[†] Stubbs, Evan. *The Value of Business Analytics: Identifying the Path to Profitability*. Hoboken, NJ: John Wiley, 2011. Print.

Analytics is any data-driven process that provides insight. Common examples include:

- Discovering which customers match certain characteristics through *querying.*
- Summarizing organizational performance through *reports.*
- Understanding sales performance through *trending.*
- Grouping similar sets of customers together through *segmentation.*
- Identifying what product a customer is most likely to be interested in through *predictive modeling.*

Importantly, each of these are based on:

- Data rather than opinion.
- Quantitative rather than qualitative techniques.

Analytics, when applied to data, creates insight. At its most broad, it encompasses a wide range of disciplines including business intelligence, statistics, data management, and data science. For example, *advanced analytics* and *machine learning* is a subset of analytics that focuses on drawing out greater insight through mathematical techniques. It often tries to understand why things are happening and predict what will happen rather than just summarize what already happened.

Once created, insight needs to be acted on to create value. Where analytics creates insight, business analytics is concerned with taking that insight and using it to create value. The major difference between the two lies in understanding the value of insight and convincing an organization to change the way it does business.

Without a desire to change, most people will revert to their preferred approach.* This is especially true when it comes to making decisions. Even when not under pressure, "confirmation bias" can lead even the best thinkers to misinterpret or even outright reject the evidence in front of them.† Because many decision makers will go with what they believe even if the data tells them otherwise, even the best evidence is rarely enough. Rather than making decisions based on experience, *people need to be convinced to trust data as well as informed recommendations.*

---

* Kotter, John P. *Leading Change.* Boston, MA: Harvard Business School, 1996. Print.
† Nickerson, Raymond S. "Confirmation Bias: A Ubiquitous Phenomenon in Many Guises." *Review of General Psychology* 2.2 (1998): 175–220. Print.

Section Summary

Analytics helps extract insight from data. Without action, however, this insight rarely leads to economic return. More than anything else, business analytics is about making this change happen. By definition, novel analytically based insights usually identify opportunities to do things differently. Because of this, the heart of business analytics is *change management*, not just creating insight. And, without the ability to identify the *value* of making a change, thereby generating sufficient cognitive dissonance to warrant re-examining one's perspective, getting people to agree to change is near impossible.

Questions
- What are some examples of analytics?
- What is the difference between analytics and business analytics?
- Why do people not act on insight?

What Are the Challenges?

Convincing people to behave differently is difficult. It is indicative of how resistant people are to change that some argue that the majority of all change initiatives fail.[*]

Supporting change requires:

- A reason to change.
- An understanding of what the change means.
- Trust that the change can be achieved.
- Belief that promises made will be delivered.

While nothing is guaranteed, four things increase the odds of success more than anything else. These form the virtuous circle of business analytics as shown below.

---

[*] Kotter, John P. *A Sense of Urgency*. Boston, MA: Harvard Business, 2008. Print; Beer, Michael and Nitin Nohria. *Breaking the Code of Change*. Boston, MA: Harvard Business School, 2000. Print.

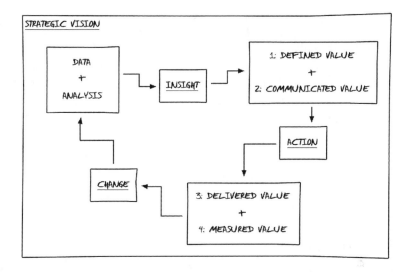

Data, when analyzed, creates insight. Insight alone rarely results in action. For insight to result in action, the value of the insight needs to be defined and communicated.

Action, in isolation, rarely in turn leads to sustained change. To create a reason to change, trust is needed. Trust is built through delivering and measuring the value that was promised. This trust then helps fuel more analysis which, when acted on and validated, supports even greater change.

This cycle of change, when aligned to a strategic vision, helps create competitive differentiation.

To create a reason to act and support ongoing change, every business analytics initiative needs to:

- *Define the value*, thereby building support and avoiding a lack of interest.
- *Communicate the value*, thereby building understanding and avoiding confusion.
- *Deliver the value*, thereby enabling tactical gains as well as long-term competitive differentiation.
- *Measure the value*, thereby supporting ongoing transformation rather than one-off successes.

They require different skills to traditional analytics. Where data scientists are excellent at extracting insight from data, "value architects" are experts at using those insights to justify change.

Defining the Value

Without defining the value, it is impossible to justify action. Organizations are economically driven, politically motivated entities. Every organization, regardless of how well funded or profitable it is, has a limited budget. Investments need to be prioritized to maximize return.

Prioritization requires comparison. For most decision makers, the benchmark is expected *value*, any outcome that has a real and measurable positive impact on an individual or the organization. *In this sense, value is not an abstract concept. It needs to be realized.* Recommendations or predictions might well be accurate; however, they create no value until they are acted on.

Communicating the Value

Knowing the value is only the start. The next step is convincing people that the value is worth the actions necessary to realize the value. Building support involves making sure the case for change is understood. Organizations are often referred to in the abstract as entities in their own right. This is misleading; organizations are pluralistic entities populated by individuals with their own views, agendas, and opinions. Truth is subjective and dependent on one's point of view. Because of this, the case for change needs to be tailored to others' preferences.

Communicating value comes from presenting information in a way that eases understanding. By tailoring one's message to an audience's preferred communication style, relating it to their understanding of value, and going into an appropriate level of detail, change agents build a stronger case for action.

Delivering the Value

One-off benefits are valuable. And, actually delivering the value of business analytics is essential. However, these tactical benefits rarely lead to competitive differentiation. *Competitive advantage comes from creating and sustaining deep operational differences.* This is more than just a successful project; it is about creating and delivering a vision. It requires being able to effectively link limited resources to both tactical activities and strategic gains. Every benefit needs to map into a longer-term plan that progressively moves toward true differentiation. Having this vision and building trust through delivering the value helps create and sustain ongoing change.

Measuring the Value

Finally, maintaining momentum and investment requires demonstrating continuous successes over time. We trust that which we believe is "safe." It is impossible to build this level of trust unless the returns that were promised can be measured and proven. *Debate without data is nothing more than speculation.* At best, further investments will be delayed until political consensus can be achieved. At worst, entire programs of work can be delayed, undermined, or outright canceled. The fastest path to success in business analytics comes from demonstrating ongoing successes.

Section Summary

The key things to remember are that results need to be measurable, they need to be contextually relevant, they need to link into a strategic vision, and their successful completion needs to be demonstrable. This "value architecture" process helps justify a reason to act. When teams do not follow these four simple principles they inevitably struggle to demonstrate the value of business analytics. When combined, insight and value enable business analytics, as shown below.

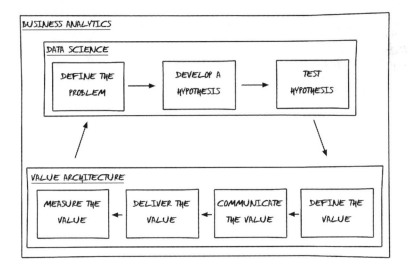

The remainder of this chapter focuses in more detail on how to define the value of business analytics as well as communicate the value.

Questions

- Within business analytics, what is needed to support ongoing change?
- What are the four activities that always need to happen?
- Why are these activities important?

TECHNIQUES AND ISSUES

Understanding and communicating the value of business analytics requires a blend of technical, domain, and soft skills. Many of these cannot be taught without the benefit of direct experience. There are, however, some key skills which, when understood, set a strong foundation for success.

Defining and Quantifying the Value of Business Analytics

Understanding the value of business analytics starts with defining what *value* means. This is a complex topic, one wrought with metaphysical implications. Within this chapter, value is any measurable improvement as perceived by a targeted beneficiary. This has two significant implications. First, it is an absolute measure: if it cannot be quantified, it is not value. Second, the perceived importance of an arbitrary quantum of value will vary from person to person: different people will weight value differently based on their context.

Benefits versus Value

Given this definition, it is helpful to highlight the difference between benefits and value. Benefits describe general improvements. Value, on the other hand, is specific; it describes measurable outcomes. For example, a business analytics initiative may improve customer satisfaction and overall productivity. While great, these are at best benefits; they remain undefined. To shift focus to value, they need to be measurable. Their value equivalents might be a 10% improvement in net promoter score and a 15% reduction in required resource levels to deliver the same outcome. Even better, the initiative might deliver millions of dollars of return through reducing service cancellations.

Benefits and value are both important. Benefits help build support; they are easily communicated and are powerful persuasion tools. Even in situations where value is unpalatable, benefits may still be attractive. For example, the only way to financially recognize productivity gains is through letting staff go. Without doing this, the organization still carries the same level of fixed costs as it did before it realized the productivity gains.

Direct managers often prefer not to downsize for a variety of political and personal reasons. On one hand, many organizations correlate power to the size of one's budget. On the other, forced redundancies often have a variety of personal and social costs. Because of this, those same managers may not even want to acknowledge the direct value of improved productivity.

This reluctance to acknowledge or support certain types of value does not necessarily translate into outright rejection of the benefits of improved productivity. While they may be unwilling to let people go, they will likely appreciate reduced stress levels, improved flexibility, and the ability to extend their work. While they might reject change based on measurable outcomes, creating a case for change involves understanding the balance between benefits and value. Where value justifies investment, benefits build support. The solution involves framing things appropriately.

Building a reason to act starts with defining the benefits and value of business analytics. It involves mapping out who will benefit, how they will benefit, whether or not they will care about the benefits they will receive; and if those benefits are measurable, what the expected value will be.

Quantifying the Value of Business Analytics

The starting point for value involves understanding three measures:

- Money
- Time
- Rate of return

Financial return is a going concern in any organization. In the private sector, business analytics might enable better customer retention, improved sales, or greater operational efficiency. These drive revenue or profitability. In the public sector, business analytics might reduce future taxpayer liabilities, fraudulent use of public services such as childcare rebates, or operating costs. All of these can be translated into financial measures, which are then directly comparable against other competing investment opportunities.

Time, being limited, is another major concern. Faster and better decisions enable better results. Algorithmically driven answers are highly scalable and repeatable. Because of this, business analytics significantly reduces the time needed to make decisions or otherwise drive outcomes. Banks that understand their risk can make decisions whether or not to offer credit cards in seconds rather than days. Retailers that understand their customers can make offers at point of sale rather than a month later. The closer an accurate decision to the point of data capture, the less the time to deliver a return on investment.

Finally, managing scarcity starts with managing opportunity costs. Given limited resources, a decision to invest in one project means deciding not to invest in another. Quantifying these opportunity costs starts by comparing the degree to which a dollar invested in one project will generate a greater return than another project. Ignoring the scale of return and the relative risk profiles, a project that doubles its investment is easily preferred over one left unquantified.

When it comes to formally quantifying the value of business analytics, the core measures used by many organizations are:

- Total cost of ownership (TCO)
- Return on investment (ROI)
- Payback
- Net present value (NPV)
- Internal rate of return (IRR)

The best business analytics teams have a deep understanding of what these measures mean, how to use them, and how to apply them. By being able to quantify their worth they make it easy for their organization to invest in their vision. And, by being able to track the value they deliver using the same set of measures, they build trust and justify ever-increasing investments in their team. Being able to quantify the value of business analytics helps organizations support a reason to act.

The Role of Value in Organizational Decision Making

Organizations exist for a variety of reasons. Common goals include maximizing shareholder, stakeholder, or social return. Regardless of the context, all exist to add value in some way and because of this, the opportunity to create value creates a case for change. Given unlimited resources, the value an organization can create is infinite. Unfortunately, given constrained resources, creating value involves coming to terms with scarcity.

All resources are limited. Cash reserves and liquidity requirements constrain investment potential. Resourcing availability constrains project delivery. Technology and capital constrain what an organization is capable of doing. In practice, most organizations spend far more time trying to balance these constraints than actually adding value!

For organizations rich in data, business analytics offers a tantalizing opportunity. Analysis can identify opportunities to create value and those opportunities, when realized, can deliver economic returns. This approach is, however, only one path to realizing value. Projects require money. That money could also be used elsewhere to create other sources of value. That same money could be spent hiring more staff, offering sales incentives, or diversifying business operations. From the perspective of the Chief Financial Officer or Financial Controller, all of these projects are largely interchangeable. Their intent may be irrelevant; what is important is their ability to generate returns and mitigate risk.

It is for this reason that being able to define the value of business analytics is so critical. In the absence of regulatory requirements or strategic commitments, projects that focus on immeasurable and intangible benefits are almost always deprioritized. While being able to make better decisions through having easy access to relevant information is a worthy goal, it is also one that is hard to measure. Faced with a choice between two projects, one that offers "insight" and one that will strip millions of cost out of a relatively inefficient supply chain, most decision makers will correctly back the one that creates measurable return.

Explaining the economic value of business analytics stops attention and investments being channeled toward other projects. This is valid and fair: the only way to deal with scarcity is to prioritize. By defining the value of business analytics, organizations can make objective decisions about where investments will create the greatest return.

Section Summary

Change agents interested in moving beyond benefits to value start by focusing on how to quantify the value of their change. Quantifying the value of business analytics starts with establishing a common set of comparable measures. Without the ability to make comparisons, measures are meaningless. For example, which is better: productivity gains resulting in twenty minutes more time a day or greater confidence in one's data?

Incomparable measures force subjective decisions. Taking one point of view, it is easy to argue that twenty minutes extra time might be more valuable than anything else. Over a year, a team might gain an extra two weeks' worth of time. It is equally valid to argue that without confidence in one's data, an organization cannot make effective decisions. Regardless of productivity gains, garbage inputs can only create garbage outputs. Both perspectives are valid but unless the organization has enough resources to support each, a choice needs to be made.

There are always situations where the "right" thing to do is not necessarily the most measurable one. What quantification does, however, is encourage focus. By establishing and understanding a core set of comparable measures, organizations simplify decision making in most situations.

Questions

- What is the difference between benefits and value?
- Why are they both important to organizations?
- How do many organizations measure value?

Communicating the Value of Business Analytics

Quantifying the value is never enough. People need to agree with that value. And appreciating value is subjective. Communication preferences vary and unless messages are framed appropriately, the content can easily be lost. Rather than see this as an obstacle, high-performing teams see this as an opportunity. By tailoring their message to their audience, they increase the odds of successfully communicating what they are trying to say.

Somewhat counter-intuitively, the structure that many organizations enforce in creating and submitting business cases can actually act as a deterrent to creating an effective communication plan. By constraining focus to a small set of pre-defined measures, the temptation is to become complacent and focus on "completing a form" rather than persuading an organization to change.

When trying to communicate the value of business analytics it helps to consider how an audience prefers to interpret a message. Given a diverse audience, the more the message spans a variety of different perspectives the easier it becomes to get the audience on-side.

Framing an effective message involves matching the message to the audience through four perspectives, as shown below.

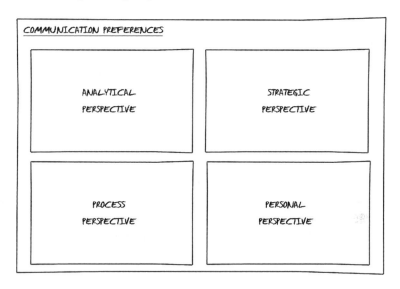

The Analytical Perspective

Some people primarily care about the facts. Unsurprisingly, most people who work in business analytics tend to favor this perspective. They like logic, rigor, and taking a rational perspective.

People who prefer to communicate using this perspective tend to focus the most on value, outcomes, and other fairly tangible measures. They will often willingly have an argument not because they dislike the concept but because they seek the truth. Catering for this perspective involves focusing on how things will work, what the project will deliver, and how the approach is justified. Dodging detail can be seen as a weakness.

The Process Perspective

Other people primarily care about the steps needed to achieve the outcomes. Rather than focusing on justifications, they may be more interested in how things will be delivered. They may equally be interested in detail; it is just a different type of detail.

People who prefer to communicate using this perspective tend to focus the most on quality, governance, and process. They will often be interested in knowing how things will change and how that change will be managed.

Catering for this perspective involves focusing on execution and planning; managing risk will often be a key concern.

The Personal Perspective

Others prefer to focus on how the change will impact people, positively or negatively. While everyone needs to demonstrate tangible benefits in some form, they may well be interested in knowing the intangible personal benefits associated with initiatives such as improved job satisfaction or better internal exposure.

People who prefer to communicate using this perspective tend to focus the most on trust, interpersonal relationships, and collaboration. They may decide not to support the change because they think it is a bad idea, but simply because they fear it may hurt their teams. Catering for this perspective involves focusing on their team's interests and how their careers might be developed.

The Strategic Perspective

Finally, some people tend to focus on the strategic implications of the proposed approach. This may be through competitive differentiation, a long-term vision, or strategic transformation. Without the ability to describe the "bigger vision," these types of people may actively resist change simply because they feel there might be better options elsewhere.

People who prefer to communicate using this perspective tend to focus the most on strategy, abstract concepts, and the simplification of detail. They will often be interested in conceptual linkages and visual representations of complex ideas. Catering for this perspective involves focusing less on structured methods of communication and more on transformative outcomes.

Section Summary

Defining the value of business analytics forms half of the reason to act. The other half is making sure the targeted value beneficiaries understand that value within their world context. By having a general communication framework that helps tailor communication strategies to a broad set of communication preferences, organizations can greatly improve the odds of building support to act on insight, thereby realizing their targeted value.

Questions

- Why is communicating the value of business analytics important?
- What are four common perspectives?
- How would each perspective prefer to view the same value proposition?

Case Study

Telecommunications

Every industry has countless examples of how business analytics can be used to drive tangible and intangible value. This section highlights two examples of how business analytics can create value within telecommunications, specifically focusing on *customer retention* and *social network analysis*.

CUSTOMER RETENTION

Most telecommunications companies see the majority of their revenue come from retail services. Consumers tend to pay through one of two payment structures:

- *Subscription* revenue (often referred to as *postpaid* plans), where minimum payments are fixed and payable on a set schedule and usage is capped at a set consumption level where excesses are charged at pre-agreed rates.
- *Usage* revenue (often referred to as *prepaid* plans), where payment is made ahead of time and consumed based on pre-agreed rates.

The split between these varies by geography. Some countries, such as Australia, have a strong bias toward subscription services. Other countries, such as India, have a significant bias toward usage revenue.

Regardless, all telcos face a common challenge: *churn*. Churn occurs when a customer cancels their services and moves to another provider. Reasons vary, but common factors include network or distribution characteristics (such as unique high-speed connectivity or exclusive rights to specific phones), service variability (such at network reliability), or simply, price.

Reducing churn is one of the fastest ways a telecommunications company can improve financial results. While churn is a natural part of the market, it also represents a key lever which, when controlled, can lead to significant growth in market share.

In a typical OECD country, churn rates on postpaid services might range from 2% to 8% per month. Over the course of a year, anywhere from 15% to 60% of a telco's customer base might move to a different provider. Scarily, churn rates on "pay-as-you-go" plans are often significantly higher!

Offsetting this loss is a happy counter-force: every other company is losing customers at an equivalent rate. As long as churn rates remain in equilibrium and new customer acquisition remains constant, every telco maintains a stable market share. Equally though, a telco that is better at retaining customers in a profitable manner instantly gains a competitive advantage. Holding everything else constant, every month that they beat the industry average increases their proportional market share.

A well-known principle is that it is easier to sell to an existing customer than it is to acquire a new customer. This is especially true when it comes to preventing churn. By understanding how customers normally behave, a telco has the ability to determine when they are likely to start looking around for a different provider.

Retention modeling drives significant value in telecommunications. Regardless of whether one is looking at fixed-line telephony, mobile telephony, or Internet services, business analytics helps reduce cancellation rates. Blending predictive modeling and operational analytics allows organizations to:

- Identify those most probable of canceling their services.
- Understand when they are likely to cancel their services.
- Integrate predictions with outbound contact processes.
- Track the efficacy of predictions and actions to demonstrate value.

Predicting when someone is likely to cancel or stop using their service involves profiling typical usage patterns. In aggregate, the vast majority of people exhibit common behaviors. For most people, phone usage remains fairly constant from month to month. Major changes from our normal patterns often indicate a change in consumer preference.

While different sets of people may show different patterns, these commonalities can be identified through techniques such as *microsegmentation*. Once people have been grouped into common sets, analytical models can be used to identify a baseline behavioral pattern through algorithms such as *decision trees* and *logistic regression*.

Typical inputs into these models include factors such as when their commitment ends,[*] how their usage changes over time,[†] and how their interactions might have influenced their impressions.[‡] These are normally converted into a variety of quantitative measures and fed into statistical models to identify which, if any, of these measures have a significant impact on a customer's probability of churn.

The output of these models are customer-level, probability-based predictions of likelihood to churn, usually normalized to be between 0% and 100%.

---

[*] Unsurprisingly, most people become extremely interested in better deals when they have the opportunity to look elsewhere at no cost.

[†] Major changes in recent behavior tend to be a leading indicator of a commercial change. In telecommunications, organizations often compare the last three month's worth of behavior against the previous year's to identify shorter-term behavioral changes.

[‡] Bill shock is a significant leading indicator of churn. Poorly handled customer interactions can damage loyalty, in turn increasing the odds of moving to a different service.

A customer with a churn probability of 100% is almost guaranteed to move to a different provider in the upcoming month. Equally, a customer with a churn propensity of 0% is almost certainly not likely to cancel their service.

Given an infinite budget, the company could contact every one of these people and make an attractive counter offer. In practice, however, retention often depends both on contacting the person at the right time as well as making the right offer. Sometimes, the right offer involves a discount in some form, hurting profitability. This trade-off forms a major operational challenge; how much should a telco offer to retain a customer who only has a certain probability of canceling their service?

By being able to predict the long-term value of a customer (also known as *customer life-time value*) as well as their likelihood of churn, the telco can make an appropriate offer at the right time. When delivered better than competitors, this helps minimize any margin losses while also driving market share improvements, a rare situation involving no real trade-offs.

SOCIAL NETWORK ANALYSIS

On one hand, it is true that in aggregate, people tend to exhibit common behaviors. On the other, however, it is also true that not all decisions are made based purely on internal considerations. We are influenced not just by how we feel or what we know, but by who we interact with. External factors also have an influence and unfortunately, are rarely represented in raw transactional data. Understanding these interactions, also known as *social network analysis* (SNA), is another significant source of value in telecommunications.

It is often said that banks and other financial institutions know what you are worth. Retailers know what you like doing on a day-to-day basis. Content and search providers know what you are interested in. The hidden strength of telecommunications is that they know whom you know.

To connect people who want to talk, SMS, or otherwise message each other, the telco needs to know the originating and receiving parties. In aggregate and over time, this transactional data maps social relationships across entire countries. One of the most interesting things about this social map is that it includes not only customers (often termed *on-network*) but also people who are not subscribers (often termed *off-network*). This may seem strange but it is eminently logical; without this counter-party interconnection, it would be impossible to link one network to another.

Give this unique perspective, it is not uncommon for a market-leading telco to have visibility over a majority of (if not all) originating and destination numbers across an entire country. While they may only legally be able to retain personal information about current subscribing customers, they may still be able to visualize and explore an entire country's social graph. When combined with business analytics, this creates a unique opportunity.

Highly scalable analytical processing allows some telcos the ability to determine the strength and directionality of interpersonal relationships. This can then be algorithmically reduced into communities, breaking down an aggregate social graph of hundreds or thousands of millions of relationships into thousands or millions of communities.

These communities are often defined based on their collective relational strength. While a person may call a distant relation once a year, it may not mean that they have a deep or influential relationship with them. By identifying communities within the overall social graph, the company can algorithmically identify leaders, followers, and influencers within those communities. Common indicators include directionality, frequency, and type of contact. Inter-generational preferences can have a significant effect on influence: frequent inbound voice calls may not represent significant influence for people between the ages of ten to twenty-five. Equally though, frequent inbound SMS traffic with occasional outbound SMS traffic may indicate a strongly influential relationship for this same cohort.

The power of this analysis cannot be understated. Given a destination number with no associated customer data, it is possible to determine their likely age to within a few years based on their relationships, typical calling patterns, and message choice (for example, SMS versus voice).

In aggregate, this social graph is simply too large to analyze interactively. There are simply too many relationships to visualize in any meaningful form. Business analytics offers an attractive alternative. By algorithmically decomposing the social graph into communities and tagging individuals with their dominant community characteristics, the telco can both better understand their customers as well as feed their results into their existing propensity models.

For example, people with a direct connection to an influencer who churns to a different provider may have a statistically significant higher probability of churning in subsequent time periods. Equally, people who are not directly connected to an influencer within a given community may also see their probability of churn rise as their indirect connections to those who have churned in that community increase.

By including this information in the telco's existing propensity models, the telco can incorporate the social network into their retention, cross-sell, and up-sell models. This lifts overall accuracy and provides another source of competitive differentiation. While the incremental gains may not be as significant as the original move to propensity models, they still represent an additional improvement. And as with all numbers games, small improvements can create big differences over time.

EMERGING TRENDS

The importance of extracting value from Big Data will only continue to grow. While the field is a rapidly expanding one, there are two important trends to be aware of.

The first is part of the ongoing push to turn insight into operational execution. Scaling business analytics happens through automation.

Rather than requiring direct interaction every time a decision needs to be made, organizations are increasingly embedding analytics into operational processes, sometimes going so far as creating real-time analytically based recommendations.

The second is the need to test different approaches in the absence of historical data. Compared to many other sources of data, social media data and social network data are relatively new. There is relatively little guidance as to what works and what does not. Because of this, many organizations are focusing on creating agile test and learn processes that allow for rapid in-market experimentation prior to choosing a particular approach.

Scalable Value Creation: Operational Analytics and Real-Time Decision Making

Simplistically, data science/analytics involves three major activities. First, data scientists need to define what the problem is and develop a hypothesis as to what the answer might be. Once defined, they need to test their hypothesis against their data. This usually involves a variety of analytical techniques ranging from visualization right through to advanced forms of predictive modeling or optimization.

Assuming the data supports their hypothesis, they have one last important task: to make sure their answer is acted on. Without action, all their effort was wasted. In this context, data scientists are often seen as the path to the answer. They spend their time doing research and answering questions, supporting exploratory and explanatory analysis. This presents an obvious problem: the only way to scale business analytics is to hire more data scientists.

Organizations interested in applying business analytics across their entire operations are instead moving more toward operational analytics. Rather than treating analytics as an interactive process, they emphasize the need to translate these insights into mathematical formulas or rules that can be embedded in data warehouses and other decisioning systems.

The role of the data scientist in this context shifts from answering questions to creating and deploying analytical assets. These assets might help identify people with a high probability of canceling their subscription services, entities likely to be committing fraud, or people likely to be interested in a particular product.

Importantly, because these assets are mathematically based and not reliant on interactive use, they can be used as frequently as needed. In some cases, this might be as infrequently as a monthly job where the formulas are applied to all customer records. Once "scored," the highest scoring customers are then automatically passed across to the contact center for follow-up. In other cases, this might be in real time where transactions are "scored" as they occur. One example might involve flagging fraudulent transactions in real time, and blocking the financial transaction from completing if it has a high probability of being fraudulent.

This move toward operational analytics represents a significant turning point. It is usually the first time an organization sees significant returns from the use of business analytics. It is also the point where organizations start to scale their application of business analytics. Best practices do exist, even if most organizations are not necessarily aware of them.* As more organizations come to terms with capturing Big Data and start shifting their attention to creating value out of Big Data, their need for operational analytics correspondingly grows.

Test and Learn: In-Market Experimentation

One of the biggest advantages of Big Data is the breadth of insight it allows. Social media, full-text customer conversations, and social relationships all offer new opportunities to generate insight. Unfortunately, this new data also presents a challenge. Because it is so new, it is often hard to validate predictive relationships to a high degree of confidence using historical data.

The traditional approach to developing and testing a hypothesis involves setting aside historical examples and testing the ability of a model to predict what actually happened. A good model will create accurate predictions where a bad model might create predictions no better than random chance.

This approach offers a number of advantages. First, it can be tested without running the risk of irritating customers or otherwise exposing the organization to risk. It is also comparatively inexpensive. Because predictions can be validated against real-world data, the organization need not change operational processes or otherwise impact field activity.

A common example involves credit scoring. Financial institutions are willing to offer certain customers access to credit in exchange for interest on credit used. Doing so requires being able to distinguish between good and bad credit risks. Offer the wrong customer credit and they will likely

---

* Stubbs, Evan. *Delivering Business Analytics: Practical Guidelines for Best Practice.* Hoboken, NJ: Wiley, 2013. Print.

default, making the financial institution lose money. Reject a good potential customer and the institution loses market share, sacrifices revenue, and hurts profitability.

To create and test these predictions, most risk groups take all the credit offers they have made historically and flag those who did and did not default. They will then set aside a certain percentage of all customer records. Using those that are left over, they will build a model that attempts to use behavioral and socio-demographic data to predict the odds of a person defaulting.

To validate the model, they will apply the model to the records they set aside and generate a series of predictions. They will then compare the predictions against reality, testing to see how well the model's predictions matched historical reality. A good model might have over 95% predictive accuracy, correctly identifying over 95% of good and bad debts. A bad model might be no better than random chance.

The biggest limitation of this approach is that it requires historical data. Without enough history to test against, it can be hard if not impossible to validate a potential model for accuracy. Many of the ways we interact simply did not exist even a decade ago. Online banking, social media, and large-scale digitization of contact center interactions are relatively new sources of information and may not always have enough historical data available to fully test a hypothesis.

This acceleration in data variety is only getting faster. Because of this, there is an ongoing push to create highly flexible, low-cost, in-market experimentation processes. Where historical data is unavailable, rather than guess which model might generate the best predictions, organizations are moving toward test and learn processes where business analytics processes are tested against each other using champion/challenger methods. While this philosophy is well established in some verticals such as debt management, the biggest shift is in its breadth of application.[*]

Through establishing control groups and doing comparative in-market testing, organizations eliminate many of the problems that go along with trying to quantify the real value of business analytics. Rather than having to make assumptions, they can scientifically isolate and measure the impact of business analytics on the final outcome. While this is still largely

---

[*] Antony, Jiju. *Design of Experiments for Engineers and Scientists*. Oxford: Butterworth-Heinemann, 2003. Print.

the domain of the most advanced organizations, it is increasingly being replicated by less mature organizations.

Assignment

As part of a group, the goal of this exercise is to develop a business case to improve a nominated organization's business analytics capabilities. It reinforces the following learning objectives:

- How value creates a reason to act and support change.
- The link between business analytics and value.
- Different types of value and how they influence decision-making.
- How to take communication preferences into account when communicating value.

You are free to choose any currently trading organization or existing government department and are recommended to review recent press releases, competitive information, policy statement, and news to help build context and relevancy.

The business case must relate to building some data-driven, decision-making capability, ideally one that relates to improvements in operational analytics or that will otherwise drive economic returns. Like in most organizations, there is no right or wrong answer. Your "success" will be based on your ability to build a persuasive argument that the returns will outweigh the investment needed.

To provide appropriate context, inform the assessor well ahead of time of:

- Your chosen organization
- The initiative you will be proposing
- Your targeted audience

In building your business case, be sure to consider:

- The investment needed to support changes in skills or capabilities, processes, data, and technology. While these can be justified by explicitly defined assumptions where necessary, these assumptions should be based on defensible grounds.
- The expected strategic and tactical rewards of investing in the initiative. These should be as specific as possible.

- The tangible and intangible benefits of the initiative. Where appropriate and possible, these should ideally be explicitly calculated in economic terms.
- The relative importance of personal and organizational value in your audience's mind given the organization's context.
- How the audience's communication preferences might influence their decision-making.

In building the most effective business case possible, it will be important to keep in mind the following:

- The more the business case relies on intangible or strategic value, the more persuasive and visionary the business case will need to be to justify the change needed.
- The more the business case relies on tangible or tactical value, the more it will need to align to immediate organizational imperatives and pressures.
- The best business cases maintain a balance between the two, painting a vision of what's possible while still linking strategic benefits to shorter-term tactical benefits.
- Because of the difficulty in predicting an audience's communication preferences ahead of time, the most effective presentations move through all four communication preferences quickly and repeatedly.
- Decision-makers appreciate simplicity based on complexity. Presenting needless complexity simply to demonstrate intelligence is often (but not always) considered irritating and time wasting. Given limited time, their interest is rarely in being impressed. Instead, it is in coming to the right answer as quickly as possible while still being confident in the results.

2

Producing Insights from Information through Analytics

Frank Stein and Arnold Greenland

CONTENTS

Learning Objectives

- Introduce the value of business analytics to organizations, whether they are commercial, non-profit, or government organizations.
- Highlight various real-life examples of how business analytics can provide insights using advanced analytical techniques that will be described in later chapters.
- Outline a process that practitioners and organizations can follow to assess and harvest the insights that business analytics can generate.

INTRODUCTION

Goals of Business Analytics

The primary goal of business analytics is to provide better insight to businesses and organizations, which allows them to achieve a higher level of performance. In common usage, the term *insight* refers to gaining an understanding of a person or situation; however, in the context of business analytics, we mean to gain an understanding of a business situation that allows a manager to make the best possible decision where *best* refers to a numerically measurable business outcome that is consistent with the goals and objectives of the organization in question. Typically this requires obtaining hard information or data about the business, the business dynamics, business relationships, and the set of choices that are available to the decision maker, and performing an analysis, maybe using a mathematical or statistical model, that forms the basis of the decision.

There are many collateral benefits of applying business analytics. For example, using analytics to analyze a company or organization's data will generally reveal patterns of behavior that bring deeper knowledge of the organization, clarify the metrics on which management should focus, and supports making the right decisions at the right time.

Another key point is that the application of analytics has proven repeatedly to be superior to decision making, which relies solely on the intuition or experience of the executives. We should be clear here: there is no substitute for excellent and talented management as leaders of an organization and decisions should always be ultimately in the hands of those managers. However, business analytics adds value to the organization by arming managers with the tools to make demonstrably better decisions, which in turn improves the organization's performance or results in ways that would not have been possible (at least with the same level of confidence based on evidence) before the analytical methods were applied.

Analytics should be pervasive within an organization. It should be applied to understand those specific situations or problems that an organization is having, and it should be used on an ongoing basis to monitor the performance of the organization to indicate potential problems.

The next section covers some of the types of problems that business analytics are good at solving.

The Need for Business Analytics Is Growing

Businesses have recognized that to cope with the vast amount of information that they are faced with, they have to resort to a new set of tools. Central among them is the use of more sophisticated approaches to analyze data and make better and quicker decisions. It is estimated that by 2020, the amount of digital information will grow to 40,000 exabytes or 40 zettabytes (a single exabyte is the equivalent of 1 billion gigabytes). The pace of growth is staggering, as it is estimated that digital data is doubling about every two years.[1]

There are a number of other interesting events that are happening at the same time as the massive growth in the volume of information. They include:

- Organizations will be faced with bigger and more complex business problems requiring even more efficient and creative algorithms to support decision making.

- In the same instance, the timeline that businesses have to make decisions is shrinking dramatically. The demand for decision-making speed has already outpaced what humans can do, and it will soon require the use of massively parallel computing environments to be able to maintain the speeds required by the most elementary business activities, such as real-time procurement decisions.
- The types of data that organizations encounter are changing dramatically. Nearly 80% of all "data" is now unstructured, such as text, audio, video, and image data. These new types of data require new analytics to extract, structure, and use to make decisions.
- The sources of information are also changing. With mobile devices so pervasive (nearly 80% of the world's population has a cell phone), and the use of social media sites to record and store information about people's "real" lives, new ways of ingesting this information and using it appropriately is desperately needed.
- Automated analytics approaches will help to address this conundrum and provide the insights needed to drive modern businesses and organizations.

The ROI of Analytics

If analytics are producing new insights for organizations, these organizations should be reporting improved performance either financially or in accomplishing their mission. A number of studies have been done that do indeed show this result.

For example, the IBM Institute for Business Value has conducted a survey of organizations using analytics for the past three years, and has found that 63% of the respondents report that the use of information and analytics is creating a competitive advantage for their organizations.[2] By comparison, this percentage was just 37% in 2010.

While this is self-reported data and may represent the aspirations of the respondents rather than true results, two professors from MIT and one from Wharton have employed a direct measurement approach leveraging available data to study the return on investment from analytics. They examined whether performance is higher in firms that emphasize decision making based on data and business analytics (which they term a *data-driven decision-making approach* or DDD).

Using detailed survey data on the business practices and information technology investments of 179 large publicly traded firms, we find that firms that adopt DDD have output and productivity that is 5–6% higher than what would be expected given their other investments and information technology usage…. Furthermore, the relationship between DDD and performance also appears in other performance measures such as asset utilization, return on equity, and market value.[3]

The consulting firm Nucleus Research has studied 60 analytics projects to try to understand the ROI for individual projects. They have found that analytics pays back $10.66 for every dollar invested in technologies such as business intelligence, performance management, and predictive analytics.[4] Their analysis included audits of projects from customers using analytics software from many of the leading analytics vendors. Analytics produced a high ROI for organizations by providing improved visibility and decision making around:

- What customers are buying and why, and their price sensitivities, thus supporting an increase in revenue generation.
- Costs of products and margins.
- Operating expenses.

They also found that projects that integrated three or more data sources had on average a higher ROI than those that use fewer data sources.

Analytics Maturity Model

An analytics maturity model helps organizations to understand the state of analytics in their organization and to consider steps to strengthen their analytics culture and capabilities. To date, there is no agreed upon model although INFORMS (Institute for Operations Research and the Management Sciences) announced plans to create one in 2013. IBM has produced the model shown in Figure 2.1.[5] In the lower left corner, we have companies that operate on heroics, where individuals do amazing things—gather information from disparate locations, collect them, and turn them into insight.

The next level is organizations that institutionalize this process and make it foundational to the business. It then becomes information-based decision making that is differentiating the company from the competition.

In the upper right corner, we find those organizations that are at the highest level of analytics maturity, predicting outcomes using advanced analytics, and are able to immediately react and turn insight into action. IBM labels the organizations at this level of Analytics as "Breakaway Organizations."

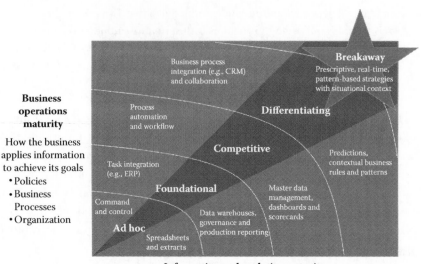

Information and analytics maturity
How the business manages information and learns from it

FIGURE 2.1
IBM's Analytics Maturity Model. (Printed with permission, Breaking Away with Business Analytics and Optimization: New Intelligence Meets Enterprise Operations at http://www.935.ibm.com/services/uk/gbs/pdf/Breaking_away_with_business_analytics_and_optimisation.pdf.)

Analytics maturity is related to both how the organization uses analytics (the horizontal axis) and how the organization takes that insight, the analysis, and leverages it for the benefit of the organization. It is important we recognize that this is a long journey and requires that organizations have foundational capabilities in order to progress.

TYPES OF ANALYTICS AND THE BENEFITS THEY PROVIDE

Descriptive Analytics identify, classify, and count objects or events like money spent or number of widgets manufactured in the past time period. They are critical for knowing how the organization is performing—your current situation. For example, they let you know if you are above or below budget, or are performing up to standards. This category is also called *Business Intelligence* (BI) and includes reports, dashboards, scorecards, and canned and ad hoc queries.

Predictive Analytics look at the trend of past events to anticipate possible future outcomes. This allows the organization to better plan for the future—deciding what actions to take that can improve the future results. For example, predictive analytics can:

- Discover patterns and correlations in data that might be missed by the human eye.
- Predict future spending or performance assuming no changes and then build a plan to try to "bend the curve" to improve results.
- Build a model that will allow "What if" analyses to decide on the best course of action.

Prescriptive Analytics focus on achieving the best possible outcome by going beyond the forecast to actually determine the optimal decision to make. For example, this would help an organization answer how best to allocate capital, people, and facilities to achieve business results such as reduced time or cost, or increased return on investment. Prescriptive analytics leverage optimization methods to obtain their prescriptive results. When the optimization is done while considering uncertainty (e.g., under different economic assumptions), it is called *Stochastic Optimization*. Prescriptive analytics helps customers:

a. Discover best options or approaches that may not be obvious due to the number of choices to be considered or the amount of data to be analyzed.
b. Automate routine decision-making tasks such as scheduling of staff or routing of vehicles.
c. Gain further insights in the trade-offs that must be made since optimizing one resource may impact another one. For example, reduced staffing may impact customer response times, or with the design of a fuel-efficient car, one might trade off various engine characteristics with aerodynamic considerations.

Text Analytics allow normal text documents to be used as the source data for some of the analytics described above. For example, emails to a company's complaint department can be analyzed to determine trends about the volume or subject of complaint. More detailed examples will be provided in the section below.

TYPICAL BUSINESS PROBLEMS WHERE BUSINESS ANALYTICS ARE APPLIED

This section will highlight how analytics can help solve various business problems, while the next section will give several case studies. The focus of many of these business problems starts with the Line of Business (LOB) executives responsible for the execution of the mission of the company or organization. These executives want to first understand how they are doing and then to understand what they should be doing to improve their business. Analytics helps them solve both problems.

Helping Organizations Know Their Customers/Constituents/Citizens

For the Chief Marketing Officer or Director of Sales, understanding your customers can give you a competitive advantage. Companies that understand why their customers are their customers can fine-tune their products/services, promotions, pricing policies, store locations, and other marketing levers to retain and grow their installed base, enhance customer loyalty, target the most profitable customers, and improve customer satisfaction.

The next time you buy something, take a close look at the receipt. A large number of receipts will say something such as "Take our survey for a chance to win $1000." The cost of the prize is small in comparison to the value that companies gain in receiving your feedback. Consider it an exchange between your time and information, and the chance for you to win money. The company can use the information you provide to quickly detect any problems you may have experienced with your buying experience (see the next section on reputation) and to enhance the appeal of the products and services they provide to you.

Retailers find that customer analytical data is not only valuable for their internal planning purposes, but can be sold to generate additional income. For example, product manufacturers may find the detail that retailers have on their customers to be of interest. This could include the demographics of the consumers of their products, as well as a comparison of these consumers vis-à-vis the demographics of their competitor's consumers.

Reputation Management

Another means by which companies collect data about consumers is social media. Marketers collect information that people post publicly on sites such as Reddit, StumbleUpon, Pinterest, Facebook, and Twitter. With this information, companies can detect negative opinions being expressed about their company or products and take proactive steps to address the problems and to build on positive opinions.

An excellent example of the use of social media analytics is the presidential election campaign of 2012 between President Obama and Mitt Romney. Obama was very successful in leveraging the social media to both put out messages and collect data on what people were saying.

> We may equate data harvesting with large online presences such as Google or Amazon, but they aren't the only ones mining user data. The ability to collect and analyze data on a large scale allowed the Obama team to model behaviors and coordinate and target communications best. They could, for example, predict which types of people could be persuaded by which forms of contact and content. The Obama field offices ranked call lists in order of persuade-ability allowing them to predict donor behaviors and to mobilize volunteers to get people out to vote, particularly in the critical swing states.[6]

Improve Operational Efficiency

Chief Operating Officers (COOs), responsible for the daily operations of a company, have traditionally been major users of analytics. COOs must make sure their business operations are efficient and effective in order to deliver the right product/service at the right price at the right time and place. In today's competitive, "do more with less" business environment, data analytics can provide the competitive edge. Business intelligence systems can provide the COO with detailed reporting on operating performance, margins, and rates of return on investments. Operations management can make extensive use of data forecasting methods (predictive analytics) to better align operations and production capabilities with demand. What if analysis can be performed by the operations staff to show the impact of changes in external environment (closing of an airport) as well as company decisions (e.g., price increases)? This can help the organization to take advantage of emerging opportunities.

These forecasts, along with optimization methods, can be used to improve the operational efficiencies of the firm's global supply chain. For example, decisions can be made on the amount of raw material or finished inventory to stock at global, regional, and local facilities.

Financial Management

Data and analytics allow the CFO to gain more visibility and control over the organization's financial performance including revenue, expenses, capital expenditures, and profits/losses. Modern financial management systems reduce the time spent collecting and validating numbers, allowing more time to be spent on analysis. While monthly and quarterly processing of financials has been typical in the past, companies are striving to automate their financial management systems so that financial analysis can provide an up-to-date view of an organization's financial posture.

Analytics can help the CFO track and evaluate the organization's performance through standard and ad hoc reports, color-coded dashboard displays, and "drill-down" business intelligence (BI) systems. Organizations can put in place Key Performance Indicators (KPIs)—a small number of important indicators of the organization's performance to provide focus for the executives. The KPIs may reflect financial as well as other measures of performance (e.g., number of cars produced this month, amount of cars in inventory). The reporting and grading of the results helps to align results with goals, and execution with plans.

When there is a mismatch between goals and results, analytics can help to clarify the results, for example, what impacted this quarter's profitability, and what can be done to correct the situation. What-if scenario modeling can be used to analyze various courses of action.

Manage Waste, Fraud, and Abuse

The U.S. federal government lost $261 billion, or 7% of total spending, to fraud and waste in 2012, according to Rep. Darrell Issa (R-CA) during a February House committee hearing.[7] Banks lost $6 billion in 2012, according to NBC News.[8] Insurance companies lose vast sums to fraudulent medical claims. What can be done about these losses? Analytics can provide a minimum visibility into the losses, and some analytics can be used to prevent the losses from occurring.

Algorithms have been developed to characterize transactions as being normal or suspicious. For example, credit card companies have sophisticated software that has characterized customer typical purchase patterns and can trigger an alert if the transaction is larger than normal or from a store that you do not typically frequent. Medical insurance companies are actively developing computer programs to stop the normal industry practice of "pay and chase" (paying claims first and then investigating later for fraud). By building profiles of typical claim amounts for different ailments, and also learning patterns of fraud such as buying drugs at a pharmacy some distance from one's home, insurance companies are able to build predictive models of which claims are fraudulent.

Proactive Risk Management

Organizations face risks from the external environment, such as variations in interest rate or weather disruptions to their business, and from internal sources such as project delays or failures. A recent new form of risk comes from computer attacks on an organization's IT (information technology) infrastructure.

The goal of risk management is to allow organizations to make risk-aware decisions that improve business performance. Quite often, the risk is evaluated or communicated by judgment (e.g., using a set of colors to define risk, or evaluating it as high/medium/low). The reason that these judgmental approaches are used is that these organizations do not have the capability of quantifying the probability of these risks. In some cases, it is because they do not have the data needed to estimate the risk probabilities. In other cases, it is because they are not leveraging advanced analytics methods to do it. Analytics can help to mitigate risks by bringing together data from throughout the organization and environment to identify the risks, using predictive tools discussed in the fraud, waste, and abuse section above, and then use the analytics method to quantify those risks and the implications to the organization. Descriptive analytics can be used to create Key Risk Indicators (KRIs), while predictive analytics can be used to predict what might happen. While these techniques may work where there is sufficient occurrence of events on which to make a prediction, for so-called black swan events—very low probability of occurrence events with very large impact—modeling and simulation may be employed to get an understanding of the business impact. Today, many organizations have

Enterprise Risk Management (ERM) departments and chief risk officers to provide competency in risk management.

Analytics in Education

Analytics are increasingly being used in education, sometimes called *educational data mining* or *learning analytics*. Schools have a wealth of data about their students including past and current test scores, teacher grades, and socioeconomic data. This data can be ingested into a business intelligence system to allow teachers and administers to more efficiently manage their schools and help their students succeed.

More sophisticated analytics can be applied to the student's raw test results to provide more insight into the learning and missed learning of the student. Massive Open Online Courses (MOOCs) are starting to use these deeper analytics to provide a better learning experience for the students. Trends within the data and careful test design can attribute incorrect answers to the particular cause, thereby providing more constructive feedback to the student, and even the instructor.

Testing analytics are already implemented in many schools and universities, although they have not reached their full potential. Statistical software analyzes student responses to detect instances of cheating. This is similar to the analytics used to detect fraud, abuse, waste, and noncompliance with regulations and standards.

EXAMPLES OF ANALYTICS PROJECTS

We believe that the best way to convey the value of analytics is through examples. Great analytics is not new. There are examples of such groundbreaking work going back decades. What is new is that the interest and acceptance of the value of this sort of thinking is growing.

Descriptive Analytics Example

Case Study: Clark County Family Services
Business Intelligence System[9]

Clark County, Nevada is home to Las Vegas and has more than 2 million residents as well as 42 million visitors a year. In 2004, as a result of state legislative action, the county assumed responsibility and staff from the state to provide services for child welfare, foster, and adoptive services. The Family Services department had limited visibility into case processing and case loads and needed a Business Intelligence (BI) system that could provide:

- A better way to input, retrieve, and share information within each sector of the department.
- A method to better manage the status of both pending and active cases.
- A way to ensure and prove that it was in compliance with federal and state regulations.
- A way to support and claim funding for activities like targeted case management, which is reimbursable from the federal government.

The department implemented a BI system to meet these requirements. Starting with the development of departmental scorecards, they moved onto On-Line Analytical Processing (OLAP) cubes, and finally to data marts to support dashboards and reporting for departmental tasks. Using this system, the managers could look at measurements such as whether open investigations were being completed in a timely fashion, how many face-to-face contacts had taken place with victims of abuse and neglect, and the average length of stay for children in out-of-home placements. The "solution has been instrumental in helping us identify more federal revenue sources. In fact, since September 2009, we've generated about $4M in new revenue—a significant amount that is especially needed in today's economic climate."[10]

The BI system now allows supervisors to monitor their caseworkers' activities in real time, improves information available for case management, and improves compliance. Nucleus Research has calculated that the ROI for this solution is 245% with a 9-month payback.[11]

Predictive Analytics Examples

Case Study: Predictive Policing

Police departments nationwide are using analytics to help predict where and when crime will occur and are using this information to improve their patrol schedules. Dr. Richard Janikowski, Professor of Criminology at the University of Memphis, worked with the Memphis Police Department to "focus police resources intelligently by putting them in the right place, on the right day, at the right time."[12] The project, called *Blue Crush* (Crime Reduction Utilizing Statistical History) has been very successful. Part One crimes, which include homicide, rape, aggravated assault, and car theft, have decreased 27% from 2006 to 2010.[13]

Predictive policing systems such as the Blue Crush system use past data on crimes to predict future crime. The data includes not just information about the date and place of the crime but also contextual data about the day of the week (crime had a different pattern on weekends), time of day, the weather, whether it was pay day or the day social security checks arrived, and what other events were going on in the city, such as a concert. This data is then used to make predictions about when and where future crimes will occur. The LAPD uses a rather sophisticated prediction model based on an earthquake aftershock prediction algorithm (which assumes that aftershocks occur in both a spatial and temporal distribution around the main shock or crime).[14] This information is then fed into a geographic information system (GIS) to create hot spot maps for each police shift. The predictions are dependent upon having a sufficient number of similar crimes to feed into the algorithms. Frequent crimes, such as drug crimes, bike thefts, and battery, are easier to predict accurately than infrequent crimes or unpredictable crimes such as crimes of passion.

The shooting at several military installations in the Northern Virginia area in 2010–11 provides another example of the use of predictive analytics. Someone fired shots at the National Museum of the Marine Corps, the USMC Museum, the Pentagon, and USMC and Coast Guard recruiting facilities. A team assigned to the Virginia Fusion Center created a geospatial predictive model of the first four shootings to "identify the locations that the shooter would most likely target next, based on areas that were geospatially similar to the first four events. Given the size of the area of interest (AOI) and potential resource constraints, the thresholds on the model were set to capture the top 2% most likely areas for a future shooting."[15]

This allowed the police across the region in multiple jurisdictions to allocate their resources to the areas most likely to be attacked. In June 2011, the suspect was apprehended at Arlington National Cemetery, which was one of the hot spots identified by the model. He had planned to desecrate the graves of Iraq and Afghan veterans. This example shows the value of using predictive analytics and "underscores the role that information-based approaches can play in operational law enforcement decision making and resource allocation."[16]

Case Study: Edelman Winning Project with
the General Motors Corporation

The Franz Edelman competition is one of the most interesting technical competitions in the world. The competition, which is sponsored by the Institute for Operations Research and the Management Sciences (INFORMS), attracts a large number of practitioners in the field of Operations Research who vie for this coveted annual award. This competition is a great place to find outstanding examples of analytics projects of exceptional value. One that we would like to highlight is the General Motors (GM) Corporation submission and winner in 2005. The project is entitled "General Motors Increases Its Production Throughput."[17] This paper described a critical business challenge for GM. As discussed in the paper, the competitive environment of the 1980s in the automotive industry was being driven by increased imports by competitors, increased expectations on the part of customers for quality of their automotive purchases, and slow growth in the overall market. This situation led to a very competitive pricing environment, which in turn led to lagging profits for the corporation. Furthermore, the company had fallen behind the competition in their productivity and needed to respond to a critical situation.

The GM research and development (R&D) organization took on the challenge to create tools to turn around the productivity and a related throughput problem in their manufacturing operations. The primary tools they had to bring to the table were advanced analytics. However, this was not an overnight activity. The R&D organization realized that they needed improvements in the availability of data, the models that they used to analyze that data, and improvements in the manufacturing processes (related to throughput). This ended up being a nearly 20-year activity. However, the results were outstanding for the company.

The core analytical methodologies that the R&D organization used were simulation of the manufacturing processes. In some cases they developed their own proprietary tools, and in some cases they used off-the-shelf simulation tools. The manufacturing detail built into these models was quite incredible, as they analyzed production lines, job routing, different types of processing, and conveyance systems. They investigated uncertainty in these processes as well as timing issues that could have negative impacts on the total throughput. In building their own proprietary tools, they were able to integrate the modeling capability into systems used by the managers, and brought them a much expanded set of metrics related to throughput, allowing much stronger and better management of the production process.

One of the other aspects of this work focused on the data. Typically, when one thinks about analytics projects, the focus is on models; however, it is clearly the responsibility of the analytics professional also to be thinking very hard about the data, and in some cases to take on the task of acquiring data that has not been available in the past. Often, at the beginning of a project, the right data is simply not collected. In many cases the data is created and exists for a short period of time in some system, but is not saved. The problem with the production line data that GM needed was that it was massive. The research team had the challenge of defining the right amount of data to retain. Furthermore, in many cases they had to seek the collection of new data that had not been obtained previously. One example, in the referenced paper, was the existence of robotic welders, stamping presses, numerically controlled machining centers, and parts conveyance systems. These pieces of equipment experience a massive number of "production events" which had historically not been monitored or counted. One of the many contributions of this work was to create systems that would obtain counts of these critical production events, and to use this information in the simulation models described above.

These years of work had major impacts on the productivity of GM's manufacturing processes, and have been a strong legacy of continued growth and success for the corporation since their implementation in the middle of the first 10 years of this century.

Text Analytics Example

Case Study: Seton Healthcare

The Affordable Care Act established the Hospital Readmissions Reduction Program, which requires CMS (Centers for Medicare and Medicaid Services) to reduce payments to hospitals with excess readmissions. In response to this and other pressures, Seton Healthcare, a healthcare provider in central Texas, decided to try a data-driven approach to identify those patients with congestive heart failure that might end up back in the hospital within 30 days.

Aware of IBM's Watson, the Jeopardy!-playing computer, Seton approached IBM to see if some of the technology could be of value. Watson made extensive use of natural language processing along with machine learning to answer the questions posed in *Jeopardy!* Could a similar approach be used to analyze all the data that Seton had on patients? Three years of data from Seton was ingested for analysis including electronic health records, cost data, and administrative data.[18] From the medical literature, a list of over 100 predictors was identified for consideration. Some of these were from structured data such as blood pressure and heart rate, while others came from the doctors and nurses notes. A Natural Language Processing (NLP) system was developed to process the unstructured data to extract words and their frequencies and correlations from these notes and other text.

After analyzing 113 predictors, Seton learned that the unstructured data provided the key to predicting which patients would be readmitted. Many of the factors they had anticipated being useful, were not helpful. The factors they did find to be useful, such as smoking indications, were more accurate in unstructured information than in the structured information—if it existed at all in the structured information. The amazing thing to us is how much it is things outside, not necessarily the lab values or clinical measures, that are big predictors... A physician may note that [lack of a transportation] when interacting with patient, but in a traditional electronic medical record, there is no place to put that piece of information, according to Ryan Leslie, VP for Analytics and Health Economics at Seton.[19] "Seton's analysis revealed that social factors were contributing to whether or not a patient was readmitted, namely assisted living and alcohol abuses."[20] This information was only available from the unstructured data, such as notes from the clinical social worker.

NLP and text analytics provide the ability to do analytics on material that was originally developed for human consumption only, such as the doctor's notes. Therefore, a much broader range of information is available to analyze. In addition, these techniques are more flexible for handling new predictive factors, since they do not require the creation of new relational databases or the modification of old ones, with their schemas and database administrator expenses. Seton Healthcare is now in the process of evaluating NLP and text analytics for other applications.

Prescriptive (Optimization) Analytics Example

Case Study: Edelman Winning Project with the Memorial Sloan–Kettering Cancer Center

Another example we are highlighting is also a Franz Edelman prize winning project that was work done by Professor Eva Lee of the Georgia

Institute of Technology and Marco Zaider of the Memorial Sloan–Kettering Cancer Center.

Their work, "Operations Research Advances Cancer Therapeutics," was the Edelman winner in 2007.[21] In their submission and as described in the paper, they explain how optimization was used as a tool in the battle against prostate cancer.

As described in the paper's Introduction, prostate cancer is "the most common form of cancer diagnosed in men and remains the second cancer killer of men in the United States." In addition, nearly every currently used treatment for this disease has a very high likelihood of devastating side effects including incontinence and sexual dysfunction. The stated goals of this work were "(a) to reduce cancer-related mortality ..., and (b) to lessen treatment-associated morbidity." This truly groundbreaking work was able to meet both of these goals, and the primary tool that Lee and Zaider brought to the table was analytics in the form of optimization.

The specific treatment that these researchers were focused on was the method called *brachytherapy*, whereby radioactive "seeds" are placed inside the prostate at the site of the tumor. The challenge was to determine the optimal placement of the seeds in real time so that plans can be done in the operation room, eliminating pre-operation knowledge, discrepancies, and thus reducing the chance of the debilitating side effects mentioned above. In addition, the new approach allowed physicians to re-optimize rapidly and dynamically during the course of the implementation, for example if one of the needles could not reach the originally intended location. Such rapid reconfiguration allows for better planning and improved outcomes.

The specifics of the methodologies used are well beyond the scope of this chapter; however, for those who are interested in the details, they are contained in the cited paper. The key message, however, is that advanced analytics can have a huge impact on solving problems, and even in areas that one does not typically think of for the use of such tools. The computational problems were actually quite challenging, but the researchers solved the problem and produced a tool that could be used in a clinical setting. The paper documents the clinical outcomes and the improvement over conventional methods. The method became standard practice across the country.

Mixed Predictive/Optimization Analytics Example

Case Study: TSA Combines Optimization and Simulation to Schedule Officers at Airport Checkpoints[22]

The following quote appears in the Website of the Transportation Security Administration:

> Following September 11, 2001, the Transportation Security Administration (TSA) was created to strengthen the security of the nation's transportation systems and ensure the freedom of movement for people and commerce. Today, TSA secures the nation's airports and screens all commercial airline passengers and baggage. TSA uses a risk-based strategy and works closely with transportation, law enforcement and intelligence communities to set the standard for excellence in transportation security.[23]

Each day approximately 2 million people interact with this agency as they board airplanes in the United States. The job of making sure that there are the right number of TSA officers, the more than 50,000 professionals who are stationed at the more than 750 check points and more than 1,000 baggage screening locations at the roughly 400 major airports in the country, is very complex. On one hand, there needs to be enough staff so that the waiting time to move through the extensive security processes is reasonable. On the other hand, this is a government activity that is funded by taxpayer dollars, so the agency has a responsibility to spend the taxpayer's money wisely. To ensure that the most efficient yet cost-effective decisions are being made with regard to staffing, the TSA turned to business analytics to help them approach this challenging problem.

An unusual and interesting aspect of this problem is that it was solved using a mix of two major analytics tools. Simulation was used to develop the demand profiles of arriving passengers. Then optimization was used to determine the most efficient starting and stopping times for shifts, and the associated number of people on each shift, so that the total cost was minimized subject to the constraints related to service levels. This is a commonplace type of problem for advanced business analytics. It does not mean that the solution was easy, because such problems can become quite large and difficult and lengthy to solve. However, in this case the solution was both timely and elegant.

The simulation component of the project created a demand profile using discrete event simulation. The basic idea of this model is to use the most updated information about the number of flights and the number of new passengers entering each of those flights. For the flight information the model accessed the Official Airline Guide (OAG), a data source that can be updated daily. For the passenger information, the TSA was able to access statistical data from the U.S. Bureau of Transportation Statistics, which records information on the numbers of passengers by flight (the fill rate) and the number of those passengers that were transitioning (changing from a different plane) rather than originating. Additionally, TSA incorporated information about behavioral patterns of arrival, that is, how many passengers historically arrive 120, 90, 60 (etc.) minutes before a departing flight. Finally, the model used specific data on the number and type of machines and the number of available lanes at each checkpoint. Combining all of these data into a model allowed the estimation of a typical arrival profile throughout the day. As needed, they can provide a weekly average profile, or profiles to specific days of the week, or a specific day of the year.

Having these profiles, the next question is: how many staff are needed? This used standing business rules for the number of staff needed to process the predicted passenger demand in each time period of interest. This was combined with the work rules relating to such things as the number of split shifts, full time shifts, and so on that are allowed to compute the optimal number of shifts needed and the number of each type of worker.

The models that were developed have been deployed at all 400 airport management organizations and are used as well as centrally by the TSA headquarters management. The tools are used centrally for budgeting and planning, and locally by the TSA local airport managers.

THE ANALYTICS PROCESS

This section provides a general methodology for implementing an analytics project. It is based on the well-known CRISP-DM (Cross-Industry Standard Process for Data Mining) 1.0,[24] with some modifications to make it applicable to many types of analytics projects.

The lifecycle of an analytics project consists of the seven phases shown in Figure 2.2.[25] While the phases look like they must be performed in a rigid order, this is not what is intended. Iteration will be required among the phases. The arrows indicate the strongest dependencies between the

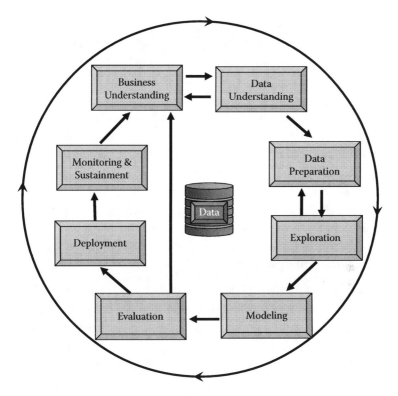

FIGURE 2.2
The Analytics Process. (Adapted from CRISP-DM SIG Workshop, 2007.)

tasks, but in reality the practitioner will move back and forth between the phases, refining the phases in the process.

Before Starting an Analytics Project

Preparation is key. Understand the organization—spend time in advance of the project to acquire this understanding. This will involve comprehending the current processes and why these processes are not producing the outcomes that the managers of the organization desire. Understand what has already been tried but did not work.

Phase 1: Business Understanding

This phase focuses on understanding the project objectives and requirements from a business perspective, and then using this understanding to define the analytics problem that will be solved. The project objectives must be clearly defined along with a way to measure success down the road. Understand what is currently inhibiting the customer from achieving their strategic goals and what information would help their decision process.

Additionally, this phase needs to include planning for the follow-on phases. Who are the end users of the analytics and how might they interface with the analytics? How should the results be visualized? Organizational change management issues and business process re-engineering should be carefully studied. Of particular importance is to plan for the future deployment of the system into operation. Considerations include performance monitoring, compliance requirements, scalability, and user training. This phase may be the single most important one. All the other phases are dependent on the successful completion of this phase.

Phase 2: Data Understanding

This phase begins with initial data collection and includes activities to get familiar with the data, identify data quality problems, understanding data access issues and the data environment, and all data definitions. In this phase, the first steps are taken to find out what insights might be gained from the existing data, and what data is missing that must be acquired.

Phase 3: Data Preparation

This phase includes all activities needed to convert the incoming raw data to data that can be used by the analytics. A key aspect is to be able to relate the analytics requirements to the available data. Tasks may include table, record, and attribute selection, defining the data model, and transforming and cleansing the data so that it can be used in the following steps. What practitioners quickly learn is that the data understanding and preparation phases (often called *data cleansing*—which might also include data acquisition within the organization) is the longest in duration, and often the most politically challenging aspect of a project. It is politically challenging because ownership/stewardship of data within organizations can become very tricky, even emotional, therefore the time and care required to get it done is longer than most people expect it to be.

Phase 4: Exploration

This phase was not in the original CRISP-DM methodology but is becoming increasingly popular with practitioners. The goal is to start exploring the data to gain an understanding of what might be possible with the data, investigate various analytics approaches to the problem, and reduce risk to the following stages. Look at options (including ones that do not include analytics) to bring deeper understanding. This is the hardest part of being successful in analytics (avoid the "hammer looking for a nail" syndrome). It is important to get the business user to provide feedback at this point on both the insights that might result and the implementation approach.

Some iteration with the data preparation phase might be necessary.

Phase 5: Modeling

This phase is where the mathematical analytics work is performed. If the Exploration phase above is not done, this is where various modeling techniques are tried, tested, and applied. Later chapters of this book provide more information on the specifics of these methods. Once the decision is made on which of the approaches to use, this phase is where the actual model is built.

Phase 6: Evaluation

Analytics projects are complex, and there are many opportunities for errors to occur. In this phase, the model is thoroughly evaluated and the data and algorithms are reviewed to ensure that the model is behaving properly and producing correct results. One of the most important aspects of this phase is to evaluate that the business objectives are being achieved. Does the model meet the objectives laid out in Phase 1?

Phase 7: Deployment

In this phase, the analytics are integrated into existing systems and deployed to the organization for use. It will usually involve applying the analytics within the business processes (automated or manual) and systems that drive the organization's decision-making processes. The organizational change management efforts investigated in Phase 1 will now be put into use, including training of end-users and the support team. Care must be taken to ensure that the users understand how to use the analytical results to perform their jobs and that they do not incorrectly interpret the results.

This phase usually includes production of the final documentation and a final report. This report must help to communicate the value of the analytics and how it supports the business objectives. The report and documentation will help management understand the benefits of the system, and users to utilize the analytics to perform their mission.

Phase 8: Monitoring and Sustainment

This phase was also not included in the CRISP-DM 1.0 model, which assumed it would be part of Deployment. However, to emphasize its importance, many projects break this into a separate phase. This phase should include performance measurement, monitoring how well the analytics are working, and plans to refresh the model perhaps including additional data sources. Over time, the analytics must be adapted to changing needs in the organization; the analytics team must learn of these needs and modify the analytics appropriately.

SUMMARY

The goal of this chapter has been to demonstrate that great business or organizational insights can be obtained by the use of analytics. We hope that the examples provided have made this clear. We also hope that the range of areas that can be benefited is quite broad, from public safety to healthcare and manufacturing.

To bring value, a business or organization needs a number of things. First, leadership must recognize the need and put in place the resources that can deliver this value. Second, the plan created by this management level, which would include the people, responsibility, and management guidance, must be implemented. Finally, there is the data. As mentioned above, the data work is often the "long pole" in this tent—requiring the most time and possibly the most budget to complete. However, the benefits can be amazing, ranging from safer and happier citizenry, healthier and longer lives for medical patients, to outstanding business successes.

Learning Exercises

1. Suppose you are the COO of a large manufacturing organization. While you have been in this business for multiple decades, your company is beginning to lose market share. You have heard that analytics is making a difference for businesses. Describe the steps you would go through to turn this business around.

2. Describe three hypothetical organizations, one a government agency, one a retail business, and the other a professional sports team. Include information such as the goals and objectives of the business, the operating situation, the number of employees, where they are located and their "market" or "constituency." For each of these organizations, describe how you would measure "value."

3. For each of the organizations you created in Step 2 above, describe an analytics project that can bring insight to the business.

4. In the movie *Moneyball*, manager Billy Bean uses a predictive model to determine how best to win the 99 games he believes is needed to secure the pennant despite a paltry payroll. Develop a predictive model for the sport of your choice, or if you prefer the salary of a Fortune 100 CEO, based on company size, earnings, and so forth.

5. Use the Analytics Process to plan a hypothetical analytics project.

ENDNOTES

1. Gantz, J. and Reinsel, D., IDC, "The Digital Universe in 2020: Big Data, Bigger Digital Shadows, and Biggest Growth in the Far East," December 2012.
2. IBM Institute for Business Value, "Analytics: The Real World Use of Big Data," *IBM*, October 2012.
3. Brynjolfsson, Erik, Hitt, Lorin M., and Kim, Heekyung Hellen, "Strength in Numbers: How Does Data-Driven Decision Making Affect Firm Performance?" April 22, 2011. Available at SSRN: http://papers.ssrn.com/sol3/papers.cfm?abstract_id=1819486.
4. Nucleus Research, Research Note, "Analytics Pays Back $10.66 for Every Dollar Spent," *Nucleus Research*. Document L122, 2011.
5. IBM, www.ibm.com/gbs/intelligent-enterprise.
6. Rutledge, Dr. Pamela, "How Obama Won the Social Media Battle in the 2012 Presidential Campaign," *The National Psychologist*, January 2013.
7. Petty, A. "Federal Government Continues to Lose Billions to Waste, Fraud, and Abuse," Capital Business, *Washington Post*, March 10, 2013.
8. "Bad Guys Are Getting Better at Credit Card Fraud," *NBC News*, June 15, 2012.
9. Nucleus Research, "ROI Case Study: IBM Business Analytics Clark County Family Services," *Nucleus Research*, September 2010, Doc K46.
10. IBM, "Clark County Family Services Department Selects IBM Cognos BI to Improve Reporting and Compliance," *IBM*, 2010.
11. Nucleus Research, "ROI Case Study: IBM Business Analytics Clark County Family Services," *Nucleus Research*, September 2010, Doc K46.
12. "Harnessing Statistics to Combat Crime," *IBM* IMC141541USEN-02.
13. Ibid.
14. Friend, Zach, "Predictive Policing: Using Technology to Reduce Crime," *FBI Law Enforcement Bulletin*, April 2013.

15. McCue, Colleen et al., "The Northern Virginia Military Shooting Series: Operational Validation of Geospatial Predictive Analytics," *Police Chief Magazine*, April 2013.
16. Ibid.
17. Alden et al., "General Motors Increases Its Production Throughput." *Interfaces* 36(1), January–February 2006, pp. 6–25.
18. Feldman, Susan et al., "Unlocking the Power of Unstructured Data," *IDC Health Insights*, June 2012, #H1235064.
19. Groenfeldt, Tom, "Big Data Delivers Deep Views of Patients for Better Care," *Forbes*, January 20, 2012.
20. Ovum, "Unlocking the Potential of Unstructured Medical Data," *Ovum*, May 11, 2012.
21. Lee, Eva K. and Zaider, Marco. "Operations Research Advances Cancer Therapeutics." *Interfaces*, 38(1), January–February 2008, pp. 5–25.
22. Coffman, Michael and Greenland, Arnold. Integrated Simulation and Optimization of Airport Security Resources. Presented at INFORMS Business Analytics and Operations Research Conference, Huntington Beach, California, April 15–17, 2012.
23. Transportation Security Administration at http://www.tsa.gov/about-tsa.
24. Chapman, Peter et al. CRISP-DM 1.0, SPSS, 2000, CRISPMWP-1104.
25. Adapted from CRISP-DM 2.0: Special Interest Group (SIG) Workshop, January 2007.

3

Executive/Performance Dashboards

Patrick Yurgosky

CONTENTS

Learning Objectives

After completing this chapter, you will be able to:

- Articulate the past, present, and future of dashboards.
- Articulate what a dashboard is, how it differs from reports and scorecards, and the key considerations when building a dashboard.
- Effectively communicate types of dashboards and how they should be structured.
- Define a KPI and how it should be displayed on a dashboard.
- Understand the key design principles and media considerations when creating a dashboard.

Businesses are rapidly changing, faced with new pressures to reduce costs and develop new opportunities within constantly changing markets, all while being more socially responsible. To achieve these results, organizations are increasingly adopting a "data driven" culture to increase the transparency within their operations, to better understand and engage their customers, and to manage toward a strategic vision.

Making sound decisions on data is easier said than done. While many organizations have adopted a "data driven" culture, the reality is that over one-third of managers still make decisions based on judgment or gut feeling, and nearly 50% do not provide the necessary transparency about how key decisions are made.[*] To overcome the challenges of developing a true data driven culture, organizations are increasingly adopting performance dashboards to monitor markets, manage their business, and drive strategy.

By some estimates nearly two-thirds of organizations are adopting dashboard tools, yet the failure rates are incredibly high; 56–80% of business

---

[*] Harvard Business Review Analytic Services. "The Evolution of Decision Making: How Leading Organizations Are Adopting a Data-Driven Culture." Harvard Business School Publishing, 2012.

intelligence projects fail.* These abysmal figures are a result of a two-pronged failure: (1) misalignment between the strategy of the organization and the data points used for management and (2) inappropriate visual display of the data making managing to numbers confusing and difficult.

This chapter is designed to dramatically increase your chances of successfully overcoming these hurdles through the use of dashboards. To do this, we focus on the two primary reasons for failure by discussing how to successfully create and implement strategic metrics (KPI) and how to use the most compelling media and dashboard design to display those metrics.

HISTORY

Dashboards began as Executive Information Systems (EIS) in the 1980s. These systems were based on the mainframe computer model and numbered only a few, as the complexity and price made them only accessible to large organizations. The visuals were simple and primarily focused on financial metrics; however, these systems set the stage for the burgeoning business intelligence and visualization market.

The late 1980s gave rise to Business Intelligence (BI), which built upon EIS but incorporated more advanced technology—such as data warehousing and online analytical processing (OLAP)—to overcome some of its previous barriers. By the 1990s the systems were becoming more widespread and were adopted by a variety of industries to manage financial, operational, and other business departments.

In 1992, Robert Kaplan and David Norton wrote their famous article in the *Harvard Business Review*: "The Balanced Scorecard—Measures That Drive Performance." The concept of the balanced scorecard, which ties together metrics from all the core aspects of a business—financial, operations, sales, marketing, etc.—to develop leading and lagging indicators of success, gave rise to the study of Business Performance Management, or BPM. By the late 1990s, the rise of BPM, coupled with the new business

---

* Michael K. Allio, "Strategic Dashboards: Designing and Deploying Them to Improve Implementation," *Strategy & Leadership*, Vol. 40 Issue: 5, pp. 24–31, 2012; 56%—(From André A. de Waal and Harold Counet, "Lessons Learned from Performance Management Systems Implementations," *International Journal of Productivity and Performance Management*, Vol. 58 Issue: 4, pp. 367–390, 2009); 70%—(From Andy Neely and Mike Bourne, "Why Measurement Initiatives Fail," *Measuring Business Excellence*, Vol. 4, Issue: 4 pp. 3–7, 2000); 70–80%—(From *Gartner Business Intelligence Report*, January 2011).

intelligence technology, made dashboards more useful to data-driven executives.

Wide adoption of dashboards began in the early 2000s prompted by two major events: the Enron scandal and the economic downturn.[*] The Enron scandal ushered in a suite of new government regulations, which required executives to have more acute knowledge of their organization's day-to-day activities. Additionally, the economic downturn spurred organizations to incorporate new technology to more efficiently manage business processes. These two events led to substantial growth of the dashboard market and a plethora of new tools designed to keep executives "in the know."

In the mid/late 2000s, the use of cloud computing and open APIs[†] made data management and collection more accessible by reducing infrastructure and knowledge costs. It also allowed more sharing of data across platforms for greater market insights.

In the late 2000s and early 2010s, advances in technology for both data collection and storage led to the rise of *Big Data*—an enormous amount of data created and stored by organizations every second of every day.[‡] However, this growth led to new technical challenges in analyzing the data.[§] In response to the technical shortfalls, there was a renewed focus on the business user and on the "right" metrics to analyze, rather than just more metrics and more data.

QUALITY DASHBOARDS

A good dashboard focuses its viewers' attention on what matters to quickly identify trends, issues, and anomalies, which allow staff at every level of an organization to make better decisions in line with the organization's strategy. In order to achieve this, dashboards must be concise—fixed to one page—and updated frequently enough where the user can make actionable decisions.

---

[*] Few, Stephen. *Information Dashboard Design*. p. 7. O'Reilly Media, Sebastopol, CA, 2006.

[†] Application Programming Interfaces (APIs) allow different technology to connect to share and use data.

[‡] 2.8 zettabyes of data created in 2012 alone (IDC Digital Universe, John Gantz and David Reinsel. "The Digital Universe in 2020: Big Data, Bigger Digital Shadows, The Biggest Growth in the Far East," IDC, Framingham, MA, 2012); this number is expected to grow 300 times by 2020 (Ibid).

[§] Only 3% of this data is tagged and able to be analyzed and only 0.5% is currently analyzed in 2012 (IDC Digital Universe, John Gantz and David Reinsel. "The Digital Universe in 2020: Big Data, Bigger Digital Shadows, The Biggest Growth in the Far East," IDC, Framingham, MA, 2012).

Effective dashboards are tailored to fit the audience's role and offer key metrics that tie to the organization's strategic mission. While everyone is looking at the same metrics, how the data is displayed should be tailored to the specific decisions the viewers must make. Additionally, the frequency of updates should cater to the urgency and types of decisions that need to be made. For example, a stockbroker needs his/her dashboard updated more frequently than the CEO of a paper company.

There are three key attributes that drive a good dashboard:

Quality Metrics—Displaying metrics that are not tied to strategic goals and are not appropriately tailored to the decisions the dashboard's audience must make results in bad decisions and poor strategic execution. The quality of the individual data is also important. If the data generated (and displayed) is not consistent and accurate, the most well-designed metrics are ineffective.

Integrated Metrics—No metric lives in a vacuum; key metrics that drive successful strategy relate to many aspects of the business and strategic execution. Every metric on a dashboard should complement another metric in order to offer greater insight and drive better decisions. It is important that key metrics are on the same screen so the relationships are easily identifiable.

Visual Design—Metrics must be presented in a format that is easily understood at a glance. As we will discuss later, different media offers different perspectives of the data and leads to different insights. If the right metrics are displayed in the wrong way, bad decisions are made.

WHAT IS A DASHBOARD?

Conceptually, a dashboard can be thought of as a story complete with a plot, supporting cast, and descriptive "language," with each work in concert to engage an audience and prompt action. The best dashboards are elegantly simple, consisting of well-designed metrics presented in a format that is accessible and packed with nuanced information.

There are many different definitions of what constitutes a dashboard. The definition we will use here is that a dashboard is a consolidated, visual display of an audience's most important indicators updated as frequently as possible and working in concert to improve the quality of decisions relating to specific objectives. Let's deconstruct this definition.

Consolidated—Dashboards should be designed to fit a single page. The fewer metrics on the dashboard, the better.

Visual—Dashboards consist of different types of media that describe the metrics. The media should be concise and display as much information as possible in every pixel.

Most important indicators—If an indicator does not directly support decisions that impact the strategic goals of the organization, it should not be on the dashboard. There are different opinions of how many metrics constitute too many, but a general guideline is 5–20.

Updated as frequently as possible—Dashboards require the right information at the right time. The sooner information can populate a dashboard, the better. The best default is real time. Only when the cost of a real-time solution outweighs the benefit should another frequency be considered.

Working in concert—Metrics do not live in isolation on a dashboard; they work together to allow viewers to quickly identify how activity in one segment of the business impacts outcomes in another segment.

Specified objectives—Dashboards are about focusing the viewer's attention to make a decision, even if that decision is to do nothing. Every dashboard should be designed with specific decisions in mind.

REPORTS, SCORECARDS, AND DASHBOARDS

Reports, scorecards, and dashboards are all similar, but they have some key differences.

Reports—A report displays static, historical information about a specific item or metric. Reports offer more in-depth analysis on the metric—for example, revenue—to make a specific management decision. Because of their nature, they tend to be updated less frequently.

Scorecards—The scorecard was originally developed by Robert Kaplan in 1992 and is designed for a 360° view of a business. While a report is focused on a single metric or indicator, scorecards include a variety of indicators tied to a strategic objective with defined goals.

Scorecards are meant to track the progress toward a goal and various sub-goals, and identify areas needing attention. Because they track progress toward a goal, scorecards are updated regularly, and generally used by executives who must monitor performance across many different verticals of a business.

Dashboards—Dashboards are often described as scorecards. They are similar insofar as they display key metrics and track their progress to goals, but they tend to be updated more frequently (default to real time) and they cascade through the organization's hierarchy through tailored metrics and goals that are directly tied to strategy. While they were once relegated to only the highest corporate executive, any person in an organization may now use dashboards. They are predominantly used by staff in roles that require the monitoring, management, and analysis of business processes.

DASHBOARD STRUCTURE

Dashboard Types

Defining dashboard types is important, as it gives sufficient context for the dashboard audience and the included metrics and structures. Here, we discuss four major types—strategic, tactical, operational, and analytical.* Each type of dashboard is designed to answer questions through unique metrics and data for a specified audience. Although each dashboard type focuses on a certain audience, it is common for different types to be accessible to multiple audiences within an organization even though a single type is most relevant.

Each type of dashboard serves a specific purpose and a specific audience. While independent, the dashboards, through common measures, shall give a comprehensive view of the health of an organization from different levels. The dashboards fit into a hierarchy that is defined by how summarized the data is and the insight the audience is looking to garner from the data.

---

* Gail La Grouw also describes an "Individual" dashboard, which we will not include here. In theory, any of the types of dashboards we outline could be meant for an individual.

Before we define each type of dashboard, we will discuss the different terminology.

Strategy—An organization's strategy is defined by its long-term, high-level goal. It is often referred to as the *organization's vision*.

Tactics—An organization's tactics are shorter-term goals that support the strategy. These are usually specific initiatives or projects that are focused on an area within the organization.

Operations—An organization's operations are specific, physical activities being performed to pursue its strategic and tactical goals. Without operations, the organization would cease to exist; therefore, these activities occur frequently and regularly.

Executives set the strategy, middle managers execute the tactics, and front-line staff manages operations. In practice, the strategy allows middle managers to make better decisions when choosing between different tactics and the tactical goals allow operations staff to make better day-to-day decisions. For instance, if an organization's strategy is to be the market-leader in customer service, a middle manager faced with a myriad of options might execute a tactic to increase the organization's online sentiment rating, prompting front-line customer service staff to encourage customers to post good experiences online. Table 3.1 illustrates the types of dashboards and how they compare.

Later in this chapter, we discuss the specific metrics on each of these dashboards and how to establish a succinct hierarchy of indicators across different types of dashboards. While a person within a certain strata of the organization generally uses each type of dashboard, they can be applied to any role. Let's look at each type of dashboard independently.

TABLE 3.1

Dashboard Types, Insight, and Data

	Strategic	**Tactical**	**Operational**	**Analytical**
Insight	What	When and Where	Who and How	Why
Data	High-level Summary	Mid-level Summary	Transactional	Transactional

Source: Adopted from Table 2: Levels of BI, La Grouw, Gail, "Effective Dashboard Design," p. 20. *Electrosmart*, Auckland, NZ, 2012.

Strategic Dashboards

Strategic dashboards are otherwise known as executive dashboards. These dashboards display the most high-level summary data and are focused on monitoring an organization's progress to achieving strategic goals and identifying potential threats. They have traditionally been used by executives but are increasingly being adopted by staff at all levels within an organization to promote increased transparency. These dashboards are also described as scorecards because their metrics display progress toward specific strategic goals across different verticals within the organization.

The metrics displayed on these dashboards tend to be the most summarized and are designed to quickly identify if a strategic metric is currently above/below its goal or if there is a possible future threat. Strategic dashboards should offer drill-down capability for a structured view of each of the tactics. While with new technology many dashboards are constantly updated, in practice these dashboards need updating less frequently than other types of dashboards.

Tactical Dashboards

A tactical dashboard is meant to manage the tactics an organization has chosen to achieve its strategy and help identify potential opportunities to better do so. As previously described, tactics and strategy are differentiated by scope. The same is true for strategic and tactical dashboards. Tactical dashboards tend to be used by middle management and are focused on managing people and projects.

Tactical dashboards usually contain comparative metrics that allow viewers to understand what/who is driving success or failure. For example, while a strategic dashboard might contain a metric of revenue to date, a tactical dashboard might contain revenue by geography or by sales unit to date.

Operational Dashboards

Operational dashboards allow front-line workers to monitor and manage the day-to-day activities of an organization. These dashboards tend to be transactional in nature—that is, the number of cars painted, the number of service requests received, etc.—and must be refreshed more frequently than strategic or tactical dashboards.

Operational dashboards are designed to monitor several processes at once to keep operations moving as efficiently as possible. Each metric on the dashboard will typically have a threshold, or minimum value, as well as a goal. For example, an operational dashboard for a front-line, assembly-line manager might monitor paint levels in each machine on a car painting line. When a machine's paint level drops below a threshold the manager knows that he needs to add additional paint to keep the line moving efficiently.

Analytical Dashboards

Stephen Few, one of the originators of dashboard design, describes analytical dashboards as using information that "demands greater context, such as rich comparisons, more extensive history, and subtler performance evaluators... more sophisticated display media... [and] interactions with the data." With these dashboards, "it is not enough to see that sales are decreasing; when your purpose is analysis, you must be made aware of such patterns so you can explore them to discover what is causing the decrease and how it might be corrected." Few, Stephan. "Information Dashboard Design: The Effective Communication of Data." O'Reilly Media, Sebastopol, CA, 2006. p. 41.

Analytical dashboards are used for exploration of data; therefore, they should be less structured than the other types of dashboards. They require the most sophisticated drill-down capabilities, so analysts can discover the underlying cause of an issue when the more formal structure of other types of dashboards does not suffice. Since analytical dashboards are for exploration and discovery, real-time updates are not a requirement. However, as issues are identified on other dashboards these dashboards must be updated with at least the same frequency. Put another way, analytical dashboards should be updated at least as frequently as the most frequently updated dashboard within an organization in order to accurately research issues. When in doubt, default to real-time updates.

Layers of a Dashboard

Like an onion, effective dashboards contain layers of information. Each layer allows the audience to obtain greater detail about a metric (or series of metrics) to better understand or identify a problem. Wayne Eckerson formalized a structure of information layers called *MAD.*[*] MAD is an

---

[*] Eckerson, Wayne. *Performance Dashboards: Measuring, Monitoring, and Managing Your Business*, 2nd ed. p. 13. Wiley, Hoboken, NJ, 2011.

abbreviation for Monitor, Analyze, and "Drill to Detail", however, *drill to detail* is also commonly described as *detail.*

Within the MAD structure, the Monitor layer represents the highest-level view of a metric within a dashboard. These metrics help the dashboard's audience identify emerging trends, anomalies, and issues as early as possible. When the audience wishes to see more detail about a metric, they would be taken to the Analyze level to view segments of the information.

The Analyze level displays greater details about a metric but remains in a summarized format. These sub-metrics should vary depending on the dashboard's audience, as different levels of the organization will have different requirements and different questions about the information. For example, an executive might have a metric on their dashboard for sales above (or below) a target for the week. If the executive sees that they are below target, clicking on the metric would display sales by region. However, a regional sales manager might click on the metric and view sales by product or by a more detailed geography. Sometimes, the Analyze level could also be a tactical dashboard.

The most detailed layer is aptly described as *Detail.* This layer will often include transactional data or another level of more detailed information that is relevant to the audience. Using the example above, the executive might drill to an additional layer that displays sales/quota by salesperson, which would be sufficient level of detail to understand who to speak to about a problem. However, the regional sales manager might view each realized sales order over the week against its projected amount.

Dashboards should have as many layers of information as necessary for their audience. However, the MAD structure provides a sufficient guidepost to use across different types. One core goal in dashboard design is to keep the information elegantly simple; each layer of information adds an additional layer of administration and complexity. Therefore, allowing users to drill through more than three layers of information is generally not a good idea unless it an analytical dashboard.

INDICATORS

Good data is at the core of every effective dashboard. This does not just mean accurate data, it also means metrics and indicators that are aligned with the organization's strategy and that work together to promote more effective decision making. Without metrics that provide action-able insight, the dashboard's audience is left with little more than a nice-looking Website. In this section, we discuss dashboard metrics, how to create them, and how they are used to drive performance.

Metrics and Indicators

Metrics are numerical values that represent a defined attribute at a point in time or within a time frame. They are measured using four different categorical scales: nominal, ordinal, interval, and ratio.

Nominal—Differentiates data by name only; there is no other defined order (for example, a list of products sold).

Ordinal—Differentiates by rank or order (such as first, second, third, etc.) without defining the extent of the difference between each ranking; the order allows them to be compared and sorted. For example, in a foot race the first-place finisher may have finished an hour ahead of the second-place finisher, but on an ordinal scale we would only know that they were first.

Interval—Differentiates based on the degree of the difference, such as temperature (100°C is twice as hot as 50°C).

Ratio—Identifies a level of magnitude of an attribute based on another attribute or value and incorporating a zero value. For example, 50 pennies is 50% of a dollar.

Indicators are metrics that compare results against a baseline or target of performance that *indicates* if the metric's result is good or bad. Indicators are used to evaluate the failure or success of an aspect of the organization—a key project, operational efficiency, etc.

There are two types of indicators: *leading* and *lagging*. Leading indicators are predictive because they are a precursor to a defined outcome and drive performance. Lagging indicators are reactive because they are reminiscent of an activity (or result of an activity) that has already occurred. Leading and lagging indicators are also described as *predictive* and *reactive indicators*.

Many indicators can be both leading and lagging at the same time depending on the context in which they are displayed. Think of a traffic light. A yellow light is a *lagging* indicator to a green light, as it occurs after a light has been green but before it turns red. But the yellow light is also a *leading* indicator of a red light, as it allows drivers to know that the light will soon turn red. A red light is a lagging indicator of the yellow light.

If this sounds confusing, you are not alone. When a group of participants were described a scenario and given a metric, 50% described the metric as leading and 50% described it as lagging. To overcome this, David Parmenter has proposed to redefine metric types as *past, current,* and *future* metrics to clarify how they are meant to be used across an organization's hierarchy.* For example, if an organization wanted to drive sales, a dashboard may display sales over the last month (past), pending sales (current), and future sales based on the current pipeline, stage, and probability (future).

Types of Indicators

There are four primary types of indicators we will discuss here: KRI, KPI, RI, and PI. Each of these types differs in the scale of their impact on the organization's strategy and whether they indicate past performance or drive future performance. In many cases the category of a metric will be up to you, but it is important to understand these categories, as it will help you to tailor indicators for specific audiences.

Key Results Indicators

Key Results Indicators (KRI) display key past performance. These indicators are the *results* of a strategy (lagging indicator) and are generally used for the Board, as they indicate how well management has performed against the organization's goals. Examples include last quarter's total sales, YTD net profit, and overall customer satisfaction in the previous fiscal year (FY).

Key Performance Indicators

A Key Performance Indicator (KPI) is used to drive an organization's progress toward a strategic goal. These are leading indicators that directly impact the organization's strategy. They are used throughout the organization, but are defined and monitored by the executive team.

---

* Parmenter, David. *Key Performance Indicators for Government and Nonprofit Agencies.* pp. 79–80. Wiley, Hoboken, NJ, 2012.

Focusing an organization on a strategic goal requires alignment of indicators across all levels and functions within an organization. To achieve this alignment, organizations focus business units on a concrete set of KPI that "cascade" across all dashboards at every level, from the executive's strategic dashboard to the front-line staff's operational dashboard. This alignment of indicators is called *cascading indicators*, which we discuss later in the chapter.

Every organization's KPIs are unique, since every organization's operations and strategy are unique. However, all successful KPIs contain the same key attributes:

Owned—There should a person who is responsible for the KPI at every level and every vertical of an organization. When issues or questions arise, it is clear whom to speak with.

Understandable—Staff at every level of the organization must understand how a KPI is calculated. This will allow them to innovate how it measures performance and how to create organizational processes to better drive its success. The simpler, the better.

Actionable—Staff should know what to do to influence a KPI. The KPI should prompt decisions, not additional questions. When staff can clearly state their role in influencing a KPI, they can manage to it.

Measurable—The KPI must be a single metric that can be benchmarked and plotted over time.

Leading—The KPI must indicate future performance.

Timely—The data must be able to be sufficiently refreshed to make the KPI actionable.

Strategic—The KPI must be tied directly to the organization's vision and be able to be acted upon by everyone in the organization—from the CEO to front-end staff.

Each of these attributes is equally important as they work in concert to support one another to drive the success of a KPI. There is not a magic number that produces the best results, but in all cases, the fewer KPIs, the better. Fewer KPIs signal a more focused strategy that allows staff to better align their efforts to understand and support it. Many organizations create as many KPIs as their dashboards can hold, which is counterproductive. Every metric added to a dashboard erodes the individual impact of all the other metrics that are in place.

One of the most famous examples of using KPIs to drive a successful strategy comes from British Airways (BA) in the 1980s, when Lord King took control as chairman. At the time, BA "was inefficient, overstaffed and reported a loss of nearly $1 billion."*

To make BA profitable again, King hired consultants to help him identify the organization's KPI. The consultants came back with a single focus: the timely departure of planes. Lord King was not amused, as every airline attempted to leave on time as frequently as possible. In response, the consultants noted that while there were many critical factors that lead to success, this was *the* critical factor that leads to success.†

Timely flight departure became BA's KPI. It was simple to understand, it could be "owned," it was easily measurable and actionable, and it was a leading indicator of the core metrics that drive profit—it resulted in lower operating costs and higher revenue through repeat business.

In practice, Lord King "was notified, wherever he was in the world, if a BA plane was delayed. The BA manager at the relevant airport knew that if a plane was delayed beyond a certain 'threshold,' they would receive a personal call from the BA official. It was not long before BA planes had a reputation for leaving on time."‡

The strategy led to decreased costs through less airport surcharges and less overnight accommodations for passengers on missed flights; it led to higher revenue through greater customer satisfaction due to less missed flights, and fewer employee issues because they did not need to deal with disgruntled customers.§ "By the fiscal year that ended in March 1987 [six years after King came onboard], its profits were among the industry's highest at $284 million."¶

Other Indicators—RI and PI

There are many other more nuanced indicators that are important but do not fit the attributes of a KPI or KRI. These indicators, termed

* Martin, Douglas. "Lord King, Who Remade British Airways, Dies at 87." *The New York Times*, 2005. http://www.nytimes.com/2005/07/13/business/worldbusiness/13king.html?_r=0.
† Parmenter, David. *Critical Success Factors*. 30 April 2010. http://csf.davidparmenter.com/.
‡ Parmenter, David. *Key Performance Indicators for Government and Nonprofit Agencies*. p. 74. Wiley, 2012.
§ Parmenter, David. *Key Performance Indicators for Government and Nonprofit Agencies*. p. 75. Wiley, Hoboken, NJ, 2012.
¶ Martin, Douglas. "Lord King, Who Remade British Airways, Dies at 87." *The New York Times*, 2005. http://www.nytimes.com/2005/07/13/business/worldbusiness/13king.html?_r=0.

Results Indicators (RIs) and *Performance Indicators* (PIs), are instrumental in day-to-day operations and are used by front-end staff and middle managers, but do not directly influence strategic initiatives. These indicators are often more individually focused, allowing staff to monitor their own performance against their peers or manage to a threshold to keep operations moving.

Similar to KRI, RI are *lagging* indicators that display historical results. These indicators may impact profit or some other positive outcome that is worth monitoring but are not directly tied to the current strategy. Examples may include the number of calls to a customer service center, gallons of fuel used in a shipping fleet, and kilowatts used in the last 48 hours in a data center.

Similar to KPI, PIs are *leading* indicators that allow staff to focus efforts to achieve a specific goal. These indicators may relate to an organization's KPI but do not directly tie to the current strategy. For instance, BA may have had a performance indicator for liters of fuel used per flight; the indicator does not directly tie to their strategic focus, but does impact expenses as more fuel usage decreases profit.

The Magic Number of Indicators

The number of KPI, KRI, PI, and RI on a dashboard can greatly influence what gets tracked and managed. Every additional indicator added to a dashboard decreases the impact of all the other indicators of the dashboard. Therefore, there has been a lot of discussion to determine the optimal amount.

Because every organization is different, it is difficult to apply fixed number of indicators for success. However, a smaller number of indicators generally result in a more focused strategy, easier implementation, and greater impact on the organization's bottom line. David Parmenter created a 10/80/10 rule. He suggests that every organization should have about 10 KRI, 80 RI/PI, and 10 KPI.* The 10/80/10 rule can also be thought of as a *ratio* of indicators. Therefore, if an organization chose 10 indicators to track on a dashboard, 1 would be KPI, 1 KRI, and 8 PI/RI.

As a rule of thumb, any new indicators should have a greater impact than the average impact of all the other indicators on the dashboard.

---

* Parmenter, David. *Key Performance Indicators for Government and Nonprofit Agencies.* p. 81. Wiley, Hoboken, NJ, 2012.

Abiding by this rule will ensure that dashboards continue to become increasingly effective.

Data Organization and Terminology

The value of an indicator to a given audience is fueled by the data that it presents; however, more data records do not necessarily make an indicator more valuable. To understand the best summation of data within an indicator, we need to first understand what data is and how it is aggregated.

Dashboards display information that has been collected and stored in a database. Here we discuss the most basic aspects of how data is stored in a database—columns and rows. Think of a Microsoft Excel spreadsheet. Within the spreadsheet you have cells, and each cell has a location that is defined by the intersection of a corresponding column (A,B,C,D, etc.) and row (1,2,3,4, etc.).

A new transaction—such as a sale, a car assembled, a plane departing—creates a new row in the database. These rows are called *records*. Records can either be created by humans manually entering data or by machines programmed to create them when certain activities occur. Records represent a point in time when some type of data is collected. Every row or record contains columns, which provide descriptive information about the transaction or activity. These columns are called *fields*. For instance, if a record represents a new sale, the columns might be the amount, the client, the products sold, date of sale, etc.

Displaying all of an organization's records on a dashboard would be counterproductive, so we use indicators to summarize the records based on fields, such as the transaction date, client, etc. The amount of records, and thus field data, that is summarized in the metric should vary depending on the dashboard's audience because the amount of records summarized in an indicator can dramatically change its meaning. In the next section, we discuss how different audiences value different amounts of data within indicators.

Summarizing Data to Provide Maximum Value to the Audience

As you know, there are different types of dashboards that specialize in informing decisions for different audiences. If the amount of data summarized within an indicator is not properly tailored to its audience, it can result in confusion, misalignment of strategy, missed opportunities, poor adoption rates, and other issues. Therefore, the better the alignment between the indicator's data and the dashboard's audience, the greater the value the indicator has on the organization's strategic success.

As data ages and aggregates, it becomes less useful for front-end staff who are closer to the transaction. Transaction-specific data, present on an operational dashboard, provides the greatest value to front-end staff. For example, if a hospital's KPIs were created to decrease patient wait time, a reception room manager would likely find specific data about how long an individual patient has been waiting more useful than aggregate data about the average wait time in the last 24 hours.

The closer the dashboard's intended audience is to operational transactions, the fewer records should be included in their dashboard's indicators. However, as records age and are aggregated with other older records, they become more useful for executives on their strategic dashboard. As a single KPI summarizes more records, the more valuable it becomes for strategic insight and thus for an executive audience. Figure 3.1 offers a graphical display of this relationship.

Meanwhile, for an executive driven by strategy, the cascading KPI on his or her dashboard would display the same data, yet with more records and over a broader time frame, because strategic dashboards are meant for tracking progress toward a goal. For this audience, the waiting room KPI would be most effective by displaying aggregate records so the executive could track if waiting room times are increasing or decreasing over time.

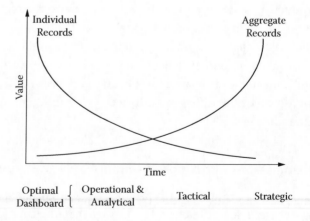

FIGURE 3.1
Record value over time.

Implementing Performance Indicators

Now that we have discussed what performance indicators are, the types of indicators, their key attributes, and how data summation plays a role in their success, we will discuss the core phases of adopting dashboards throughout an organization. The three phases* are:

1. Information insight and transparency
2. Strategy
3. Repeatable process

In the **information insight and transparency phase**, metrics are collected and shared throughout the organization. At this point, the metrics are likely defined by different managers at various levels within different verticals. The information has historically been kept in spreadsheets, deemed proprietary, and sharing did not readily occur except in special occasions on a summary level. During this phase, the indicators are recorded, and similarities and redundancies become apparent. Different verticals learn from one another and best practices begin to be defined. This phase is usually facilitated by consultants with significant executive involvement.

In the **strategy phase**, an organization usually embarks on a strategic planning process, which defines the organization's strategic goals and analyzes the outputs of different departments. Metrics are then streamlined and tied to the strategic goals. This phase is also generally facilitated with consultants with heavy executive input. During this phase, the goal is to make sense of the many metrics collected in the first phase, determine which metrics are critical to success, and then rank them according to their strategic impact to form a unified suite of KPI, KRI, RI, and PI that cascade throughout the organization.

Finally, the organization begins the **repeatable process phase**. During this phase, the strategic metrics are implemented across the organization, dashboards become commonplace, and everyone is aware of how their day-to-day processes impact the organization's strategic goals. The importance of this phase cannot be overstated. This is where many organizations fail, as defining the indicators is not enough; organizations are made of people and it is the front-line staff and middle management that will make

* La Grouw, Gail. "Effective Dashboard Design: Design Secrets to Getting More Value from Performance Dashboards." p. 27. *Electrosmart*, Auckland, NZ, 2012.

this endeavor a success or failure. This phase generally requires input from change-management consultants, and continues to require heavy executive leadership. Because this phase is based more on understanding and adoption, it requires much more face-to-face interaction, training, and communication.

EFFECTIVE DASHBOARD DESIGN

So far, we have discussed the types of dashboards and how they are structured, structuring indicators and data for maximum value and the implementation phases. Next, we focus on visual design. Identifying the right indicator is only part of the process. The best indicator, if improperly displayed, can be difficult to understand at best and completely misleading at worst, resulting in ineffective decision making and a misaligned strategy. Meanwhile, a KPI that is effectively displayed has transformative powers that can fundamentally change an organization.

In this next section, we discuss how to visually design a dashboard and display indicators for effective decision making. We discuss human perception, design principles, and specific media types that best convey different sets of data to an audience.

Memory Types and Information Processing

Before we discuss different media to convey indicators, it is important to understand how we, as humans, perceive different media—specifically, how the information displayed on a screen becomes transferred to our memory for analysis.

Much like a computer, our brains have a hierarchy of memory that stores different types of information, which is shifted from one level to another based on the level of importance. Understanding this hierarchy allows dashboard designers to exploit it for maximum speed of perception, retention, and understanding. This hierarchy is composed of three levels:

Iconic memory (the visual sensory register)
Short-term memory (working memory)
Long-term memory

Each level stores information for a specific period of time during which it is processed by our brain. Dashboards are focused on exploiting iconic and short-term memory.

Iconic memory is also called the *visual sensory memory*. Iconic memory acts as a buffer to our short-term memory, storing everything our bodies sense before it is moved to short-term memory or discarded. All visuals are subconsciously stored in iconic memory and subject to a type of neural processing called *preattentive processing*, which determines if it is important enough to warrant focus and a move to short-term memory for more in depth processing.

Short-term memory stores information during conscious processing, otherwise known as *attentive processing*. Much like a computer's RAM, short-term memory only stores information temporarily before it is either moved to long-term memory or discarded (forgotten). The information is stored temporarily because of limited capacity. The information in our short-term memory is grouped into three to nine pieces of specific information. These groups are determined by the nature of the objects we are seeing, their design, and our familiarity with them.

A dashboard's media can help an audience's brains group the information to make analysis easier and more effective. For example, information displayed as a number on a dashboard is grouped into a single piece of information by our brains. However, when we transform that number into a line graph that displays that same metric over time alongside another metric—such as profit and loss—our brains also perceive that as a single group. Both the single number and the graph are processed at the same speed but are comprised of vastly different amounts of information. The same holds true for the dashboard as a whole. When multiple relevant groups of information are separated and require scrolling or are relegated to separate pages, our short-term memories cannot group them effectively and analysis becomes significantly more difficult.

The goals of a dashboard's visual design is to:

1. Display information using the most effective media possible so it can be easily perceived using preattentive processing.
2. Organize the information as concisely as possible so our short-term memory can optimally group and analyze it as quickly and accurately as possible.

98734979027564790289472862409240603707057027907280320802900730250127023700837408207872027200708324780260270379377570970737797066746209709470278092797970972309723097959275092727979873497260802 7

FIGURE 3.2
How many fives are in the list? (Adopted from Figure 4-1, Few, Stephen, *Information Dashboard Design*, p. 81. O'Reilly Media, Sebastopol, CA, 2007.)

The difference between the two types of processing is striking. Preattentive processing is performed quickly and subconsciously, while attentive processing is significantly slower because it requires conscious thought. One of the best examples to demonstrate the difference comes from Stephen Few. Take a moment to analyze Figure 3.2. How many fives can you identify?

The correct answer is six, but regardless of if you got the right answer, it took you awhile because the process involved attentive processing. Try it again using Figure 3.3.

Much faster, right? This time, the list exhibited preattentive attributes to distinguish the fives from the other numbers, making them easier to spot. Saturation is one of the preattentive attributes, but why wasn't it easier to distinguish by shape? Simply, the shapes of numbers are too elaborate to process preattentively. We can quickly distinguish geometric shapes, such as circles and squares, but complex shapes require using attentive processing.

Table 3.2 shows the types of design attributes that leverage preattentive processing. Embedding these attributes in a graph or other form of media allows viewers to more quickly distinguish trends and anomalies.

While the features in the table allow us to leverage our preattentive processing, there are also some key limitations, which need to be identified.

98734979027564790289472862409240603707057027907280320802900730250127023700837408207872027200708324780260270379377570970737797066746209709470278092797970972309723097959275092727979873497260802 7

FIGURE 3.3
Now, how many fives are in the list? (Adopted from Figure 4-1, Few, Stephen, *Information Dashboard Design*, p. 81. O'Reilly Media, Sebastopol, CA, 2007.)

TABLE 3.2

Preattentive Attributes

Position	Size	Saturation
○○○ ○○	○○○○◯	◌◌◌◌●
Enclosure	**Marking**	**Color**
○○○○[○]	○○○○⊗	◌◌◌◌◌
Line Width	**Line Length**	**Orientation**
○○○○◯	‖‖‖‖ı	□□□□◇
Shape	**Flicker**	
○○○○□	Two attributes alternating between one another – black to white, circle to square, etc.	

Number of attributes—We are only able to perceive five expressions of any preattentive attribute at a time.* For example, if every metric on a dashboard is flickering, viewers become overwhelmed and not drawn to one metric over another.

Color—It is common to use greens and reds in dashboard indicators. However, these do not work for the 10% of males and 1% of females that are colorblind as fully saturated reds and greens look like the same color. It is a best practice to use black (instead of green) to indicate a non-issue. Additionally, when more than five colors are applied to a single graph, they will be grouped together, and we lose the ability to quickly identify individual trends.

Saturation—Fully saturated colors are best used for emphasis, whereas muted colors are best used to display standard data. The greater number of fully saturated colors—bright reds, greens, etc.—the more difficult it is for a dashboard's audience to quickly identify anomalies or differentiate data of greater importance. And, the additional benefit of saturation is the fact that colorblind individuals are able to differentiate saturation levels, regardless of color.

---

* Few, Stephen. *Information Dashboard Design.* p. 89. O'Reilly Media, Sebastopol, CA, 2006.

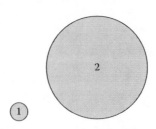

FIGURE 3.4
Size and volume. (This example was taken from Figure 4-7, Few, Stephen, *Information Dashboard Design*, p. 87. O'Reilly Media, Sebastopol, CA, 2006.)

Shape—As highlighted in the 5s example, complex shapes do not leverage our preattentive processing.[*] Our brains must process every angle of every shape and when there are many shapes together with many angles, we cannot separate out differences quickly and must delegate the work to short-term memory and attentive processing.

Size—When we assign a graphic object to represent a quantitative value, we lose some precision. This is because our brains have a very difficult time gauging differences in volume, which is related to size. For instance, in Figure 3.4, how much larger is bubble #2 than bubble #1? While you are aware that bubble #2 is significantly larger, it is nearly impossible for you to distinguish the actual number of times larger.[†] It is important to weigh the level of precision needed when graphically displaying key metrics using size.

Gestalt Principles of Visual Perception

In 1912 the Gestalt school of psychology began researching how our brains group observations to form patterns in order to make sense of them. The product of this research, the Gestalt principles, was a fundamental shift in our understanding of how our brains group information in our short-term memory. Today, we use the principles as a cornerstone in dashboard design to weave together different pieces of information to make it quick and easy to analyze for all audiences. There are six core Gestalt principles that are used in dashboard design:

---

[*] Few, Stephen. *Information Dashboard Design*. p. 89. O'Reilly Media, Sebastopol, CA, 2006.
[†] Bubble #2 is six times larger than bubble #1. This example was taken from: Few, Stephen. *Information Dashboard Design*. Figure 4-7. p. 87. O'Reilly Media, Sebastopol, CA, 2006.

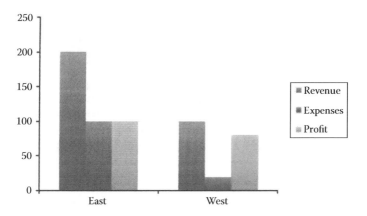

FIGURE 3.5
Proximity perception.

Proximity—We naturally group items that are closer to each other to the same group. Conversely, items that have more blank space between them than others are also separated into different groups. For example in Figure 3.5, we immediately associate the values to each category, without needing to read the labels.

Closure—Our brains will naturally "close" an open square or circle. For example in Figure 3.6 we will naturally see the shape on the left as a rectangle, not two angled lines. Likewise, we see a circle on the right, not two curves. In practice, on a dashboard, we do not need to add borders, colors, etc., around each graphic to define the space. In the figure, you can see that our brains do it for us.

Similarity—We group items that are similar size, shape, color, or orientation together. In Figure 3.7, even without a line, your brain immediately associates certain data points with others.

Enclosure—Items are grouped based on the background shading or surrounding lines.

FIGURE 3.6
Shape closure.

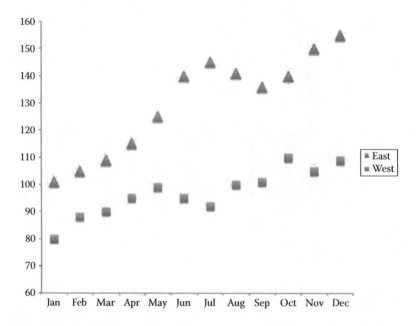

FIGURE 3.7
Similarity of shapes and colors.

Connection—Objects that are tied together by a line or other form of identifier are seen to be part of the same group. For example, in text, a hyphen connects two separate words. We also connect words with lines in a thought-map.

Continuity—Our brains will naturally connect lines or dots that are left open. For example, a dotted or dashed line can form a full line to display a trend.

Data-to-Ink Ratio

Edward Tufte, in his 1983 book *The Visual Display of Quantitative Information,* outlines the importance of each and every drop of ink on a graphic. The modern day equivalent to ink is pixels on a dashboard. Dashboards have two types of pixels—(1) *data pixels,* which represent key data; if these were removed, insight would be lost; and (2) *non-data pixels,* which provide some visual context such as grid lines, shading, enclosures, etc. Because the goal of a dashboard is to allow its audience to make better decisions based on data, our goal on a dashboard is to increase the data pixels and decrease the non-data pixels. Edward Tufte describes this relationship as the data–ink ratio (a.k.a. the data–pixel ratio).[*]

The data–pixel ratio can be calculated a few different ways[†]:

= Data pixels/total pixels used to display the graphic.

= Proportion of a graphic's pixels devoted to the non-redundant display of data-information.

= 1.0—Proportion of a graphic that can be erased without the loss of data-information.

Your goal when designing a dashboard is to have the highest data–pixel ratio possible. There are two effective strategies to do this. The first is to remove all the pixels possible that are not directly tied to data information, for example, grid lines, non-relevant boundaries, inappropriate shading, etc. The second strategy is to condense information into summaries and exceptions. For example, if the audience only cares about projects that are over budget, do not display projects that are within budget.

Dashboard Media

In this section we discuss various types of media for displaying quantitative information and how each can be effectively leveraged for quick decision making. When creating a dashboard it is important to ask a few key questions:

1. What decision does the viewer need to make?—i.e., do I need to do anything?
2. What action does the viewer need to take?—i.e., should I call someone? Who?
3. How should the viewer feel?—i.e., "this is important!" or "everything is copacetic."

There are numerous types of media. The media you chose for your dashboard should be the most effective at answering these questions using the smallest amount of non-data pixels. Here, we focus on the most popular four dashboards—text, icons, organizers, and graphs.

---

[*] Tufte, Edward. *The Visual Display of Quantitative Information.* p. 93. Graphics Press, Cheshire, CT, 1983.
[†] Ibid.

Text

Text is the most precise form of media. Any time that a single metric must be displayed precisely and without comparison, text should be used. Just like other media, text should be enhanced using preattentive attributes—such as color or flicker.

Icons

Icons are simple images that convey a defined message and garner attention. The two most popular types for dashboards convey good/bad or up/down sentiment.

> *Good/Bad* icons are the typical green and red images that highlight if an indicator is above or below goal. It is important to remember the color preattentive attribute, and that colorblind people cannot differentiate between fully saturated greens and red.
>
> *Up/Down* icons are usually displayed as arrows or triangles pointing in either an up or down direction. These icons build upon the good/bad indicators by offering a direction of progress—that is, an indicator might be above goal (indicated by a green color) but trending down (indicated by a downward facing triangle).

Organizers

Organizers help to organize other display media on the page. The most prevalent examples are data tables and spatial maps.

> *Data tables* arrange text metrics into rows and columns. These are commonly used when the same, precise metrics are required to be divided into different segments, for example, revenue and expenses by regions.
>
> *Spatial maps* arrange information geographically. This media tends to be most effective for high volume information that contains different detailed spatial coordinates. They do not work well to summarize data as there can be a lot of non-data pixels. For example, if a franchise had thousands of stores across the United States, instead of using a data table, which would take up significant space and require scrolling, profitability could be color-coded and displayed for each store on a single map.

Graphs

Graphs are the most popular media on dashboards, and for good reason—they do an excellent job at summarizing information to identify trends and anomalies, both of which are key to making decisions. Some graphs accomplish this better than others. While there are many different types of graphs, in this section we discuss only the most popular ones: pie, bar, line, scatterplot, and sparklines (a relative newcomer).

Pie Graphs are the least useful graph for conveying quantitative information. They are meant to display proportional pieces of a whole for comparison; however, as displayed in Figure 3.8, the human brain has difficulty comparing area volume, so it is much more difficult to identify the difference in size of the different pieces. A better graph for displaying proportion is the bar graph, which combines multiple preattentive attributes to allow viewers to more easily compare the size differences of different slices. For example, which graph in Figure 3.8 is best to determine which product is bestselling?

The data on each of the graphs in Figure 3.8 are the same, but it takes significantly longer to identify the bestselling product in a pie graph. The one thing pie charts do convey quickly is that each section makes up a piece of a whole; however, a sufficiently labeled bar graph could fulfill this requirement.

Bar Graphs organize data along an XY-axis where the length of the bar indicates a quantitative value. They are used to compare categorical data and can be organized horizontally or vertically. Where bar graphs excel is in displaying nominal data categories for

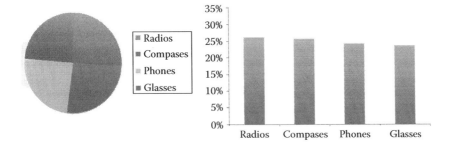

FIGURE 3.8
Pie versus bar chart. (Adopted from Figure 6-22, Few, Stephen, *Information Dashboard Design*, p. 135. O'Reilly Media, Sebastopol, CA, 2006.)

comparison—such as for comparing the amount of items sold over a set period.

Line Graphs, similar to bar graphs, organize data along an XY-axes and connect the data points to provide a visual shape of the data through defined intervals. While bar graphs make comparison between categories easy, line graphs are most useful for displaying trends and continuity of data. Line graphs should only be used on data that is categorized on an interval scale, meaning that there is a defined progression (usually time) from one interval to another along the X-axis. These intervals could be individual data points (such as seconds) or groups of data points (such as months or quarters).

Scatterplots display individual, unconnected data points along a plane where both the X and Y axes are interval scales. They are used to visualize clustering of data points across two different but related variables. This allows viewers to identify correlations between variables within large data sets. For example, if we wanted to identify if there was a correlation between time spent studying and GPA, we might survey 500 students and plot the data on a scatterplot. In this case, the students each have two variables: hours studying and GPA. From there, we could easily visualize a correlation while displaying precise data.

Sparklines are word-sized graphics that are typically displayed without axis to show basic data trends. While sparklines could be line graphs, bar graphs, or other types, they are unique because of their size and simplicity. They were created in the early 2000s by Edward Tufte and began widespread usage in 2010 when Microsoft Excel added them as an optional chart type. Sparklines are powerful because they give viewers quick insight into data across time, while taking up very little space. They are most powerful when paired with text indicators in a list or table, giving the viewer not just specific numbers but also a historical trend of each indicator requiring minimal space. Figure 3.9 is an example of a sparkline.

 YTD: $40M

FIGURE 3.9
Example of a sparkline. Legend: YTD: $40M.

Dashboard Real Estate

Different areas of dashboards have different real estate values, and should be used accordingly to display information of similar value. Areas on the upper left and middle of a dashboard grab a viewer's attention first: this is where the most important information should be focused. The upper-right and lower-left areas of the dashboard command less focus, while the lower right area is the least valuable. The reason the viewer's eyes focus on the upper left and center first is mostly because western languages read from the upper left to the bottom right.*

DASHBOARD TRENDS

Dashboards are changing dramatically, not just by the data that they collect but also how they present the data. Below are the four emerging trends that are shaping the industry.

Aggregating external data—While dashboards have traditionally displayed internal data for internal analysis, increasingly they are able to tap into open data sources using open APIs (Application Program Interfaces). APIs allow different technology to communicate and share data. There has been significant growth in the number of "open APIs," moving from close to 0 in 2005 to over 8,000 in 2012. Meanwhile, over a quarter of all new applications plan on incorporating an open API so other applications can access the data.† This growth is significant because it allows organizations to better understand their market segments and tailor operations appropriately. For instance, if a company sees a significant increase in positive tweets about a product in China, they could proactively increase production to meet the estimated demand.

Predictive analytics—Dashboards are increasingly incorporating complex algorithms to analyze leading and lagging indicators, external data, and other internal metrics to project future outcomes. For example, a police department dashboard may include a feature that analyzes social media with an algorithm that projects future protests based on word association within that media. The dashboard might then display current and required staffing based on the estimated size and location of an illegal protest being planned through Twitter.

* Few, Stephen. *Information Dashboard Design.* p. 114. O'Reilly Media, Sebastopol, CA, 2006.
† DuVander, Adam. "8,000 APIs: Rise of the Enterprise." *Programmable Web.* 26 November 2012. http://www.slideshare.net/mjskok/2013-future-of-open-source-7th-annual-survey-results.

Exploratory and machine-generated analysis—Dashboards are increasingly being developed for hypothesis-driven exploration (acting on a "hunch") and interactive analysis for the business user to arrive at insight. To achieve this, new dashboard products are focused on exploratory analytics. They are cultivating the hypothesis by performing machine-generated analyses and pushing results to the viewer. For example, a dashboard might display text that says that yesterday, "sales of product X dropped by 8%, the largest drop in 4 years" and may estimate lower sales and larger inventories than anticipated, lowering the quarterly profit by a certain percent. A business user would then analyze social media, customer service requests, and other factors to identify what was driving the drop and either work to reduce production or possibly increase sales through a new advertising campaign and pricing strategy. These insights, garnered through machine developed analysis and forecasting, are increasingly allowing non-technical users to monitor, manage, and analyze complex businesses.

Technology and data—Dashboards and the data they display are increasingly running in the cloud. They are accessed through computers and other Internet-connected devices, such as mobile phones and tablets. Increasingly, the data is pushed to the device's memory, which allows it to be very responsive for quick drill-down. However, while the technology to allow in-memory analysis is improving, the amount of data required for analysis is growing exponentially.[*] The amount of data generated is expected to grow 300 times in the next seven years, which poses new technical challenges. The vast majority of this data is unstructured and untagged, making searching and analysis difficult. New forms of databases, analytical tools, and dashboards are emerging that help us access and structure the trillions and trillions of data records to make sense of them.

SUMMARY

1. Performance dashboards are a product of the combination of business intelligence technology, and balanced scorecard methodology, which became widely popular in the 2000s after the economic downturn and Enron scandal.

---

[*] "2.8 zettabytes of data created in 2012 alone" (IDC Digital Universe, John Gantz and David Reinsel. "The Digital Universe in 2020: Big Data, Bigger Digital Shadows, The Biggest Growth in the Far East," IDC, Framingham, MA, 2012).

2. A dashboard is a consolidated visual display of an audience's most important indicators, updated as frequently as possible and working in concert to improve the quality of decisions relating to specified objectives.

3. There are four types of dashboards: *strategic, tactical, operational,* and *analytical.* Each type—ranging from strategic to operational/analytical—provides a less summarized view for data in each indicator. Each type is designed to fit a specific role within the organization: strategic dashboards are focused on executives, tactical dashboards are focused on middle managers, operational dashboards are focused on front-line staff, and analytical dashboards are focused on analysts. It is becoming more popular to transcend the hierarchy and *also* use another dashboard—for instance, an executive might also use an analytical dashboard to "dig into the numbers" on his or her own.

4. Dashboards display indicators to help their audience make decisions. These indicators should be focused on a strategy set by executives and cascade throughout the organization on different dashboards. The four types of indicators are *Key Performance Indicators* (KPI), *Key Results Indicators* (KRI), *Performance Indicators* (PI), and *Results Indicators* (RI). KPI and KRI directly relate to a specific strategy, while PI and RI do not but are still important to track. KPI and PI are *leading indicators*, meaning that they are a precursor to a desired outcome and therefore drive performance. Meanwhile KRI and RI are *lagging indicators*, meaning that they display past performance and are used to assess whether a strategy is working, and to evaluate staff performance.

5. Indicators are comprised of records in a database. While every dashboard in an organization should display the same indicators, the amount of record summation within the indicators should vary based on the type of dashboard and audience. Operational dashboards should summarize the records the least, as they provide the most value to their viewers through greater data granularity. Tactical dashboards should offer mid-level summation, as they need to track various indicators and directly relate them to specific strategic goals. Strategic dashboards should offer the highest level of record summary, as executives need to focus on strategy, not individual transactions.

6. There are three stages an organization goes through when implementing a suite of dashboards: (1) *information insight and transparency*, (2) *strategy*, and (3) *repeatable process*. In the first stage, organizations aggregate metrics, share them across internal verticals, to learn and

adopt. In the second stage, organizations form a succinct strategy using the data garnered in stage one and couple it with the organization's vision, thus defining the KPI, KRI, PI, and RI for each vertical and department. In phase three, the organization implements the indicators and dashboards to develop strategic alignment throughout the organization.

7. Preattentive attributes leverage our brain's iconic memory, making it easier to quickly identify anomalies and potential issues. To effectively display indicators, dashboards should leverage these attributes: position, size, saturation, enclosure, marking, color, line width, line length, orientation, shape, and flicker. These attributes draw the eye and make it easy to spot an issue. However, they should be used sparingly; using more than five will be counterproductive, as the eye will not know where to focus.

8. After preattentive attributes draw our eyes to certain information, it is sent to our short-term memory for analysis. The Gestalt principles leverage our brain's short-term memory's attentive processing, which groups pieces of the information together to analyze it in batches. The principles—proximity, closure, similarity, enclosure, connection, and continuity—make it easier and quicker to group information resulting in faster and more effective decision making.

9. There are two types of pixels on a dashboard: data pixels and non-data pixels. Data pixels display important data for the viewer; if these pixels were removed, information would be removed. Non-data pixels support the data pixels by giving context through attributes such as grid lines, borders, shading, etc. Data pixels are important to making effective decisions, while non-data pixels can make decisions more difficult as our brains must process every pixel on a dashboard and determine if it is worth analysis. To make dashboards more visually effective, increase the data pixels and reduce the non-data pixels, or increase the data–pixel ratio. The data–pixel ratio was developed by Edward Tufte and is calculated by dividing the total data pixels by the total pixels used to display the graphic.

10. When choosing the type of media to display information on a dashboard, ask yourself: What decisions does the viewer need to make? What action does the viewer need to take? How should the viewer feel? The four types of media discussed are text, icons, organizers, and graphs. Text should be used when the information must be very precise; it can also be combined with other media such as icons and

organizers. Icons are simple images that convey a defined message to draw attention. Organizers arrange information on the page, either through a table or a spatial map. Graphs are excellent for identifying trends and anomalies but not for displaying precise numbers. Because it is difficult for us to assess volume, pie graphs should be used sparingly. Instead, bar graphs are faster and easier to read; they should be used to display nominal and ordinal data. Line charts should display interval data and are best to display trends. Scatterplots are best at identifying correlations between values. Finally, sparklines have a minimal pixel–data ratio and are data graphics into text to identify historical information.

11. Dashboards are increasingly being designed to handle more data such as machine-generated data and data from external sources using APIs. They are becoming more business-user centered, providing better options for drilling down/up for exploration and offering machine-generated insights and analysis. There is also a significant focus on predictive analytics and forecasting of outcomes using embedded algorithms that automatically monitor an organization's data to predict future events.

Exercises

1. What type of dashboard is in an automobile and why?
2. Review the graphic below:

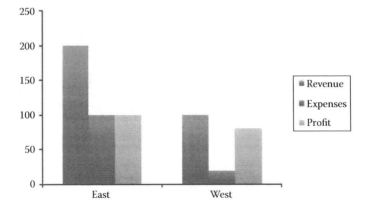

a. Which preattentive attributes are present?
b. Which Gestalt principles are employed?

3. We discussed that British Airways used the amount of time a flight was delayed as a key indicator with a threshold of 2 hours. If Lord King's dashboard had text that displayed the current number of flights more than 2 hours late, would that be a *leading* or *lagging* indicator (KPI or KRI)? What other indicators could precede or result from it?

4. How many KPIs should be included on an executive dashboard and why?

5. A retail equity brokerage company would like to offer an online dashboard for clients to monitor their portfolios. The dashboard will include a list of stocks that are currently owned or being watched. The CEO has proposed displaying the current trade price and a circle icon that displays red if the stock is trending down, or green if it is trending up. Is this the best way to display this information? What other information might be useful to a client? What is your recommendation for including that information in this media?

ANSWERS

1. Operational. An automobile dashboard is used to monitor the current state of the car and operational dashboards are used to monitor current business processes. The information on an automobile dashboard is constantly updated and is not aggregated by defined intervals—for example, it does not display an average speed over the last 30 minutes. The information is not compared to goals, but does display specific thresholds; for instance, the dashboard does not display an optimal amount of fuel, but does display a warning when fuel drops below 1/8th of a tank.

2. a. Preattentive attributes:

   Color—Different bars display different colors indicating that they are different information.

   Size—Bar size indicates that one data point is greater or less than another.

   Position—We know two groups are displayed because of the large gap between them.

   Line length—The lines displayed around each bar are longer/shorter/equal to their counterparts; meanwhile, the horizontal lines across the tops of the bars do not draw attention.

b. Gestalt principles:

Proximity—We group items that are closer together, in this case to compare regions.

Closure—We instinctively close boxes, there is no need to close the graphic's top horizontal line or a right vertical line.

Similarity—Items that display a similar attribute (in this case color) are grouped together. We instinctively group the different colors together to define the categories of information—revenue, expenses, and profit.

3. A metric that displays past performance is a Key Results Indicator (KRI) and a metric that drives future performance is a Key Performance Indicator (KPI). As described in the traffic light example, indicators are many times both KPI and KRI depending on the audience's goals. On Lord King's dashboard, a metric that displays planes over 2 hours late would be a KPI because his goal is to increase profits and that indicator impacts expenses and customer satisfaction. However, the BA airport manager would likely view the same indicator on his dashboard (filtered for only his airport) as a KRI because his goal is to have planes leave less than 2 hours from their scheduled departure time and therefore it displays the *result* of his efforts.

4. The absolute minimum. Fewer KPIs signal a more focused strategy. There are opposing views on how many work best such as the 10/80/10 rule or absolute numbers such as 5 or 20; however, everyone agrees that less is always more. It is never a good idea to compromise strategic success to display less information on a dashboard; however, dashboards are about focus and the more indicators and thus variables make focus more difficult.

5. Instead of a circle, we could include a triangle that is pointed up or down based on the current trend and color-coded green if the position is profitable and red if it is a loss. This enhancement would increase the information in the metric without increasing non-data pixels. A client that is monitoring an equity portfolio would likely want to see the current stock price and historical performance, if there has been a profit or loss since the position was opened, *and* if the stock is trending up or down. We could also display the current price as red if the stock is down for the day or green if it is up for the day. Additionally, we could include a sparkline next to the current trading price to show the last 30 days of performance.

4

Data Mining: Helping to Make Sense of Big Data

Barry Keating

CONTENTS

Learning Objectives

After reading this chapter, one should be able to:

- Distinguish "data mining" from online transaction processing.
- Define data mining.
- Explain the four categories of tools available in data mining.
- Relate common data mining terminology to standard statistical terminology.
- Use R.A. Fisher's linear classifier technique.
- Interpret the output from a k-Nearest-Neighbor model estimation.
- Use and explain the two most common diagnostic statistics in data mining.

INTRODUCTION*

One apocryphal story about the origin of statistics (and hence analytics in general) describes a tale going back to the 17th century in London. During the plague that decimated London and the surrounding area, it became popular to declare oneself dead in order to avoid paying taxes (even though one was very much alive). To prevent this practice, the king required a death certificate including some basic information. A routine report was prepared for the king summarizing recent mortality details. In the preparation of the report (the Bills of Mortality), patterns were discovered; this was reportedly the first instance of noticing patterns in data as opposed to seeing patterns in nature (e.g., the stars in the night sky, leaf structure in plants, and the tides of the sea). Mortality cropped up again in the analytics literature, when Benjamin Gompertz discovered the pattern of exponential deaths as age increases in fruit flies. The pattern he wrote about is a special case of the generalized logistic function used in present-day data mining.

The Bills of Mortality may be the first recorded instance of data mining. The early data miners of London who created the document let the data display the patterns important to them. Data mining is quite different from what most of us know as standard statistical techniques (sometimes called *frequentist statistics*). In most forecasting situations, for instance, the model imposed on the data to make the forecasts has been chosen by the forecaster. In most business situations we assume that our data will, or could, exhibit the patterns commonly found in most business data: trend, seasonality, and cyclicality. We then choose a model that we believe will represent the data well, say a Holt–Winters smoothing model; we may believe this is appropriate because we have observed all previous forecasts to include these patterns. In a word, we selected and imposed the pattern on the data.

Data mining is an altogether different way of viewing the world and the data in it. IBM is fond of using the term *Big Data* to represent this distinct view. But the term *Big Data* does not belong to just IBM, it is a term commonly used in place of data mining. If there is any distinction between

---

* The author would like to thank Professor Eamonn Keogh of the Department of Computer Science & Engineering at the University of California, Riverside; Keogh has provided Web readers with excellent examples and explanations of data mining tools and issues. This chapter draws on some of his examples.

the two terms it is this. Big Data refers to seeing things by using large-scale data, things that cannot be seen at a smaller scale. Data mining refers to the tools and techniques that are used in this large-scale, or Big Data, arena. In the physical world we are used to using tools like the telescope or the microscope to see the dimensions we are unable to examine with the naked eye. In more recent history the radio telescope (a non-optical instrument) and the electron microscope have allowed us to see physical data in dimensions we could only previously hypothesize about. In much the same way, data mining tools use Big Data to make sense of what was previously unable to be seen.

With data mining, the tables are turned. We do not know what pattern or family of patterns may fit a particular set of data. Sometimes we do not even know what it is we are trying to predict or explain. This should seem strange to a traditional forecaster; it's not the method of attacking the data we have been pursuing throughout our frequentist statistics texts. To begin data mining and using Big Data we require a new mindset. We need to be open to finding relationships and patterns we never imagined existed in the data we are about to examine. To use data mining is to let the data tell us the story (rather than to impose a model on the data that we feel will replicate the actual patterns in the data).

Data mining traditionally uses very large data sets, often far larger than the data sets we use in business forecasting situations. But Big Data is not defined by the size of the data set so much as it is defined by whether we are using a sample of the true population or are using all the data (i.e., the population). Sample statistics were created at a point in time when our supply of data was limited; it may have been impossible to collect or use the entire population. Today, the tables are turned; we have so much data (all of it) that we seem sometimes to be attempting to drink from a fire hose. The sample statistics of the past were useful in working with pieces of the population; we were careful to know our sample well and were taught to make inferences from those samples. The entire game, however, is changing. Google Correlate allows us access to all the Google searches: it is Big Data not because there are so many observations (*records* in data mining-speak), but because we have all the data. The number of records equals *all*.

The tools or algorithms we use in data mining are also somewhat different than standard business forecasting tools; some of the data mining tools will be familiar but they may be used in different ways than we have used them in previous chapters. The premise of data mining is that there is a great deal of information locked up in any database (i.e., all the information): it's up to us to use appropriate tools to unlock the secrets hidden within. Business forecasting is explicit in the sense that we use specific models to estimate and forecast known patterns (e.g., seasonality, trend, cyclicality, the effects of advertising, etc.). Data mining, on the other hand, involves the extraction of implicit (often unknown) intelligence or useful information from data. We need to be able to process very large quantities of data to find patterns and regularities that we did not know existed beforehand. Some of what we find will be quite useless and uninteresting (at the moment); perhaps only coincidences. But from time to time we will be able to find true gems in the mounds of data. The objective of this chapter is to introduce a variety of data mining methods for you to consider. Some of these methods are simple and meant only to introduce you to how the basic concept of data mining works. Others, however, are full blown data mining algorithms that are commonly employed by data miners to exploit large databases. After completing this chapter you will understand what data mining techniques exist and will appreciate their strengths; you will also understand how they are applied in practice. If you wish to experiment with your own data (or that provided with a demonstration program) we recommend the XLMiner© software.* Anyone capable of using an Excel spreadsheet will find XLMiner a delightful introduction into many of the algorithms used by data miners. Be aware that it is a teaching tool created as an Excel add-in for the purpose of familiarizing the user with data mining tools; it is not a commercially used piece of data mining software and is not able to handle some of the size and complexities of real-world business data.

DATA MINING

A decade ago one of the most pressing problems for a forecaster was the lack of data collected intelligently by businesses; forecasters were limited to few pieces of data and only limited observations on the data that existed. Today, however, we are overwhelmed with data. It is collected at

---

* XLMiner© is an inexpensive noncommercial Excel add-in. Both student and full versions of the software are available from Frontline Systems (http://www.solver.com/). It provides an excellent way to learn about data mining by applying the algorithms to medium-sized data sets. For a more complete introduction to data mining keyed to the XLMiner software the author also recommends Galit Shmueli, Nitin Patel, and Peter Bruce (2010), *Data Mining for Business Intelligence*, 2nd ed., Hoboken, NJ: John Wiley & Sons.

grocery store checkout counters, while inventory moves through a warehouse, when users click a button on the World Wide Web, and every time a credit card is swiped. The rate of data collection is not abating; it seems to be increasing with no clear end in sight. The presence of large cheap storage devices means that it is easy to simply keep every piece of data produced. The pressing problem now is not the generation of the data, but the attempt to understand it.

The job of a data miner is to make sense of the mounds of data we now have available by examining the data for patterns. The single most important reason for the recent interest in data mining is due to the large amounts of data now available for analysis; there is a need for business professionals to transform such data into useful information by "mining" it for the existence of patterns. You should not be at all surprised by the emphasis on patterns; this entire text has been about patterns of one sort or another. Indeed, man has looked for patterns in almost every endeavor undertaken by mankind. Early man looked for patterns in the night sky, for patterns in the movement of the stars and planets, and to predict the best times of the year to plant crops. Modern man still hunts for patterns in early election returns, global temperature changes, and sales data for new products. Over the last twenty-five years there has been a gradual evolution from data processing to what we call *data mining* today. In the 1960s, businesses routinely collected data and processed it using database management techniques that allowed indexing, organization, and some query activity. Online Transaction Processing (OLTP) became routine and the rapid retrieval of stored data was made easier by more efficient storage devices and faster and more capable computing.

Database management advanced rapidly to include very sophisticated query systems; it became common not only in business situations but also in scientific inquiry. Databases began to grow at previously unheard-of rates and for even routine activities. The amount of data in all the world's databases has recently been estimated to double in less than every two years. That flood of data would seem to call for analysis in order to make sense of the patterns locked within. Firms now routinely have what are called *data warehouses* and *data marts*. **Data warehouse** is the term used to describe a firm's main repository of historical data; it is the "memory" of the firm, its collective information on every relevant aspect of what has happened in the past. A **data mart**, on the other hand, is a special version of a data warehouse; they are a subset of the data warehouse and routinely hold information that is specialized and has been grouped or chosen specifically to help businesses make better decisions on future actions. Data marts are usually derived from a data warehouse. The first organized uses of such large databases has come to be called Online Analytical Processing (OLAP). OLAP is a set of analysis techniques that provides aggregation, consolidation, reporting, and summarization of the data. It could be thought of as the direct precursor to what we now know by the name of *data mining*. Much of the data collected by any organization becomes simply a historical artifact that is rarely referenced and even more rarely analyzed for knowledge. OLAP procedures began to change that as data was summarized and viewed from different angles.

Data mining for many years had an altogether different connotation than it enjoys today; instead of being an analysis that finds useful patterns in data, it carried the meaning that the researcher was imposing a model on data, whether it fit or not. When someone was called a *data miner*, it was meant to be a derogatory term applied to a person who tortured data until it told the preconceived story the researcher wanted to tell. Data mining today concerns analyzing databases, data warehouses, and data marts that already exist for the purpose of solving some problem, discovering new relationships, or to answer some pressing question. **Data mining is the extraction of useful information from large databases**; it is about extracting knowledge or information from large amounts of data.* Data mining has come to be referenced by a few similar terms; in most cases they all refer to much the same set of techniques that we refer to as data mining in this chapter:

- Exploratory data analysis
- Business intelligence
- Data driven discovery
- Knowledge Discovery in Databases (KDD)

Data mining is quite separate from database management. Keogh points out that in database management, queries are well defined; we even have a language to write these queries (Structured Query Language, or SQL, pronounced as "sequel"). A query in database management might take the form of "find all the customers in South Bend," or "find all the customers who have missed a recent payment."

---

* D. Hand, H. Mannila, and P. Smyth (2001), *Principles of Data Mining*, Cambridge, MA: MIT Press.

Data mining, however, uses very different queries; they tend to be less structured and are sometimes quite vague. For example: "Find all the customers likely to purchase recreational vehicle insurance in the next six months," or "group all the customers with similar buying habits." In one sense, data mining is like statistical forecasting in that we are forward looking in an attempt to obtain better information about future likely events.

We could probably consider data mining an extension, or an advanced form, of OLAP. That would probably be incorrect. Both data mining and OLAP look at large amounts of data; it is not the absolute size of the data, however, that distinguishes one from the other. Many companies are data rich but information poor; data mining is the set of tools and techniques that can help firms to make sense of the enormous mountains of data they likely already have available. These available databases may contain customer profiles and the choices those customers have made in the past. There are likely patterns of behavior exhibited in the data, but the sheer amount of data will mask the underlying patterns and even a skilled researcher, testing for patterns she believes will be exhibited in the data, will miss a great deal of the information locked within. Some of those underlying patterns may be interesting but useless to a firm in making future decisions, but some patterns may be predictive in ways that are very useful. If, for example, you "know" which of your customers are likely to switch suppliers in the near future, you may be able to prevent them from jumping ship and going with a competitor; it is always less costly to keep existing customers than to enlist new ones. If you were to "know" which customers were likely to default on their loans in the near future you might be able to take pre-emptive measures to forestall the defaults or you might be less likely to loan to such individuals in the future. If you "know" (i.e., are able to predict) the characteristics of potential customers who are likely to purchase your product, you might be better able to direct your advertising and promotional efforts than if you were to blanket the market with advertising and promotions; a well-targeted approach is usually better than an unknowing "shotgun" approach.

What types of patterns can be mined? The answer is different from the patterns we expected to find in data with business forecasting methods such as a Winters' smoothing model. When a forecaster applies a Winters' smoothing model to time series data, the expectation is that the data contain some level variation, some trend, and some seasonal variability.

Experience with business data has taught us to expect those pattern types in virtually all business time series data.

Data mining, however, does not pre-specify the patterns. In a sense, there is no preconception of what will be found in the data with most data mining techniques. We are simultaneously searching for several different kinds of patterns in parallel. At the same time we are measuring the certainty or trustworthiness associated with the patterns we discover in somewhat the same vein as we do in standard business forecasting.

THE TOOLS OF DATA MINING

Shmueli, Patel, and Bruce use a taxonomy of data mining tools that is useful for seeing the big picture. There are basically four categories of data mining tools or techniques; they represent the four types of patterns we would like to search across:

1. Prediction
2. Classification
3. Clustering
4. Association

Prediction tools are most like the methods used in standard business forecasting; these tools attempt to predict the value of a numeric variable. We might, for example, be attempting to predict the value of a piece of residential property or the amount that an individual might contribute yearly to a particular charity. The variable we are attempting to predict in these instances could be a continuous variable, but it could also be a categorical variable. For example, we might wish to predict whether an individual will contribute to a particular cause rather than how much they might contribute, or whether an individual will make a certain purchase this year rather than how much they likely will spend on the purchase. Prediction, then, involves two types of variables: continuous and categorical.

Classification tools are the most commonly used methods in data mining. Classification tools distinguish between data classes or concepts; the purpose is to create a model that allows us to predict a class of objects whose label is unknown to us. For instance, when you present your credit card for a purchase in a retail store, the business must determine whether the impending transaction is a legitimate one (i.e., you are who you say you are, you have requisite purchasing power, etc.). The business would not find it profitable to hand over merchandise to everyone who presents a piece of plastic at the checkout counter. For this reason there is a short delay between when your card is swiped and when the receipt begins to print. In that short period of time a data mining algorithm's rules have been applied to your situation and a determination has been made; either the transaction is in the "class" of legitimate or it is in the class of illegiti-mate. In another example of the classification type of data mining, you may wish to know which characteristic of your firm's advertising of a par-ticular product is most important to consumers. Is it price? Or could it be the description of the quality and reliability of the item? Perhaps it is the compatibility of the item with other components the potential pur-chaser already owns. Classification tools may be able to tell you the answer for each of many products you sell, thus allowing you to make the best (i.e., most profitable) use of your advertising expenditures by providing consumers with the information they find most relevant in making the purchasing decision.

Clustering analysis tools analyze data objects without consulting a known class label. The classes of the objects are not input by the user; it is the function of the clustering technique to define and attach the class labels. The clustering technique generates the labels. Clustering techniques group objects based upon maximizing the intraclass simi-larity and/or minimizing the interclass similarity. Whether the clus-ters unearthed by the techniques are useful to the business manager is subjective; some clusters will be interesting but not useful in a business setting while others will be quite informative and will also be able to be exploited to advantage.

Association rules discovery is sometimes called *affinity analysis*. It is the discovery of rules attribute characteristics that often occur together in a given data set. If you have been handed coupons at a grocery store checkout counter, your purchasing patterns have probably been subjected to association rules discovery; Netflix will recommend movies you might like based upon movies you have watched and rated in the past. In each instance an association rules discovery has taken place.

We will examine a single technique from the most used data mining cat-egory: Classification. Specifically we will examine a k-Nearest-Neighbor model. Note that we are examining only a single algorithm in a single category of data mining tools (classification).

STATISTICAL FORECASTING AND DATA MINING

In statistical forecasting we seek verification of previously held hypotheses; that is, we "know" which patterns exist in the time series data we try to forecast and we apply appropriate statistical models to accurately estimate those patterns. When an electric power company looks at their load demand, they expect that past patterns, such as trend, seasonality, and cyclicality, will replicate themselves in the future. Thus, the firm might reasonably use time series decomposition as a model to forecast future electric usage. Data mining, however, seeks discovery of new knowledge from the data; it does not seek to merely verify the previously chosen hypotheses regarding the types of patterns in the data but seeks to discover new facts or rules from the data itself. Data mining allows the data itself to reveal the patterns within, rather than imposing the patterns on the data at the outset.

TERMINOLOGY IN DATA MINING: SPEAK LIKE A DATA MINER

The terminology used in data mining is a bit different than that used in statistical forecasting models; while the terms are different, their meanings are similar.

Data Mining Terminology	Statistical Terminology
Output Variable = Target Variable	Dependent Variable
Algorithm	Forecasting Model
Attribute = feature	Explanatory Variable
Record	Observation
Score	Forecast

Source: Eamonn Keogh, Department of Computer Science & Engineering, University of California, Riverside.

A DATA MINING EXAMPLE: K-NEAREST-NEIGHBOR AND R.A. FISHER

Iris Setosa   Iris Versicolor   Iris Virginica

Consider the data mining example in Figure 4.1. While it is not business related, it is easy to see the process visually. The data* used here is actually a well-known data set; R.A. Fisher collected the data in 1936. The data consists of information on three variations of iris flowers known as Setosa, Versicolor, and Virginica (see photos above). The data includes 50 examples of each of the three types of iris. For each of the 150 flowers, we know the length and width of the petals (Fisher also included the sepal length and width). The unknown is the particular type of iris. Could we use this data set to create a set of rules that would allow us to classify an iris as belonging to one of the three possible types? By seeing how this might be done graphically through trial and error we can begin to understand one of the general processes that data mining classification techniques uses.

We have only included two of Fisher's attributes in our graph for demonstration purposes. It is usually a good idea to graph the data to look for obvious relationships. We can do that here by arbitrarily placing petal length on the x-axis and petal width on the y-axis, thus creating a scatterplot of the data (Figure 4.2). The resulting plot is quite informative—the three types of flowers cluster around a particular portion of the scatterplot. While neither characteristic would do very well by itself in helping our classification, the combination of the two might quite accurately define unknown flowers.

An unknown flower appears as a star symbol in Figure 4.3. It appears to fall closest to the Versicolor flowers. But can we come up with a mechanistic way of choosing the unknown as Setosa, Versicolor, or Virginica?

---

* The data originally appeared in Fisher, R.A. (1936), "The Use of Multiple Measurements in Axonomic Problems," *Annals of Eugenics* 7, 179–188. The original dataset is available in numerous locations on the Web.

Species_No	Petal_width	Petal_length	Sepal_width	Sepal_length	Species_name
1	0.2	1.3	3	4.4	Setosa
1	0.2	1.5	3.4	5.1	Setosa
1	0.3	1.3	3.5	5	Setosa
1	0.3	1.3	2.3	4.5	Setosa
1	0.2	1.3	3.2	4.4	Setosa
1	0.6	1.6	3.5	5	Setosa
1	0.4	1.9	3.8	5.1	Setosa
1	0.3	1.4	3	4.8	Setosa
1	0.2	1.6	3.8	5.1	Setosa
1	0.2	1.4	3.2	4.6	Setosa
1	0.2	1.5	3.7	5.3	Setosa
1	0.2	1.4	3.3	5	Setosa
2	1.4	4.7	3.2	7	Versicolor
2	1.5	4.5	3.2	6.4	Versicolor
2	1.5	4.9	3.1	6.9	Versicolor
2	1.3	4	2.3	5.5	Versicolor
2	1.5	4.6	2.8	6.5	Versicolor
2	1.3	4.5	2.8	5.7	Versicolor
2	1.6	4.7	3.3	6.3	Versicolor
2	1	3.3	2.4	4.9	Versicolor
2	1.3	4.6	2.9	6.6	Versicolor

FIGURE 4.1
A portion of Fisher's original 1936 data is shown.

One method would be to look at the "neighbors" of the unknown. Which neighbors are the closest to the unknown? We could describe this process by drawing distance lines between the unknown and the neighbors. If the distance to the unknown is closest to the Versicolor (as measured by summing the distance to Versicolor neighbors and comparing this to

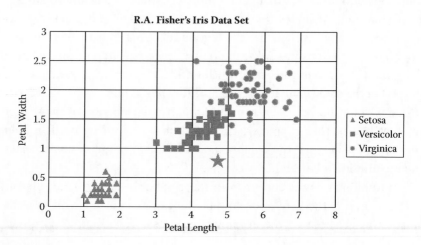

FIGURE 4.2
All 150 records of Fisher's original data set are shown with Petal Length on the x-axis and Petal Width on the y-axis.

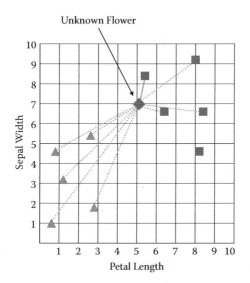

FIGURE 4.3
Looking at "neighbors" of an unknown.

the summation of the distances to Setosa neighbors), then the unknown is likely a Versicolor.

In essence, the k-Nearest-Neighbor model of data mining works in somewhat this manner. In actual practice it is not necessary to calculate the distance to every neighbor—only a small subset of the neighbors are used. The "k" in k-Nearest-Neighbor is actually the number of neighbors we optimally use to classify an unknown. In classifying many unknowns it might be optimal to use only a single neighbor, but this is unlikely. More often, two or more neighbors will be used to select the predicted classification. Data mining software employing the k-Nearest-Neighbor algorithm will use a measure of successful predictions in choosing what "k" to select and report.

When employing k-Nearest-Neighbor (i.e., selecting the number of neighbors to poll for a predicted classification) we use a subset of the total data we have available (called a *training data* set) to attempt to identify observations in the training data set that are similar to the unknown. Scoring (or forecasting) new unknowns is assigning the unknowns to the same class as their nearest neighbors. What we are interested in is classifying future unknown flowers using a rule, not the past performance on only historical data. We already know the correct classifications of the flowers in the training data set; that is why we call it a training data set.

It "trains" the algorithm to correctly classify the unknowns by selecting closeness to the k nearest neighbors. So the error rate for classification on historic data will not be very useful to determine if we truly have a good classification model (i.e., one that accurately classifies flowers as Setosa, Versicolor, or Virginica). An error rate on a training set (the known historical data) is not necessarily a good indicator of performance. To indicate how well this model might do in the real world at flower classification we should classify data that the model has not previously had access to; we need to use data that was not part of the training data set. This separate data set is called the *validation data*. In one sense, this separation of data into a training data set and a validation data set is much like the difference between using "in sample" test statistics and "out of sample" test statistics. The real test of a statistical forecast was the "out of sample" test; the real test of a data mining model will be the test statistics on the validation data, not the statistics calculated from the training data.

In order to produce reliable measures of the effectiveness of a data mining tool, researchers **partition** a data set before building a data mining model. It is standard practice to divide the data set into partitions using some random procedure. We could, for instance, assign each instance in our data set a number and then partition the data set into two parts called the *training data* and the *validation data* (sometimes researchers use a third partition called the *test set*). If there is a great deal of data (unlike the Fisher iris data), there is little trouble in using 60% of the data as a training set and the remaining 40% as a validation data set. This ensures that no effectiveness statistics are drawn from the data used to create the model. Thus, the first step in any real data mining procedure is to partition the data. It is common practice to fold the validation data back into the training data and re-estimate the model if the model performs well in the validation data.

CHURNING: A BUSINESS EXAMPLE

What would such a model look like in a business situation? We turn now to examining data related to an important issue for any company: customer attrition. Churn is the opposite of customer retention and represents one situation that businesses analyze using data mining techniques, including k-Nearest-Neighbor. We are going to define *churn* here as it is used in the cellular telephone industry; it refers to all forms of customer attrition whether voluntary or involuntary. One of the challenges faced by any firm that offers services on a continuing basis is retention of their customer base. One common view about retention is that "it is one-third as expensive to retain a customer you already have compared to attracting a new one." Television viewers are bombarded with advertising that extols the benefits of one mobile carrier or another and the services they offer, the devices they offer to you, and the always low rates they guarantee to subscribers. Since most individuals in the United States already have a cell phone, this advertising must be directed toward people who already subscribe to a competitor's service. That begs the question of how many people actually switch their cellular service providers. Judging from the volume of advertising, it must amount to a substantial portion of the installed customer base.

What if you could successfully identify which of your customers were "thinking about" switching to another provider? Would this be valuable information? You bet it would! It would allow you to approach those customers being successfully attracted by your competitors and offer them whatever it takes (within reason) to retain them. Remember, every lost customer must be replaced by new customers, and new customers are expensive to acquire and often generate less revenue now than established customers. What we are describing here is true of almost every industry that is mature and where the market is almost saturated; it is certainly true of the cellular telephone industry. In any saturated industry the response rate to these ads goes down, acquisition costs skyrocket, and the cost of attracting a new customer goes up. But your firm already has data on your present and past customers that could hold the answer to the question "which of my customers is thinking about jumping ship?"

The data we use in this example represents a company's own customer data; each record (observation) represents a single customer. These individuals have been customers of the mobile provider at some time in the past; many are current customers. The type of data is listed in Table 4.1.

The cellular carrier would like to know which customers are likely to leave the carrier (churn). Will this set of attributes predict whether a customer would be likely to churn? This is a classification problem not unlike deciding in what class to place an unknown iris type. In this case the firm would like a rule that would classify all customers as either "likely to churn" or "unlikely to churn."

TABLE 4.1

Cellular Carrier Customer Data Table

ID	Customer ID						
Bill	Current bill amount						
Average Calls	Average number of calls per service period						
Acct. Age	Account age						
Delinquent	Average delinquent days per period						
Complaint	Current technical support complaints						
Age	Equipment age						
Churn	A categorical variable equal to 1 if the customer leaves, otherwise 0						

It is appropriate to begin first by partitioning the cellular carrier data. Since each row represents a different customer we could assign a number to each row and use a random selection process to choose 60% of the data to act as a training set. All data mining software, such as XLMiner[*], will have such a partitioning option.

Note that the "Row ID" in Figure 4.4 skips from row 1 to row 4 and then from row 6 to row 9. This is because the random selection process has chosen customers 1, 4, 5, 6, and 9 for the training data set but has placed customers 2, 3, 7, and 8 in the validation data set. Examining the header to Figure 4.4 you will note that there were a total of 4,708 customers in the original data set that have now been divided into a training partition of 2,825 customers and a validation partition of 1,883 customers.

When we instruct the software to perform a k-Nearest-Neighbor analysis of the training data, the real work takes place in the software. Just as in the iris classification example, the program will compare each customer's churn experience with the remaining attributes. This example is, of course, more multidimensional since we have six attributes for each customer (as opposed to only the two characteristics we used in the iris example). The program will compute the distance associated with each attribute. For attributes that are measured as continuous variables the software will normalize the distance and then measure it (because different attributes may be measured in different scales). Different numbers of neighbors will be asked to "vote" for one classification or the other (i.e., likely to churn or

---

[*] XLMiner is not a commercial data mining software; it is designed to teach data mining principles in the form of an add-in for Microsoft Excel. Easy to use, it is an ideal first step for an individual new to data mining.

Data								
Data source	Data Short!$A$2:$H$4709							
Selected variables	Account ID	target churn	Current Bill Am	Avg Calls	Account Age	Avg Days Del	Current Tech	Equipment Age
Partitioning Method	Randomly chosen							
Random Seed	12345							
# training rows	2825							
# validation rows	1883							

Row Id.	Selected variables							
	Account ID	target churn	Current Bill Amt	Avg Calls	Account Age	Avg Days Delinquent	Current TechSupCo	Equipment Age
1	1100115	0	14210	17950	24	6.2	0	8
4	1100891	1	10594	2136	39	25.75	1	16
5	1100913	1	12712	204.6666667	23	17.6	0	23
6	1100939	0	13807	15490.33333	39	0	0	17
9	1101000	1	2847	94.66666667	39	11.2	0	19
10	1101104	0	10238	5147.666667	36	3.666666667	0	1
12	1101179	0	8082	2667	39	4	0	15
17	1101323	1	4616	4244	32	9.5	0	3
18	1101503	0	22061	12681.66667	39	7.666666667	0	10
19	1101591	0	34888	66	39	0	0	39

FIGURE 4.4
A portion of the partitioned mobile carrier customer data.

not likely to churn) and the best k given some performance measure will be selected and reported.

The accuracy measures for the estimated model are the way a data miner can tell if she has possibly found a useful classification scheme. In this instance we want to find a way to classify customers as likely to churn. Are there characteristics that could lead us to classify some customers as much more likely to churn and others as quite unlikely to drop the services of this mobile carrier? While the accuracy measures are often produced by the software for both the training partition and the validation partition, the emphasis should clearly be on those measures pertaining to the validation partition of the data. There are two standard accuracy measures that data miners use and we will examine: the **classification matrix** (also called the *confusion matrix*) and the **lift chart**. The classification matrix for the mobile carrier training data is shown in Figure 4.5.

Accuracy is measured in terms of error rate, the percentage of records we have classified incorrectly. The error rate is often displayed for both the training data set and the validation data set in separate tables. Figure 4.5 is such a display for the validation data set in the cellular carrier data. The table is correctly called either a *confusion matrix* or a *classification matrix*. In Figure 4.5 there were 655 records that were correctly classified as "class 1" (i.e., probable churn candidates). They were correctly classified because these records represented individuals that did indeed churn. However, 252 records were classified as class 1 incorrectly; these were individuals that the model expected to churn when in fact they did not historically do so.

Validation Data scoring - Summary Report (for k=5)

Cut off Prob.Val. for Success (Updatable)	0.5

Classification Confusion Matrix

Actual Class	Predicted Class	
	1	0
1	655	252
0	281	695

Error Report

Class	# Cases	# Errors	% Error
1	907	252	27.78
0	976	281	28.79
Overall	1883	533	28.31

FIGURE 4.5
Confusion matrix for the validation partition of the mobile carrier customer data.

In addition, the table shows 695 records predicted to be class 0 (i.e., not probable churn candidates). These records were classified correctly since historically these individuals did not churn. Finally, 281 records were incorrectly classified as class 0 when they actually churned. The table can then be used to compute a misclassification rate. This calculation simply shows the percentage of the records that the model has placed in the incorrect category. In this case we have 1,883 records in the validation data set and we have correctly classified 1,350 of them (655 + 695). But we have also incorrectly classified 252 records as class 1 when they were actually in class 0. We have also incorrectly classified 281 records as class 0 when they were actually in class 1. Thus, we have incorrectly classified 533 records (252 + 281). The misclassification rate is the total number of misclassifications divided by the total records classified (and is usually reported as a percentage). Most packages show the calculation and report it. The misclassification rate is shown in Figure 4.5 in the lower right-hand corner as 28.31 percent (calculated as 533/1,883 and expressed as a percentage). There are two ways error enters our cellular carrier example and although some errors may be more costly than others to a firm, the misclassification index groups these two types of error together. This may not be an ideal reporting mechanism but it is the common practice in data mining software. Some software allows the user to assign different costs to the different forms of error as a means of differentiating their impacts.

In Figure 4.5 the output indicates that the software has chosen the best k to be equal to 5, meaning that 5 neighbors (not 5 attributes) were used to classify each record. The software has taken a "vote" of the 5 nearest neighbors in order to classify each record as either likely to churn or not likely to churn. As part of the solution routine, the software actually varied the number of neighbors from small to large numbers but reported only the best results. With most software the researcher will specify the range of values for k that the software is to search. In this situation the software minimized the misclassification rate (a performance measure) when examining the various values of k that it could select.

In Figure 4.6 the software has provided a visual picture of how the optimal k was chosen. Values of k between 1 and 10 were tried and the resulting misclassification rates are reported in the "% Error Validation" column. The smallest (i.e., the best) of these is 28.31 resulting from using 5 neighbors in the vote; this is the optimal k that was reported.

Data miners often use a second way of examining the accuracy of their models, and this can be displayed for the cellular carrier data example. Virtually all data mining software will display a lift chart for the chosen solution. The lift chart for our example appears in Figure 4.7.

Lift is actually a ratio; lift measures the change in concentration of a particular class when the model is used to select from a portion of the general population. Consider why the cellular carrier is attempting to classify records as either "likely to churn" or "unlikely to churn." The firm is probably interested in contacting those likely to churn and attempt to keep them as customers. What if the mobile carrier is able to identify those

Validation error log for different k

Value of k	% Error Training	% Error Validation	
1	0.00	33.35	
2	17.98	34.15	
3	17.84	30.54	
4	21.59	29.53	
5	21.70	28.31	<— Best k
6	23.26	29.21	
7	22.62	28.89	
8	23.29	28.36	
9	23.40	28.78	
10	23.93	28.52	

FIGURE 4.6
Validation error log.

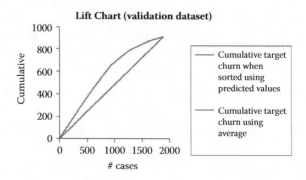

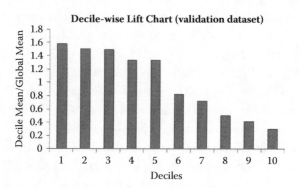

FIGURE 4.7
Validation data lift chart and decile-wise lift chart.

likely to churn before attempting to contact any of its current customers? Furthermore, what if the number of those likely to churn was far smaller than the size of the entire set of customers? The lift curve (and decile-wise lift chart) will help the mobile carrier to see how effective the model was in predicting such a classification.

Using the information about what the k-Nearest-Neighbor model predicted in every case in the validation data set and what every individual actually did, the software draws the lift chart. The lift chart shown in Figure 4.7 is correctly called a *cumulative gains chart*; it is built with the records arranged on the x-axis from left to right from the highest probability to the lowest probability to churn. The y-axis records the number of true positives at every point (i.e., the y-axis counts the number of records that represents those who churn). Examine the decile-wise lift chart shown on the right-hand side of Figure 4.7. Note that if we were to choose the top 10% of the records classified by the model (i.e., the 10% most likely to churn) the selection would include approximately 1.6 times as many correct classifications than if we were to select a random 10% from the database. That is a modest lift exhibited by this model when compared to a random selection; in many instances, the lift will be a large multiple of the success offered by a random selection.

The same information is displayed in a slightly different manner in the lift chart on the left-hand side of Figure 4.7. This form of the lift chart exhibits the cumulative records correctly classified on the y-axis with the records arranged in descending probability order on the x-axis. As the curve inclines upward above the 45-degree line, the model is said to provide lift relative to a random selection of the records. The steeper the curve deviates from the 45-degree line, the more lift is indicated for the model (i.e., the better the model is at classifying). The 45-degree line is a reference line; the line represents how well you might do by classifying as a result of random selection. If the calculated lift line is significantly above the reference line, you should expect the model to outperform a random selection. In this case the k-Nearest-Neighbor model modestly outperforms a random selection.

TEXT ANALYTICS

Of course, analytics deals not only with numerical data but also with textual data (which could be transformed into numerical data). That brings us to the need to define the difference between "discovery" and "search." The distinction applies to data mining as well as text analytics, but it is best explained with a table identifying exactly where both fit in a simple taxonomy.

The Table 4.2 taxonomy makes clear that mining, either data mining or text mining, fits clearly into the category of "discovery" (i.e., we are looking for correlations or patterns that we had no preconception of the data). Using "search" routines, however, presuppose that we had something in mind in the way of a possible pattern before we began the search. There is good reason to believe that text mining could be even more important

TABLE 4.2

Search versus Discover

	Search (Goal Oriented)	Discover (Opportunistic)
Structured Data	Data retrieval	Data mining
Unstructured Data (Text)	Information retrieval	Text mining

than data mining proper. The reason is that most of the world's data is held in an unstructured format, and hence there is much more data to "mine" in the unstructured world.

An example is provided in the *Text Mining Handbook*.[*] Francis and Flynn point out that the insurance industry is a likely user of text mining through the use of mining open-ended fields on insurance forms that customers traditionally complete (e.g., accident descriptions). These fields can be examined for word length, word usage, sentiment, word uniqueness, correspondence to Zipf's law, and so forth. The goal may be to determine the claims most likely to result in significant attorney involvement; claims adjusters might be better able to manage claims if they had such information (according to Francis and Flynn).

It seems fairly obvious that text mining is a subset of data mining which has been around a shorter time and which may be a bit less advanced simply because we have been at it for a shorter period of time. But text mining is catching up in terms of sophistication and it has good reason to, since that is where much of the data exists. The data in text is not well organized and has a different set of characteristics than the data we think of as numerical; text has characteristics associated with syntax, semantics, as well as lexical and pragmatic characteristics. Even given the unstructured challenges of text, some of the very same algorithms used in data mining are also used in text mining. Chapter 6 will discuss text mining in more detail.

SUMMARY

In this chapter, we have explained the uses of data mining and defined the four classes of data mining tools. We concentrated on the classification type of data mining tool and demonstrated an example of one data mining algorithm that aids classification: k-Nearest-Neighbor. Classification, however, is only a single aspect of data mining and k-Nearest-Neighbor is only one of a number of algorithms available for classification. In general, there is no one best classification technique; the individual data in a particular situation will determine the

---

[*] Louise Francis and Matt Flynn, (2010), *Text Mining Handbook*, 2010 Data Management, Quality and Technology Call for Papers, Casualty Actuarial Society, (http://www.casact.org/pubs/forum/10spforum/Francis_Flynn.pdf).

best technique to use. The diagnostic statistics will lead the researcher to choose an appropriate model. There may be no optimal model, only acceptable models. Other data mining tools such as clustering analysis and neural networks analysis are not covered here but there are excellent resources for those interested.

Questions

1. Explain (with a diagram perhaps) how a k-Nearest-Neighbor model works.

   Answer: A k-Nearest-Neighbor model works by selecting the classification of an unknown with reference to its "nearest neighbors." It is common to use more than a single nearest neighbor (by taking a "vote" of neighbors) to make the classification. The "k" refers to the number of neighbors used to minimize the misclassification rate.

2. Explain the difference between a "training" data set and a "validation" data set. How are the two data sets constructed?

   Answer: The historic data in a data mining situation is "partitioned" before an estimate of the model is constructed. The data is divided into three or, more commonly, two separate data sets. The three data sets are constructed by randomly selecting records in the original data set. The model is constructed from the "training" data set and usefulness is tested with the "validation" data set; the validation data set is unseen data for the model estimated. At times a third data set called the *test* data set is employed.

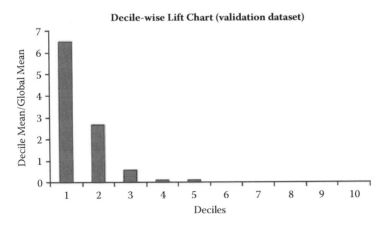

Decile-wise Lift Chart (validation dataset)

3. Consider the decile-wise lift chart above resulting from the application of a data mining algorithm (k-Nearest-Neighbor, perhaps). For the decile most likely to achieve "success," how many more times likely is this algorithm to make the correct prediction than a naïve model?

Answer: For the first decile of the validation data set (ordered in rank by the model from most likely to be in the "success" category to least likely to be in the "success" category), the model beats a naïve model by about 6.5 times as likely to correctly classify a record (as shown by the height of the left-most bar). For the second decile, the model is about 3 times as likely to correctly classify a record compared to the naïve model. This then is a very predictive model; the algorithm has done its job well!

A

Classification Confusion Matrix		
	Predicted Class	
Actual Class	1	0
1	58	920
0	30	32

B

Classification Confusion Matrix		
	Predicted Class	
Actual Class	1	0
1	32	30
0	58	920

C

Classification Confusion Matrix		
	Predicted Class	
Actual Class	1	0
1	30	32
0	58	920

D

Classification Confusion Matrix		
	Predicted Class	
Actual Class	1	0
1	920	58
0	30	32

4. Which of the confusion matrices above would match the validation data set decile-wise lift chart in Question 3?

Answer: Only the confusion matrix in "C" is consistent with the decile-wise lift chart shown in Question 3.

	Predict class 1	Predict class 0
Actual 1	8	2
Actual 0	20	970

5. Consider the confusion matrix shown above. What would be the misclassification rate associated with this data mining model result?

Answer: The misclassification rate is 2.2%.

6. Consider again the correct confusion matrix shown in Question 4 and the decile-wise lift chart shown in Question 3 (these are both from the same model). How did this data mining technique do as compared to a naïve model?

Answer: The overall (i.e., using all 1,000 records in the validation data set) misclassification rate for the naïve model would have been 5.96%. Since the estimated model reported an overall misclassification rate of 8.65% for the validation data set, it would appear that the naïve model is better. This would be correct if we were to look at the entire validation data set as a whole. That is not, however, how a data scientist compares the models.

The decile-wise lift chart clearly shows that when we allow the data mining model to arrange the records in the validation data set from "most likely" to "least likely," the rate of classifying records in the first two deciles improves dramatically (as shown by the height of the first two bars on the left side of the diagram). The model outperforms the naïve model by about 6.5 times the success rate for the first decile and by about 3 times for the second decile in the validation data set. Thus, the model appears to be quite predictive and a significant improvement from using the naïve model.

5

Big Data Analytics for Business Intelligence

Onur Savas, Tung Thanh Nguyen, and Julia Deng

CONTENTS

Learning Objectives

In this chapter, we discuss the fundamentals of Big Data analytics for business intelligence (BI). We first describe what *Big Data* is, why Big Data analytics is important for BI, what data science is, and who a data scientist is. We then discuss emerging Big Data analytics frameworks with an emphasis on cloud computing and the Hadoop ecosystem, and we discuss two important applications, online targeted advertising and recommendation systems. At the end of this chapter, we will have answered the following questions:

- What is Big Data and why does it matter for business intelligence?
- What challenges does Big Data present?
- What is data science, who is a data scientist, and what skills are required to become one?
- What technologies are available to solve Big Data problems?
- What are some important applications of Big Data analytics?
- What does the future hold for Big Data?

DISCUSSION OF THE CONCEPTS, TECHNIQUES, ISSUES, APPLICATIONS, AND TRENDS

Big Data and Big Data Analytics

The truth about Big Data is that the data *was always* big and *will always be* big. However, with the explosion of digital information, the need to crunch Big Data has been obliterated. In fact, it has been realized that the applications, algorithms, and software tools that used to work with smaller data sets are no longer efficient (and sometimes useless) to process data. Hence, we can define Big Data as *"a collection of data sets so large and complex that it becomes difficult to process using traditional data processing applications."* The important words in this definition are *large* and *complex*. While large refers to the amount of data, complex has more profound meanings, including the rate at which data is processed. To put the "large" and "complex" into perspective, we will use the "3Vs" model for describing Big Data. The three "Vs" refer to the volume (amount of data), velocity (speed of data in and out), and variety (range of data types). Some of the challenges introduced by these 3Vs are as follows.

- *Volume:* At minimum, Big Data needs to be stored, read, queried, and transmitted; for example, over the Internet. These challenges should be addressed in software and require investment in infrastructures that support Big Data.
- *Velocity:* Sometimes one minute is too late. For time-sensitive processes such as online trading or detecting fraud, Big Data must be used as it streams. This creates enormous challenges in terms of

balancing data latency in decision cycles because even small glitches in service delivery can lose companies millions of dollars.

- *Variety:* Big Data can be any type of data such as text, sensor data, audio, video, click streams, log files, and more. New insights are found when analyzing these data types together. However, analyzing different types of data demands complex software that is capable of interoperability.

In addition to these original 3Vs, many other "Vs" have been introduced. For example, *veracity* refers to establishing trust in the Big Data, and *value* refers to, well, value of the Big Data.

Big data analytics then refers to the process of examining large amounts of data of a variety of types to uncover hidden patterns, unknown correlations, and other useful information. From a BI perspective, we can argue that the primary goal of Big Data analytics is to help companies make better business decisions. This is done by employing data scientists and other users to analyze huge volumes of transaction data as well as other data sources that may be ignored by traditional BI programs. This brings us to the need for data science, and the *data scientist*.

Data Science and the Data Scientist

Harvard Business Review calls data science *"the sexiest job in the 21st century"* [1]. Given the amount of investment and expected return on investment on the Big Data, this claim is not far from the truth. But what is data science and what skills are required to be a data scientist? We answer these questions below.

Data science includes various elements and builds on techniques and theories from many fields. Some of them are shown in Figure 5.1, and include math, statistics, data engineering, pattern recognition and learning, advanced computing, visualization, uncertainty modeling, data warehousing, and high performance computing with the goal of extracting meaning from data and creating data products. Data science can be used interchangeably with competitive intelligence or business analytics. Data science aims to use all available and relevant data to effectively gain insight that can be easily understood by non-experts.

A practitioner of data science is called a *data scientist*. Data scientists are expected to have great analytical skills and solve complex data problems through expertise in some of the related fields. It is also generally expected

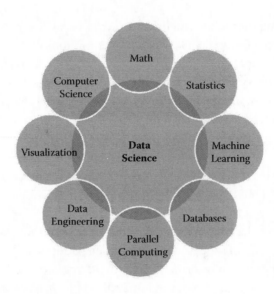

FIGURE 5.1
Some of the required skills for data science.

that data scientists are able to work with various elements of mathematics, statistics, and computer science, although expertise in these subjects is not required. However, a data scientist is most likely to be an expert in only one or two of these disciplines and proficient in another. That is the reason data science should be practiced as a team. Data science teams need people with the skills and curiosity to ask the big questions for Big Data. In fact, as of the writing of this book, 1.5 million more data scientists are needed to take full advantage of Big Data in the United States. There are a lot of opportunities for data scientists for decades to come.

BIG DATA FOR BUSINESS INTELLIGENCE: REAL-WORLD EXAMPLES

Companies have already started investing in Big Data and are serving millions of customers using Big Data technologies. Some of the amazing facts about the companies and their use of Big Data are listed below [2]:

- Amazon.com handles millions of back-end operations every day, as well as queries from more than half a million third-party sellers.

- Walmart handles more than 1 million customer transactions every hour, which is imported into databases estimated to contain more than 2.5 petabytes (2560 terabytes) of data—the equivalent of 167 times the information contained in all the books in the U.S. Library of Congress.
- One billion pieces of content are shared via Facebook's Open Graph daily.
- PayPal uses their big-data capabilities for fraud detection in line with their reputation as a secure e-commerce and payment platform.
- American Express, by contrast, uses proprietary Big Data it holds to create new services to enhance customer acquisition and retention programs for marketers and merchants.
- IBM converts 350 billion annual meter readings through Big Data to better predict power consumption.
- IBM analyzes 500 million daily call detail records in real time with Big Data to predict customer churn faster.
- Twitter uses 12 terabytes of tweets each day to improve product sentiment analysis.
- Progressive Casualty Insurance Company uses Big Data as part of its "pay as you drive" program, offering drivers the chance to lower their insurance premiums based on real-time analysis of their driving habits.

BIG DATA TECHNOLOGIES

Cloud Computing

From the technology view point, according to the official NIST (National Institute of Standards and Technology), cloud computing is defined as "a model for enabling ubiquitous, convenient, on-demand network access to a shared pool of configurable computing resources (e.g., networks, servers, storage, applications, and services) that can be rapidly provisioned and released with minimal management effort or service provider interaction."

From the business viewpoint, cloud computing can be considered a computing environment, where business owners outsource their computing needs to a third party. When they need to use computing resources such as Web server, database, emails, and so on, they access these resources via the Internet. A popular example of cloud computing is Yahoo! Mail or Gmail. When you send or receive email, you do not need any application software installed in your computer. You just need a browser and an Internet connection. Essential characteristics of cloud service include on-demand self-service, broad network access, resource pooling, rapid elasticity, and measured service.

The cloud computing model is emerging rapidly due to the benefits it brings to both consumer and provider. Cloud providers can consolidate a user's software stack (virtual machines) to improve the utilization of the system, and focus on the efficiency of their system (energy consumption, security, etc.). The biggest benefit of cloud providers is obviously the revenue generated by the service itself.

From the consumer point of view, cloud users do not have to pay for IT infrastructure installation and maintenance cost. The high up-front cost for the IT infrastructure is for devices, servers, networking equipment, and software licenses. There are also many other costs in running an IT infrastructure such as real estate, energy, cooling, IT admin staffs, management and monitoring software, servers, and so on.

A user of cloud computing only has to pay the service charges according to her usage of computing resources. She does not have to worry about software updates, installation, anti-viruses, backups, Web/email servers, and both physical and logical security of her data, and therefore can concentrate more on her core business competency. Basically, cloud computing allows its users to shift from capital expenditures to operating expenses.

Another key reason to employ a cloud solution is that the on-site IT system of a small business is usually underutilized, and it also does not scale/agile to quickly meet business demands. Cloud computing allows us to deploy new servers in minutes and pay based on hourly usage. It helps in increasing the agility, which is the ability to get up and running with new products and services faster, and provides the ability to scale on demand to handle unexpected loads, preventing loss of business due to decreased performance or downtime. It is this scalability of the cloud that enables Big Data analytics.

Other important benefits of using the cloud include disaster recovery/backup ability, carbon footprint reduction, accessibility, and collaboration improvement (people worldwide can access the cloud to synchronize, work on documents, and share applications simultaneously with the Internet).

However, there are also some issues in adopting the cloud. First, since all data is stored in the third-party infrastructure (data centers), security and privacy are obviously potential problems. Second, since most or all computing needs are satisfied by the cloud, users could feel a lack of control over their data, applications, or services. Third, due to the lack of cloud computing standards and compliance, users may be locked in with a certain cloud provider. Fourth, availability and reliability should also be a concern when moving to the cloud due to the fact that all users are sharing the same environment.

There are many different types of cloud services. We can classify them into three main categories as shown in Figure 5.2:

- *Infrastructure as a Service (IaaS)* provides the consumer with the ability "to provision processing, storage, networks, and other fundamental computing resources where the consumer is able to deploy and run arbitrary software, which can include operating systems and applications." In this category, the user or consumer does not manage the underlying IT infrastructure such as power, cooling, network, and servers. However, he or she can control the operating systems, storage, applications, and even selected networking components. Amazon EC2 is a great example of this type of service.
- *Platform as a Service (PaaS)* enables the user to deploy onto the cloud infrastructure their own or acquired applications created by "using programming languages, libraries, services, and tools supported by the provider." The PaaS consumers do not operate the cloud infrastructure, operating systems, or storage. Nevertheless, they have control over the deployed applications and even the configuration settings of the hosting environment. Google App engine, IBM smart

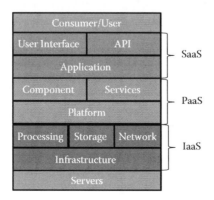

FIGURE 5.2
Cloud computing service architecture.

cloud, Microsoft Azure, RedHat Openshift, Force.com, and so on, provide this type of service.

- *Software as a Service (SaaS)* allows the consumer to use the provider's applications running on a cloud infrastructure. The applications can be accessed via either a thin client interface (e.g., Web browser) or a program interface from various client devices. The SaaS consumer also does not manage the underlying cloud infrastructure and even individual application capabilities, but he or she may have limited control over certain user specific application configuration settings. Akamai, Oracle On Demand, SAP, Salesforce.com (Customer Relationship Management), and NetSuite are some examples in this category.

Considering the installation of network infrastructure, a cloud environment can be broadly categorized into the following deployment models:

- *Private cloud:* A cloud infrastructure is deployed to be exclusively used by a single organization containing multiple business units. The organization or a third party may own, manage, and operate it. They need to set up their own data center, bear all the installation as well as maintenance costs, but they have complete control of all data. This type of cloud provides more security and privacy, but it is more expensive.
- *Community cloud:* A cloud infrastructure is deployed to be exclusively used by a specific community of organizations that share certain concerns. One or more members of the community or a third party may own, manage, and operate it.
- *Public cloud:* A cloud infrastructure is deployed to be used by the general public. A business, academic, government organization, or some combination of these may own, manage, and operate it. It normally resides on the premises of the cloud provider. It can be considered the most popular type of cloud system by cloud computing experts. Amazon Web Services and Google Apps are the two most popular public cloud computing service providers.
- *Hybrid cloud:* A cloud infrastructure is a combination of two or more distinct aforementioned types of cloud infrastructures (private, community, or public). They are bounded together by standardized or proprietary technology that enables data and application portability.

Almost all big IT companies such as Google, Microsoft, Apple, Intel, Oracle, IBM, Amazon, HP, Salesforce, Dell, Rackspace, and so forth, provide cloud computing services. There are also many open-source cloud projects available such as OpenStack, CloudStack, Eucalyptus, Nimbus, Ganeti, and OpenNebula.

Big Data Analytics Software and Services

Cloud computing provides the IT infrastructure that enables Big Data analysis but we also need an efficient and scalable programming framework and environment to develop and execute our analytic applications.

While Big Data can be analyzed by the software tools commonly used in advanced analytics via data warehouses (a database used for reporting and data analysis) such as predictive analytics and data mining, it is the unstructured data sources that may not fit in traditional data warehouses. Moreover, traditional data warehouses may not have enough processing capability to handle Big Data. Consequently, a new class of Big Data technology has emerged and is being used in many Big Data analytics environments. This is where the **Hadoop Ecosystem**, **NoSQL**, and **MapReduce** technologies come to the scene. These technologies are open source and together they form a software framework that supports the processing of large data sets on distributed clustered systems.

Potential problems of Big Data analytics initiatives include a lack of internal analytics skills, the high cost of hiring experienced analytics experts, and challenges in integrating Hadoop systems and data warehouses. Certain efforts have been taken to offer connectors between those technologies.

NoSQL

NoSQL, or Not Only SQL, database is a solution to manage data and design databases for very large sets of distributed data. It provides a mechanism to store and retrieve data using looser consistency models (differing from the strong consistency of the traditional relational databases) to achieve horizontal scaling and *higher availability*.

NoSQL is coined to solve the scalability and performance problem when processing Big Data that relational databases were not designed to handle. It is especially useful if one needs to access and analyze massive amounts of unstructured data or data that is stored in a distributed manner in the cloud. It is particularly useful when we prefer the ability to store and retrieve great quantities of data to the relationship among data.

Contrary to its misunderstood name, NoSQL does not necessarily exclude structured query language (SQL). While some NoSQL systems are entirely non-relational, others simply avoid selected relational functionality such as fixed table schemas and join operations. Instead of organizing data into tables, a NoSQL database might use objects, key/value pairs, or tuples.

There are many implementations of NoSQL databases such as Apache Cassandra, SimpleDB, Google Bigtable, Apache HBase, MemcacheDB, Voldemort, and so on. Companies that employ NoSQL include Netflix, Facebook, LinkedIn, and Twitter. NoSQL is often mentioned together with other Big Data tools such as massive parallel processing, columnar-based databases, and Database-as-a-Service (DaaS).

MapReduce

MapReduce [3,4] is a programming model for processing large data sets. The model is inspired by the *map* and *reduce* functions commonly used in functional programming languages such as Lisp and Haskell, although these functions in the MapReduce framework are not the same as the original. It is useful for tasks such as data mining, log file analysis, financial analysis, and scientific simulations.

It is well recognized that developing a parallel-executable application is very challenging and requires various specialized skills. A MapReduce implementation addresses this challenge by enabling programmers to produce parallel distributed programs in a much easier manner. The programmers only need to define the simple map and reduce functions (using the provided library), and create parallel programs that focus on the logic of their specific problem. The MapReduce framework would automatically take care of the rest, which includes marshaling the distributed servers, executing the tasks in parallel, managing communications and data transfers among components, monitoring tasks, and handling failure.

MapReduce allows for distributed processing of the map and reduction functions (operations/tasks). Normally, the mapping function is applied to different sets of data. Each of these applications is considered a task or operation. The mapping operations are independent of the others; all map tasks can be performed in parallel. However, in practice the parallelism is limited by the independency of data sources and/or the computing resource. Similarly, a set of reduce functions can be performed at the same time if all outputs of the map operation that share the same key are presented to the same reducer, or if the reduce function is associative. The parallelism enables some possibility of recovering from partial failure of servers or storage during the operation. If one map or reduce operation/ task fails, it can be executed again—assuming the input data is still available. While this process seems to be inefficient, it can be applied to significantly large data sets effectively. For example, it takes only a few hours for MapReduce to sort a petabyte of data [4].

How is a MapReduce application executed? First, it takes a list of records as an input. The records are split and distributed among the different computers in the system. Then, each split is processed by the user-defined map function to generate a list of key/value pairs. Next, the reduce function takes each set of values that has the same key and combines them into a single value. Generally, a map function takes a set of data chunks and produces key/value pairs, and a reduce function merges values of the same key to a single value.

The basic idea of the MapReduce framework is shown in Figure 5.3. The MapReduce framework operates exclusively on <key, value> pairs. The data that need to be processed is divided into "input splits." Each split contains many records in a <key, value> pair structure. The map blocks (defined by software developers based on the application business) map these input key, value pairs into other intermediate key, value pairs. This intermediate data is then sorted and grouped together based on the keys. As a result, the input of the reduce blocks is a key with a collection of values. The reduce blocks (also developed by MapReduce programmers) then produce the final results in the form of key-value pairs as well. One very

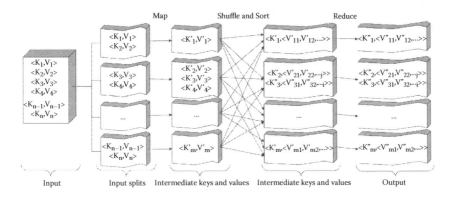

FIGURE 5.3
The MapReduce Framework. (From T. Nguyen, W. Shi, and D. Ruden, "CloudAligner: A Fast and Full-Featured MapReduce Based Tool for Sequence Mapping," *BMC Research Notes* 4:171, 2011.)

important feature enabling MapReduce to process a huge amount of data efficiently is that all maps and reduce blocks are executed concurrently. There are two main phases though: *map* and *reduce*. As we can see from the figure, all map tasks need to finish before running any reduce tasks.

Let us look at a simple example. Assume we have five text files and each line of a file contains two entities. The first one is the key that represents the name of a city and the second, called a *value*, represents the corresponding temperature recorded in that city at different points of time. Each file might have the same city represented multiple times. For example, in one file, we have the following collected data:

Toronto, 20
Whitby, 25
New York, 22
Rome, 32
Toronto, 4
Rome, 33
New York, 18

Our goal in this simple example is to find the maximum temperature for each city across all of the data files. Using the MapReduce framework, we have to define the map and reduce function. The map function takes a file as input. It goes through the input data and returns the maximum temperature for each city. For example, the results after applying the map function to the data above would look like this:

(Toronto, 20)   (Whitby, 25)   (New York, 22)   (Rome, 33)

The semantic of the functions is unchanged (the same code). However, when applied to different data sets it would return different results. In this case, we have five map tasks; each is for one input file. Let us assume the other four map tasks produced the following intermediate results:

(Toronto, 18)	(Whitby, 27)	(New York, 32)	(Rome, 37)
(Toronto, 32)	(Whitby, 20)	(New York, 33)	(Rome, 38)
(Toronto, 22)	(Whitby, 19)	(New York, 20)	(Rome, 31)
(Toronto, 31)	(Whitby, 22)	(New York, 19)	(Rome, 30)

All five of these output streams would be fed into the reduce tasks, which combine the input results and output a single value for each city. The input of the reduce function has the form of

```
<key, list of values>
```

For example, one input of our reduce task is Toronto, 20,18, 32,22,31>.

With this form of input, in the reduce function of this particular example, we only need to return the maximum in the list of values. For example (Toronto, 32).

Similarly, the reduce function is applied to all other keys (cities) producing a final result set as follows:

(Toronto, 32)   (Whitby, 27)   (New York, 33)   (Rome, 38)

This example is very simple. Real-world applications would contain millions or even billions of rows with or without a neat format. However, no matter how big or small the amount of data, the key principles still remain the same.

There are several implementations of MapReduce available in a variety of programming languages such as Java, C++, Python, Perl, Ruby, and C.

Google implemented the model with the same name (MapReduce) to index Web pages and replace their original indexing algorithms and heuristics in 2004 [3]. Hadoop [6], inspired by Google's MapReduce, GoogleFS, and Bigtable, is a free, Java-based programming framework that supports the processing of large data sets in a distributed computing environment. It is part of the Apache Software Foundation sponsored project created originally by Doug Cutting. Sector/Sphere, Phoenix, Mars, Disco, and MapR are some other implementations of the MapReduce model. From this point on, we will focus on Hadoop, since it is open source and considered the most popular implementation of MapReduce.

Generally, an implementation of MapReduce is a software framework to do distributed computing for processing parallelizable problems on huge data sets across a large number of computers (nodes). The computing infrastructure can be a physical cluster (same network and similar hardware), a grid (geographically and administratively distributed and heterogeneous hardware), or a cloud (virtual machines). The data to be processed can be stored in either a distributed file system (unstructured) or a database (structured). MapReduce can take advantage of data locality to process data on or near its storage to reduce data transmission.

Hadoop Implementation of MapReduce

Hadoop framework follows the master/slave model in which each slave (node) in the cluster is expected to report periodically with completed work and status updates to the master. If a node remains silent for longer than the specified amount of time, the master node assumes that it is failed, so it makes note and re-assigns the task to others. Therefore, the Hadoop framework is fault-tolerant.

Hadoop claims that it can run applications on thousands of nodes with thousands of terabytes of data. It comes with a Hadoop distributed file system (HDFS) that supports fast data transfer rates among nodes and is able to continue operating properly even in the presence of node failure.

The MapReduce framework is used by many giants including eBay, Yahoo, LinkedIn, Facebook, and IBM, largely for applications relating to search engines and advertising. The preferred operating systems are Windows and Linux but Hadoop can also work with BSD and OS X.

Let us look at another popular example. We would like to write a MapReduce WordCount application to count the number of appearances of each word in a given input set of documents. Assuming our input set includes two text files with the following content:

File1: "Hello World Bye World"
File2: "Hello Hadoop Goodbye Hadoop"

As we have learned, we need to define the map and reduce function for this application. However, before designing them, it should be noted that MapReduce works on <key, value> pairs. As a result, we need to identify what are key and value in each stage (map and reduce stage). A pseudo code for these [7] is as follows:

```
function map(String input_key, String input_value)
    //input_key: document name
    //input_value: document contents
    for each word w in input_value:
                EmitIntermediate(w, "1");
function reduce(String output_key, Iterator intermediate_values)
    //output_key: a word
    //output_values: a list of counts
    int result = 0;
    for each v in intermediate_values:
            result + = ParseInt(v);
Emit(AsString(result));
```

In the code, we can see that the key and value input of the map function are the document name (or file name) and its corresponding content, respectively. The key and value of the output of the map function are word and 1, respectively. Basically, the map function would split each document into words. For example, the output of applying the map function to our File1 is:

```
< Hello, 1>
< World, 1>
< Bye, 1>
< World, 1>
```

and to File2 is:

```
< Hello, 1>
< Hadoop, 1>
< Goodbye, 1>
< Hadoop, 1>
```

These outputs are called *intermediate* <key, value> pairs. The framework puts together all the pairs with the same key and feeds them to the reduce function. The key and value of the input of the reduce function in this example are the word and a "list of count," respectively. For example: <"Hello,"<1,1>>.

As such, the reduce function only needs to sum all of its input values to find the total occurrences of a word that is exactly what is shown in the code.

The following is the real Java code of the map and reduce function in the Hadoop framework.

```
public void map(LongWritable key, Text value,
          OutputCollector<Text, IntWritable> output, Reporter reporter)
          throws IOException {
     String line = value.toString();
     StringTokenizer tokenizer = new StringTokenizer(line);
     while (tokenizer.hasMoreTokens()) {
          word.set(tokenizer.nextToken());
          output.collect(word, one);
     }
}
public void reduce(Text key, Iterator<IntWritable> values,
          OutputCollector<Text, IntWritable> output, Reporter reporter)
          throws IOException {
     int sum = 0;
     while (values.hasNext()) {
          sum + = values.next().get();
     }
     output.collect(key, new IntWritable(sum));
}
```

In this real code, it is noteworthy that the key and value of the input for the map function differ a little bit from the pseudo code. The key and value in this version are the line number and the content of that line in the document. This is the default <key, value> input of Hadoop. However, the programmer can always change it according to his or her needs. The "Writable" and other classes are provided by the Hadoop framework as a library to help the programmers in developing their MapReduce applications.

In addition, in Hadoop one can specify a combine function called *combiner* (in this case, it is the same as the reduce function). The output of each map is passed through the combiner for local aggregation. For example, the output of the combiner after the first map is:

```
< Bye, 1>
< Hello, 1>
< World, 2>
```

The second map is:

```
< Goodbye, 1>
< Hadoop, 2>
< Hello, 1>
```

Hadoop also automatically sorts this output. Finally, the result of the WordCount application (job) is:

```
<Bye, 1>
<Goodbye, 1>
<Hadoop, 2>
<Hello, 2>
<World, 2>
```

Hadoop Ecosystem

Hadoop MapReduce and Hadoop Distributed File System comprise a core platform where many other software tools and services are built. Altogether, they are referred to as the *Hadoop Ecosystem*. In other words, the Apache Hadoop Ecosystem consists of the Hadoop kernel, MapReduce, HDFS, and a number of related projects such as Apache Hive, HBase, Pig, Zookeeper, and so forth. The Hadoop ecosystem is, as an ecosystem, complex and evolving. It is not easily divided clearly into neat categories. It is not easy just to keep track of all the project names in it. These projects are not meant to be used together as a whole. Some of them may even try to solve the same problem in different ways. However, the common interest they share is the scalability and power of the core Hadoop (MapReduce and HDFS).

Figure 5.4 provides a very good story that reasons and positions the Hadoop-related projects in a big picture. First, starting from (1): How does everything begin? It is from the fact that the data available on the Web is extremely large. Therefore, in order to get useful information (search) from it, some tools have to be developed and Nutch (2) was created. Another

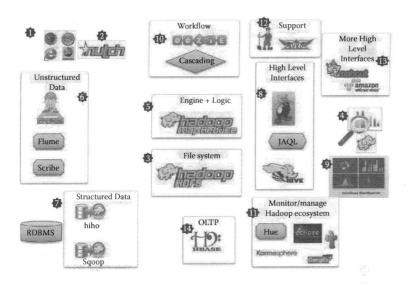

FIGURE 5.4
The Hadoop Ecosystem. (http://indoos.wordpress.com/2010/08/16/hadoop- ecosystem-world-map/.)

immediate need is storage for this large data effectively. As a result, HDFS (3) was born. After storing the data, what can we do with it (4)? MapReduce (5) was developed for coding and running analytics on it. As the work expands, one would like to add unstructured data (6) such as log or click streams to the system which results in the development of the projects such as Flume, Scribe, Chukwa, and so on. The import of structured data in the traditional Relational DataBase Management Systems (RDBMS) (7) is also taken care of by Sqoop or Hiho. To reduce the programming effort and lower the entrance barrier, a library for high-level programming (Pig, Hive, Mahout) was developed (8)(13). Next, to provide business intelligence and reporting solutions to the user based on the system, projects such as Intellicus (9) must be in place. As the system matures, we need to have tools to create and manage MapReduce workflows (Oozie) (10), tools to monitor, manage, view the system (Hue) (11), and supported frameworks (12) for serialization (Avro/Thrift) and coordination (Zookeeper). Finally, when one needs to process an extremely large table (billions of rows), one might want to try HBase (14).

We will give a little more detail of each popular project in the Hadoop ecosystem next. All the following information is obtained from the home page of each project (follow the links at Apache Hadoop [6]).

- *HDFS* (Hadoop Distributed File System), together with MapReduce, is the core of the whole system. It is a highly fault-tolerant distributed file system due to data replication and distribution of data. It is designed to run on a commodity cluster of machines. A MapReduce job typically processes data stored in HDFS. Files stored in HDFS are split into blocks and stored across nodes designated for storage, also known as DataNodes. One significant drawback to HDFS is that it has a single point of failure, which is its NameNode.
- *Avro* is a data serialization framework. It allows the user to define schema which is language independent so that data can be interchanged between different languages. Avro provides rich data structures; a compact, fast, binary data format; a container file, to store persistent data; remote procedure call (RPC); and simple integration with dynamic languages.
- *Pig* is a framework for analyzing large data sets using a high-level language called *Pig Latin*. Scripts written in Pig Latin are compiled by the framework to produce MapReduce jobs to be executed on the Hadoop cluster. Pig makes MapReduce job development easier. More than 60% of Hadoop usage at Yahoo is on Pig [9].
- *Hive* is a data warehouse system for Hadoop that facilitates easy data summarization, ad hoc queries, and the analysis of large data sets stored in Hadoop compatible file systems. It provides a mechanism to project structure onto this data and query the data using an SQL-like language called *HiveQL*. At the same time this language also allows traditional MapReduce programmers to plug in their custom mappers and reducers when it is inconvenient or inefficient to express this logic in HiveQL.
- *HBase* is a type of "NoSQL" database. HBase is very much a distributed database. Technically speaking, HBase is really more a "Data Store" than a "Data Base" because it lacks many of the features of a traditional RDBMS, such as typed columns, secondary indexes, triggers, advanced query languages, and so forth. However, HBase has many features, which support both linear and modular scaling. RDBMS can scale well, but only up to a point—specifically, the size of a single database server—and for the best performance requires specialized hardware and storage devices. HBase notable features include strongly consistent reads/writes, automatic sharding, automatic region server failover, Hadoop/HDFS Integration, Java Client API, Thrift/REST

API, Block Cache, Bloom Filters, and so forth. It is modeled after Google's Bigtable and is designed to support online transaction processing (OLTP).

- *Mahout* is a scalable machine learning library. It leverages Hadoop to achieve massive scalability.
- *YARN* of MapReduce 2.0 (MRv2) is the next generation of MapReduce. The MapReduce framework was revised to overcome the scalability bottlenecks in earlier versions when it was run over a very large cluster (thousands of nodes). The fundamental idea of MRv2 is to split up the two major functionalities of the JobTracker, resource management, and job scheduling/monitoring into separate daemons.
- *Oozie* is a scalable, reliable, and extensible workflow scheduler system to manage Apache Hadoop jobs. Oozie Workflow jobs are Directed Acyclical Graphs (DAGs) of actions. Oozie Coordinator jobs are recurrent Oozie Workflow jobs triggered by time (frequency) and data availabilty. Oozie is integrated with the rest of the Hadoop stack supporting several types of Hadoop jobs out of the box (such as Java map-reduce, Streaming MapReduce, Pig, Hive, Sqoop, and Distcp) as well as system specific jobs (such as Java programs and shell scripts).
- *Flume* is a distributed, reliable, and available service for efficiently collecting, aggregating, and moving log data to HDFS. It is robust and fault tolerant with tunable reliability mechanisms and many failover and recovery mechanisms. It uses a simple extensible data model that allows for online analytic applications.
- *Sqoop* is a tool designed for efficiently transferring bulk data between Hadoop and structured datastores such as relational databases.
- *Cascading* is an application framework for Java developers to simply develop robust data analytics and data management applications on Apache Hadoop.

APPLICATIONS

Targeted Online Advertising

Many advertisers (the companies that sell a product) and advertising agencies (the companies that show the online advertisements) rely on targeted online advertising for revenue generation. Targeted online advertising refers to the marketing or promotion of relevant products and services

over the Internet based on intelligent decisions about the user's interests, demographics, and history. For example, a considerable amount of
Google's revenue comes from showing and expecting users to be influenced
by "AdWords" in exchange for using free services such as Google search
or Gmail. In the case of Google search, Google shows relevant search ads
placed among or on top the results of a search query. In Facebook, targeted
advertisements are shown based on the factors including but not limited
to the users' interests, users' friends' interests, age, gender, and location.
The algorithms that make these decisions are well-kept secrets and part of
the company's intellectual property.

Targeted advertising has many advantages over direct placement of ads
[10], which is very similar to the advertising used by the traditional media
such as newspapers, TV, or magazines. Some of the advantages to the
advertisers, advertising companies, and users are as follows:

- Advertisers can show more "attractive" ads hence increasing the
  probability that a user will click on the ad. If Alice is looking for a
  vacation, a cruise ad is more likely to be relevant to her. Moreover, if
  she indeed clicks on the link, the advertising company will "learn"
  from this action and use this data to further improve their ad placement algorithms.
- There are various business models for ad placement. The advertiser
  can agree to pay when the ad is shown, when the user actually clicks
  on the ad, when the number of visitors to a certain Website that the
  ad is shown exceeds a predefined threshold, or simply a fixed amount
  no matter what. A company that advertises its products can negoti-
  ate a business model and put a cap on the amount of money spent.
  For example, in Google AdWords, one can set up a daily budget and
  pay only when the ad is *clicked* until the cap is reached. If the cap is
  reached, AdWords will stop showing any ads from the company.
- The ads can act as a system that recommends products based on the
  predictions about the user and user's browsing history. For example,
  Amazon shows relevant ads for its own products from its store to
  increase the probability that the customer will buy a product. This
  system essentially recommends products to the user. We will study
  recommendation systems in detail in the next section.
- While misplaced and excessive ads are generally a distraction for the
  Web user, useful ads give more information and more choices to the
  user before he/she makes a purchase.

As you might have already guessed, these algorithms use a lot of data in order to make intelligent decisions. The data can come from user's search queries (Google search, Amazon product search), professional information (LinkedIn), interests and "likes" (Facebook), purchase histories (Visa, Mastercard), check-ins (Foursquare), and login information (age, gender, location, income etc.) when registering to the Website. While it can be argued that right and honest ad placement increases the user's Web experience, the data collected by the companies also raise privacy issues. Though it is unlikely to find a solution that is satisfactory to all parties involved, the focus of this section is to discuss algorithms and challenges in the execution of these algorithms when Big Data is involved.

In addition to the Big Data, the ad placement requires intelligent machine learning algorithms and sophisticated systems that are capable of crunching data at fractions of seconds. Moreover, many advertisers want their ads to be shown to the same queries. For example, Audi might want their ads to be shown when users search for "luxury car." Mercedes would also prefer their ads to be shown when a user searches for "luxury car." This creates both a challenge (for the advertisers) and an opportunity (for the advertising companies). To cope with this competition, intelligent algorithms that maximize the revenue for the advertising company are generally employed. In particular, advertising companies are running algorithms that answer the question of "How does an advertising company decide what ads to display with each query so as to maximize its revenue?"

Before explaining the types of algorithm that are used in targeted online advertisement, let us consider a hypothetical example, where Mercedes and Audi are competing for keywords in Google search. Mercedes wants to show their ads for "luxury car" and "luxury SUV" queries, and Audi wants to show their ads only for "luxury car." For simplicity, consider there are no other competitors for these keywords. When a user searches for "luxury SUV," a Mercedes ad is going to be shown (as long as the maximum cap set by Mercedes is not attained). However, if a user queries "luxury car," either a Mercedes or Audi ad can be shown. Therefore an algorithm has to decide which ad to show considering the budget caps and what these companies are willing to pay. An intuitive approach is to show the ad of the car company who is willing to pay more for the query "luxury car." However, this approach might not be optimal if Mercedes is willing to pay more than Audi. This is because Mercedes can hit its maximum cap and when the cap is hit, the Google search can no longer show ads regarding "luxury SUV." This is clearly a revenue loss for Google. Therefore, a "balanced approach" should be used, which not only decides on who is willing to pay more but also takes into account the money spent and maximum cap. At the same time, it is impossible to exactly predict the future and what people might search. In either case, we have to rely on *what we know* until now and can only use *online algorithms* because the future is not exactly known.

An online algorithm makes decisions based only on the sequential data available until the decision moment and in a particular order. In other words, an online algorithm never has access to a full history of search (query) results because people have not searched yet. In the extreme case, the algorithm has to make a decision with the first time a query is entered. This is as opposed to offline algorithms, where the algorithm has access to all data in any order. Hence, we have to use an online algorithm for targeted online advertisement. Going back to our Mercedes versus Audi competition example, we can use all the search results from the past but we cannot know whether there is going to be a burst of searches for "luxury SUV" or "luxury car."

A popular online algorithm that is used for ad placement in the competitive environments is "bipartite matching." In the bipartite matching algorithm, we group advertisers (e.g., Mercedes, Audi) in a bin, and keywords in another bin (e.g., "luxury car," "luxury SUV"). Our goal is to "match" a keyword from the second bin to an advertiser from the first bin. This matching is performed each time a user searches for a query that is in the keywords bin, so that the advertising company's (e.g., Google) revenue is maximized. The constraint is one keyword can only be matched to one advertiser. The key to designing the algorithm is finding the correct tradeoff between the bid and (fraction of) unspent budget. Respecting this tradeoff, the algorithm in Mehta et al. [11] works the following way:

> Allocate the next query to the bidder in maximizing the product of his bid, and some function of the fraction of the bidder's budget, which has been spent so far.

The algorithm assumes that the daily budget of advertisers is large compared to their bids. This algorithm, along with many other online algorithms, is of the so-called greedy type because they make short-term decisions, which might not be best in the long term. They are generally not optimal, however given the nature of the targeted advertising problem, it is very hard to find a solution that maximizes revenue in the long term with the constraints. It should also be noted that the algorithms have to work in a fraction of seconds due to the huge volume of searches.

Recommendation Systems

A recommendation system predicts the *rating* or *preference* that user would give to an item or a service they had not yet considered. Our interest lies in the recommendation systems that involve Web applications. Before dealing with the problem and possible solutions, we present the following examples.

- *Netflix recommends videos to watch.* These suggestions are partly based on the user's previous ratings, watching habits, and characteristics of the films the user generally watches. Intuitively, if a user has similar video taste to certain groups of users, then it is more likely that the user is going to watch similar videos the group has previously watched.
- *Amazon recommends products to buy.* The recommendation is partly based on what other shoppers bought along with the current item, what the user has been recently shopping for, and the user's purchase history.
- *Pandora Radio recommends songs to listen to.* The playlist takes an initial input of songs or musicians and plays similar music with the same characteristics (e.g., same genre). The system is refined as the user skips or "likes" certain musicians and songs.

As it can be seen from these examples, the recommendation systems rely on *similarities*. The similarities can be between the users (such as having the same demographics or habits) or between the items (such as having the same genre of movies or songs). There are two types of recommender systems, content-based systems and collaborative filtering systems [10].

- Content-based systems make recommendations about an item to use based on a description of the item and a profile of the user's interest. In general, content-based recommendation systems have components that describe the items that may be recommended, that create a profile of the user that describes the types of items the user likes, and that compare items to the user profile to determine what to recommend.
- Collaborative filtering systems recommend items based on similarity measures between users and/or items.

TABLE 5.1

A Utility Matrix

	The Godfather	The Matrix	Braveheart	Forrest Gump	Star Wars
Alice	X	4/5	X	5/5	5/5
Bob	X	X	4/5	5/5	5/5
Carol	5/5	X	2/5	3/5	1/5
Dave	4/5	3/5	1/5	X	X

To study recommendation systems, we use a mathematical tool named a *utility matrix*. A utility matrix is a matrix with rows from users and columns from the items. We construct a utility matrix in Table 5.1. The rows of the utility matrix are users (Alice, Bob, Carol, Dave) and the columns are the movies (*The Godfather, The Matrix, Braveheart, Forrest Gump*, and *Star Wars*). If a user watched the movie, he/she is asked to rate the movie out of 5 stars and we put this rating in the corresponding row and column. For example, Alice gave 5 stars out of 5 for *Forrest Gump* and Dave gave only 1 star out of 5 stars for *Braveheart*. In fact, Netflix uses the same rating scheme to rate its videos. If a user has not watched the video or did not rate the video for some reason, we put an "X" in the corresponding column.

The main question we are interested in the scope of the recommendation system is "Had a user in fact watched the movie, how would he/she rate the movie?" This is not an easy question because it involves prediction. For example, we can claim that Alice would rate *Braveheart* 4 out of 5 because she gave the same ratings as Bob for the movies they both watched. However, Alice and Bob might have completely different backgrounds. If we knew Alice and Carol had a very similar background, we might have been inclined to predict that Alice would rate *Braveheart* 2 out of 5 because Carol did so.

Collaborative filtering systems use similarities to predict ratings or recommend products. In our case, a collaborative system would first weigh the similarities between the users' ratings, average them appropriately, and then assign the predictions. The solutions to collaborative filtering systems require matrix algebra and are outside the scope of this book. Implementing a good recommendation system is also very hard. In fact, Netflix offered a prize of $1,000,000 to the first person or team to beat their own recommendation algorithm, called *CineMatch*, by at least 10%. The prize was finally awarded in September 2009. The Netflix challenge consisted of a published data set, giving the ratings by approximately half a million users on approximately 17,000 movies. This data was selected from a larger data set, and proposed algorithms were tested on whether they could predict the ratings in an unpublished remainder of the larger data set. The information for each (user, movie) pair in the published data set included a rating (1–5 stars) and the date on which the rating was made.

There are also many non-trivial challenges in collaborative filtering. Cold start is one of them. As collaborative filtering methods recommend items based on users' past preferences, new users will need to rate sufficient number of items before getting valuable recommendations. This is called a *cold start*. Scalability in terms of dealing with huge utility matrices is another problem. The previously studied Hadoop ecosystem using MapReduce programming framework is one solution to the scalability problem. Also, collaborative systems should be designed carefully so that a colluding group of individuals does not create false results. This is a big problem in online Web stores such as Amazon or eBay, where fake ratings and reviews may deceive honest buyers.

FUTURE OF BIG DATA

To summarize, Big Data is here to stay, and it is going to get even bigger. In fact, 90% of all data in the world (as of 2013) has been created in the preceding two years. Data is growing at an enormous rate, given the rise of social networking and cloud computing in the last two years. Every day, 2.5 quintillion (approximately 10^{18}) bytes of data are created. As discussed before, traditional technologies cannot handle this demand and billions of investment is going into new systems such as clouds or Hadoop clusters. International Data Corporation forecasts the Big Data market will grow to $16.9 billion in 2015. This represents a compound annual growth rate (CAGR) of 40%, which is about seven times higher growth than the overall information and communication technology market.

With all these numbers and predictions, we expect data scientists to be at a premium for all business intelligence needs. Much of the current investment for Big Data currently focuses on software and data mining technologies. These include Hadoop and related open-source tools, cloud computing, and data visualization. While those are important breakthroughs, at least as important are the people with the skill set (and the mind set). Therefore, we can confidently predict that the next decade belongs to the data scientists, and we expect this chapter to be useful to those who are new to this field.

SUMMARY OF THE KEY POINTS

- *Big Data:* Big Data is a collection of data sets so large and complex that it becomes difficult to process using traditional data processing applications. Big Data has at least three dimensions in terms of volume, velocity, and variety.
- *Big Data analytics:* Big Data analytics refers to the process of examining large amounts of data of a variety of types to uncover hidden patterns, unknown correlations, and other useful information. From a BI perspective, we can argue that the primary goal of Big Data analytics is to help companies make better business decisions.
- *Data science*: *Harvard Business Review* calls data science "the sexiest job in the 21st century." Data science includes various elements and builds on techniques and theories from many fields including math, statistics, data engineering, pattern recognition and learning, advanced computing, visualization, uncertainty modeling, data warehousing, and high performance computing. Data scientists are expected to have great analytical skills and solve complex data problems through expertise in some of the related fields.
- *Cloud computing:* From the business view point, cloud computing can be considered as a computing environment, where business owners outsource their computing needs to a third party. When they need to use the computing resources such as Web server, database, emails, and so forth, they access these resources via the Internet. There are many cloud computing services including IaaS, PaaS, and SaaS.
- *NoSQL:* NoSQL, or Not Only SQL, database is a solution to manage data and design databases for very large sets of distributed data. It provides a mechanism to store and retrieve data using looser consistency models (differing from the strong consistency of the traditional relational databases) to achieve horizontal scaling and *higher availability*. NoSQL is coined to solve the scalability and performance problem when processing Big Data that relational databases were not designed to handle.
- *MapReduce*: MapReduce is a programming model for processing large data sets. It is useful for tasks such as data mining, log file analysis, financial analysis, and scientific simulations. A MapReduce implementation addresses this challenge by enabling programmers to produce parallel distributed programs in a much

easier manner. The programmers only need to define (using the provided library) the simple map and reduce functions and create parallel programs that focus on the logic of their specific problem, and the MapReduce framework would automatically take care of the rest which includes marshaling the distributed servers, executing the tasks in parallel, managing communications and data transfers among components, monitoring tasks, and handling failure.

- *Hadoop ecosystem*: Hadoop MapReduce and Hadoop Distributed File System comprise a core platform where many other software tools and services are built. Altogether, they are referred to as the Hadoop ecosystem. In other words, the Apache Hadoop ecosystem consists of the Hadoop kernel, MapReduce, HDFS, and a number of related projects such as Apache Hive, HBase, Pig, Zookeeper, and so on. The Hadoop ecosystem is, as an ecosystem, complex and evolving.

- *Targeted online advertising*: Targeted online advertising refers to the marketing or promotion of relevant products and services over the Internet based on intelligent decisions about the user's interests, demographics, and history. Targeted advertising has many advantages over direct placement of ads, which is very similar to the advertising used by the traditional media such as newspapers, TV, or magazines. Targeted ads require intelligent machine learning algorithms, which generally fall into the class of online algorithms.

- *Recommendation systems*: A recommendation system predicts the *rating* or *preference* that user would give to an item or a service they had not yet considered. Netflix movie suggestions, Amazon product recommendations, and Pandora music playlists are all examples of recommendation systems. The recommendation systems are generally implemented using content-based systems or collaborative filtering systems.

Exercises

EXERCISE 1 (DESIGNING A DATA CENTER)

In this exercise, we will build a data center to crunch Big Data. Consider you are the architect of the data center, and you can build your data center using one of the two following computers. Computer A can crunch 1 TB (terabytes) of Big Data in 1 day and costs $5,000, and Computer B can crunch 2 TB (terabytes) of Big Data in 1 day and costs $20,000. Assume everything is linear (e.g., if you can do it in 2 days with one computer, then you can do it in 1 day with two computers) and there are no other costs. Then answer the following questions:

1. Using only one Computer A, how many days does it take to crunch 1 PB (petabytes) of data? How many days does it take with only one computer B? (Hint: 1 PB = 1000 TB)
2. Using a cluster of 10,000 Computer As, how many days does it take to crunch 1 EB (exabytes) of data? How many days does it take with a cluster of 10,000 Computer Bs? What if you use 5,000 Computer As and 5,000 Computer Bs? (Hint: 1 EB = 1000 PB)
3. If you have 1 million dollars, what is the maximum amount of data you can crunch with a cluster of only Computer As in 1 day? In 1 week? In a month (assume a month is 30 days)? (Give answers in terms of either TB or PB)
4. If you have 1 million dollars, what is the maximum amount of data you can crunch with a cluster of only Computer Bs in 1 day? In 1 week? In a month (assume a month is 30 days)?
5. If you want to crunch 1 EB of data in 10 days, how much money do you need if you use only a cluster of Computer As? What if you use only a cluster of Computer Bs?

SOLUTION TO EXERCISE 1

1. 1000 days. 500 days.
2. 100 days. 50 days. 75 days.
3. 200 TB (or 0.2 PB). 1400 TB (or 1.4 PB). 6000 TB (or 6 PB).
4. 100 TB (or 0.1 PB). 700 TB (or 0.7 PB). 3000 TB (or 3 PB).
5. 500 million dollars. 1 billion dollars.

EXERCISE 2 (MAPREDUCE EXAMPLE)

Assuming we have two text files that store the information about the water level of a lake at different time points. Each line of a file contains two entities. The first one represents the name of a lake and the second one represents the corresponding water level (in meters) recorded in that lake at different points of time. The water level of a lake can be measured multiple times and stored in the same file as follows:

File1:
Superior, 182
Huron, 177

Superior, 184
Erie, 175
Erie, 174

File2:
Ontario, 74
Superior, 183
Huron, 174
Huron, 176
Ontario, 75
Erie, 173
Ontario, 73

The goal is to find the average water level of each lake. Using the MapReduce framework, we have to define the map and reduce function. Assuming you defined the map function that takes a file as input and returns the average water level for each lake in that file; and the reduce function that calculates the average water level across the two files. Now answer the following questions. (Hint: follow the MapReduce example in the chapter.)

1. What is the output when applying the map function to File1?
2. What is the output when applying the map function to File2?
3. How many reduce operations are there in total in this example (number of distinct keys feed to reduce)?
4. Give one example input for the reduce function from the given data.
5. If implemented in Hadoop, what is the possible key, value of map, and reduce function?

SOLUTION TO EXERCISE 2
1. (Superior, 183) (Huron, 177) (Erie, 174.5)
2. (Ontario, 74)(Superior, 183)(Huron, 175)(Erie, 173)
3. 4
4. (Superior, <182, 183, 184>)
5. Map Key: Line number in the file.
   Map Value: A single text line in the file.
   Reduce Key: The name of the lake.
   Reduce Value: List of water levels.

148 • *Business Analytics: An Introduction*

REFERENCES

1. T. H. Davenport and D. J. Patil, "Data Scientist: The Sexiest Job of the 21st Century," *Harvard Business Review*, October 2012.
2. Wikipedia contributors, "Big Data," *Wikipedia, The Free Encyclopedia*, http://en.wikipedia.org/wiki/big_data.
3. J. Dean and S. Ghemawat, "MapReduce: Simplified Data Processing on Large Clusters," in *Proc. of the Sixth Symposium on Operating System Design and Implementation* (OSDI), San Francisco, CA, December, 2004.
4. R. Lammel, "Google's MapReduce Programming Model—Revisited," *Science of Computer Programming*, 2008.
5. T. Nguyen, W. Shi, and D. Ruden, "CloudAligner: A Fast and Full-Featured MapReduce Based Tool for Sequence Mapping," *BMC Research Notes* 4:171, 2011.
6. Apache, "Apache Hadoop," *Hadoop*, http://hadoop.apache
7. J. Dean and S. Ghemawat, "Example: Word Count Occurrences," OSDI, 2004, http://research.google.com/archive/mapreduce-osdi04-slides/index-auto-0004.html.
8. S. Sharma, Sanjay Sharma's Weblog, http://indoos.wordpress.com/2010/08/16/hadoop-ecosystem-world-map/.
9. K.Shaikh, http://www.neevtech.com/blog/2013/03/18/hadoop-ecosystem-at-a-glance/.
10. A. Rajaraman, J. Leskovec, and J. D. Ullman. *Mining of Massive Datasets*, Cambridge University Press, New York, NY, 2013.
11. A. Mehta, A. Saberi, U. Vazirani, and V. Vazirani, "AdWords and Generalized On-Line Matching," in *Proc. of the IEEE Symposium on Foundations of Computer Science (FOCS)*, 2005, Pittsburgh, PA.

6

Text Mining Fundamentals

Luca Toldo

CONTENTS

Learning Objectives

- How to obtain structured information from unstructured text.
- How to assess the fit for the purpose of text mining solutions.
- How to do text mining with free and commercial software.
- How to find the actionable information needed, from gigabytes of thousands of files.
- How to solve problems, using several "template" examples provided in the chapter.

While business analytics is typically performed on well-structured content, narrative is the most natural way for humans to share their thoughts, feelings, and knowledge, basically to communicate with other humans. Be it news, blog, Facebook, social media, patents, emails, scientific articles, electronic health records, or other sources, a large amount of information is not structured in databases and therefore not directly usable by business analytics. Text mining enables us to automatically structure narrative and therefore it empowers business analysts to also find nuggets of value from overwhelming sources of unstructured text. In spite of the apparently impossible task of making computers understand natural language, decades of progress in research and development have only very recently made this goal largely achievable.

This chapter aims to deliver executable knowledge: an understanding of what text mining is and how to use it for business analytics. It is rooted in many years of practical experience, analysis of several dozens of cases, and an accurate reading of the relevant scientific literature. We have conceived this work as a building: good theoretical foundation, solid walls of current technology, and a roof of experiments to personalize and complete the knowledge transfer.

INTRODUCTION

"A picture is worth a thousand words." In Figure 6.1 a generalized problem-solving workflow, to be read from left to right, is depicted: the business analyst has a problem to solve, and how to tackle it using text mining is described here.

1. *Data collection.* The analyst seeks data to support her analysis, and collects it from all possible sources she has access to. This implies recorded voice messages, PDF and Microsoft Office files, photographs of posters, images from the Web, paper-only documents received from colleagues or customers, and so forth. The amount of materials and the short time available do not allow the analyst to read all of that material manually and therefore she designs a digital processing workflow.
2. *Digitalization.* All the materials need to be digitized, namely to be transformed in a way that subsequent text analysis programs can

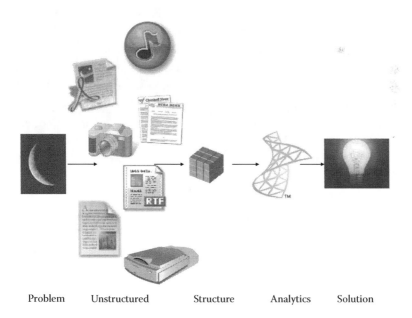

| Problem | Unstructured | Structure | Analytics | Solution |

FIGURE 6.1
Role of text mining in business intelligence.

process. Depending on the format of the data, this might imply one or more operations; for example, PDF and Microsoft Office files can be directly processed and therefore no action is needed for them. However, voice messages need to be transcribed (manually or automatically)—their content needs to be transformed into a format that a "text editor" such as Notepad or Microsoft Word could visualize. The same applies to pictures from photographs and/or from the Web: typically GIF or JPEG images need to be transformed into text. This is typically called *Optical Character Recognition* (OCR) and can be done either by humans or by software, to different extents of precision. Information contained in documents available only in printed form (a printed letter, an advertising flyer, etc.) needs to be digitized (using scanners that generate high-resolution pictures) and then processed.

3. *Text mining.* At this point, the materials are all readable by software programs that transform the unstructured content of the documents into a format that is then appropriate for analytics. From an aerial view, this is the core of text mining: assigning **meaning** to unstructured text. The rest of this chapter focuses in detail on that core activity, since *meaning* is a task-specific context and therefore there are different methods specific to each task.

4. *Analytics.* Once the *meaning* is obtained from each document, then the analyst can perform typical reporting and predictive analytics from which she should be able to draw the conclusions needed to solve the original problem. An example of reporting could be the number of times the *meaning* is found in the document collection; a predictive analytics application could then assess the correlation between the counts of *meaning* and different dates at which the *meaning* has been reported. In this case, the analytics would imply using the metadata about when the information has been collected, and the outcome of text mining. The statistical correlation between date and number of counts of *meaning* could therefore be used to identify a trend (either positive, negative, or instable) and therefore drive decision making. The same document collection can also be automatically processed to identify all occurrences of meanings and trends in its appearance, connected to time or authorship, geographical origin, affiliation, or other metadata available on the document, author, or source.

CONCEPTS

"Text mining" is an ill-defined field of applied computer science whose general aim is to make "best use" of unstructured information, namely information contained in written narrative text (technically called *plain text* to differentiate it from structured formats such as SGML or XML). The specific technical aspects of this field have changed with the advent of new technologies, and not surprisingly often have been driven by national security purposes.

Text Mining Metrics

As Lord Kelvin said, "if you cannot measure it, you cannot manage it." Metrics are essential for text mining applications. Several different metrics need to be applied to different parts of the text mining process, as described above.

Corpus Collection Metrics

The first step of text mining is to select a corpus of documents to process. Although this corpus can simply be "given" (e.g., all documents of an intranet), the largest majority of text mining applications involve the retrieval of the documents from some wider repositories.

While exhaustive retrieval based on metadata could be easily achieved in certain cases (e.g., select all patents of a specific patent class), the same task in the vast majority of cases is non-trivial (e.g., find all scientific articles published by an author) due to the lack of a single source for the data (e.g., not all scientific articles are indexed in MEDLINE or EMBASE or other literature databases) or language ambiguity. (For example, when searching for all scientific articles written by John Smith and indexed in MEDLINE, one currently retrieves almost 20,000 articles; however, since the query is "Smith J[au]" then there are many "false positives." Furthermore, Smith could have published in journals that are not included in the MEDLINE journal list.) The same kind of problem arises when seeking patents based on a *topic* that is not marked by the applicant as patent class (this is a common case of information hiding, whereby the applicant has to make the text of the patent public but wants to hide it in order to avoid competition and/or in order to exploit legal opportunities against patent infringements). A common practice today is to seek

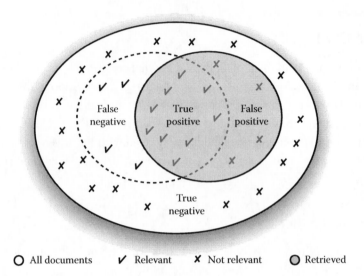

O All documents   ✔ Relevant   ✘ Not relevant   O Retrieved

FIGURE 6.2
Results of the corpus collection. (From Philipp Katz, 2010, "NewsSeecr—Clustering und Ranking von Nachrichten zu Named Entities aus Newsfeeds." Master's thesis, Dresden University of Technology, 2010.)

information from consumers/customers. Complementary to surveys, social media has emerged as an important source of data (albeit of low quality). When doing social media mining, one of the biggest hurdles is in getting access to the largest possible amount of good data; unfortunately, there is not a single database for where to search for social media content!

In each of the cases described above, and many other similar ones, the first step in text mining is indeed an information retrieval task, whereby the objective is to select all the relevant documents and only them (do not miss any document and do not include any irrelevant document). Given the complete set of documents analyzed by an information retrieval process, one can categorize those results into four main classes whose relationships are shown in Figure 6.2:

> *True negative*—The documents that the system marked as not relevant and were indeed not relevant.
> *True positive*—The documents that the system marked as relevant and indeed were relevant.
> *False negative*—The documents that the system marked as negative, and therefore did not return to the analysis.
> *False positive*—The documents that the system marked as relevant but were not relevant.

An ideal system would return 0 false negative, 0 false positive, and only true positive. In order to interpret the performance of a system, the metrics of those four classes have been combined into compacted metrics such as *Precision, Recall, F1, precision at (k)*.

$$\text{Precision} = \frac{\text{true positives}}{\text{true positives} + \text{false positives}} \qquad (6.1)$$

Equation 6.1 is a precision metric.

$$\text{Recall} = \frac{\text{true positives}}{\text{true positives} + \text{false negatives}} \qquad (6.2)$$

Equation 6.2 is recall metrics.

Precision and Recall can be intuitively understood as the *accuracy* of the finding a system detects (lack of false positives) and *thoroughness* (lack of false negatives).

Recall is a measure of completeness, and precision of correctness. When you promise to tell the whole truth, you are promising 100% recall. When you promise to tell nothing but the truth, you are promising 100% precision (Hobbs 2002). For a given system, these two measures are typically inversely correlated; the higher the precision, usually the lower the recall, and reciprocally, the higher the recall, the lower the precision.

When comparing different systems on the same task, it is helpful to use a single metric for measuring performance. **F1** is a common single metric, widely adopted by the information retrieval community, for this task.

$$\text{F1} = \frac{2 * \text{Precision} * \text{Recall}}{\text{Precision} + \text{Recall}} \qquad (6.3)$$

Equation 6.3 is the F1 metric for performance of information retrieval and information extraction systems. The F1-score is a weighted harmonic mean between precision and recall, weighted equally.

Beyond these metrics, which are used to compare a set of items regardless of their order, there are other indicators to compare ranked lists (e.g., PageRank in Google is used to deliver a list of results for which the results are sorted by decreasing relevance to the query). The most widely used indicator for a ranked sub-list is certainly the "**precision at k,**" that is, the ratio of relevant documents within the first "k" hits. For example, if a result contains in the top 10 documents only four relevant ones, then the "Precision at 10" score is going to be 0.4.

Corpus Creation Metrics

Once a corpus is collected, in order to measure the quality of information extraction techniques one needs to select a small number of representative documents, manually annotate them, and compare the efficiency of the text mining software in detecting what the human annotators have selected as relevant for the task. This phase is called *"corpus annotation"* and is mentioned also later. At this point, however, we need to introduce the metric used for that task: *observed agreement, specific agreement, Kappa.*

Observed agreement (A_o): The proportion of instances on which the annotators agree.

$$A_o = \frac{\text{agreements}}{\text{all}} \qquad (6.4)$$

Equation 6.4 is the observed agreement metric for annotators agreements.

Specific agreement: The degree of agreement for each individual category separately.

Kappa is defined as the observed agreements minus the agreements expected by chance and is normalized between –1 and 1.

$$\kappa = \frac{A_o - A_e}{1 - A_e} \qquad (6.5)$$

Equation 6.5 is a metric for measuring the agreement between human annotators. Kappa can also be extended for the case of more than two annotators. For more details, such as for the equation of kappa for more than two annotators, and on the limitations of kappa, please see Chapter 10 of Cunningham, Maynard, Bontcheva, et al. (2011).

Tagging Metrics

As pointed out by Moens (2006), often the purpose of performing text mining is beyond the text mining itself. Therefore, one can adopt *intrinsic metrics* (metrics that quantify how well the text mining performed by it) and *extrinsic metrics* (how the text mining process affected the achievement of the overall goal). Hereafter, we address only the intrinsic metrics.

The fundamental intrinsic metrics used in text mining have been derived by those developed for information retrieval tasks: Precision, Recall, and F1, as described above. In spite of its wide adoption, analytical research has shown (Makhoul, Kubala, Schwartz, et al. 1999) that by simply using F1 as a performance measure, one is making the system look like it is much better than it really is. For this reason, the Slot Error Rate (SER) has been proposed as an alternative single error measure. SER is the ratio of the total number of tag errors divided by the total number of tags in the reference: one talks of *deletion* when a tag is missed, *substitution* if it is of the incorrect type, or *insertion*, when the tagged text should not have been tagged, and *correct* if it is the right tag.

$$\text{SER} = \frac{\text{Substitution} + \text{Deletion} + \text{Insertion}}{\text{Correct} + \text{Substitution} + \text{Deletion}} \qquad (6.6)$$

Equation 6.6 is the metric for performance assessment of text mining systems. This single measure of performance of information extraction systems has the great advantage of also being adaptable to scenarios where certain types of errors may be deemed more or less important than others, thus introducing error-specific weightings so one can customize it to the task. This measure has been widely adopted by the community in performing information extraction from speech. When computing tagging metrics over a corpus, one has to specify if one considers the whole corpus as a single document (micro averaging) or whether to calculate the metrics on the individual documents and then average the results over the corpus (macro averaging). The latter tends to increase the importance of short documents.

Data Selection: Conversion and Filtering

Narrative can be available in a variety of "formats" and therefore some computational disciplines support text mining tasks. Hereafter, we convey some examples of the major sources of "pre-processing" which are required to start a text mining project as shown in Figure 6.3.

Optical Character Recognition (OCR)

Generally as it is described, *text mining* requires the text to be "understandable by computers." Therefore a first step is to convert it from *images* to *text*. This step, which involves digitization in case the document is not already scanned, is often performed by appropriately trained individuals

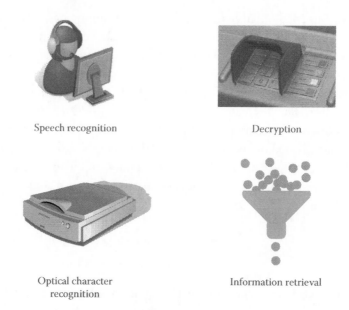

Speech recognition

Decryption

Optical character
recognition

Information retrieval

FIGURE 6.3
Pre-processing steps optionally needed for text mining.

who read the documents and type them in low-cost regions of the world. Automatic ways to perform this task, however, have been available since the late 1980s, whereby it has taken more than 100 years (first reports are from 1870) to make these techniques reliable. Table 6.1 lists some of the OCR software currently available.

Speech Recognition

Voice is a common medium for exchanging information, and the application of automatic speech recognition systems today can be seen in any task that requires a human–machine interface. It started in the 1930s, when Bell Laboratories proposed a system model for speech analysis and synthesis. Thanks to Siri and Voice Actions, they are now already deployed on common portable devices (e.g., iOS and Android). Speech messages transcribed into text then became a valuable source for text mining. Examples of speech recognition used as input for text mining are the support functions of call centers, where the dialogue between customer and operator is recorded and automatically transcribed using speech recognition technologies, as well as sales-rep visits to customers. Table 6.2 lists some of these solutions currently available.

TABLE 6.1

OCR Solutions*

Vendor	Product	License	Language	Table	User Domain
ABBYY	FineReader	Commercial	189, Chinese/Japanese/Korean/ Arabic/Farsi/Hebrew	Yes	Yes
Tracker Software Products Ltd.	PDFXCHANGE Viewer	Freeware	English	No	No
Softi	Scan to PDF	Commercial	English	No	No
FreeOCR	PaperFile.net	Freeware	10	No	No
Google	Tesseract	OpenSource	10	No	No
GNOME	OCRfeeder	OpenSource	English, Chinese	Yes	Yes
Cognitive Technologies	GOCR	Freeware	20	Yes	No
GNU	Ocrad	GPL	English	No	No
I.R.I.S. s.a.	Readiris	Commercial	137, Chinese/Japanese/Korean/ Arabic/Farsi/Hebrew	Yes	No
Nuance	OmniPage	Commercial	137, Chinese/Japanese/Korean/ Arabic/Farsi/Hebrew	Yes	Yes
Cvision	PdfCompressor	Commercial	117	No	No

*See also OCR solutions at www.simpleocr.com for more details.

TABLE 6.2

Voice to Text Vendors

Vendor	Product	License	Language	Installation	Domains
VOCITEC	V-Cloud	Commercial	Customisable	Cloud based	Customisable
NUANCE	DRAGON	Commercial	English	Local	Legal
CUSTVOX	VocBI	Commercial	Customisable	Cloud based	Customisable
GENESYS	ANGEL	Commercial	Customisable	Cloud based	Customisable
TELSTRA	VOICE2TEXT	Commercial	English	Hosted service	None
SIMPLESIGNAL	Voice2Text	Commercial			
DOLBEY	Fusion Voice2Text	Commercial			Legal, medical
Microsoft	Windows 7	Commercial		Local	None
Google	Google Chrome	Freeware		Cloud based	
Linguatec	Voice pro	Commercial	English, German	Hosted service	Legal, medical
Carnegie Mellon University	SPHINX4	Academic		Local	

Exercise 1

Using Google Chrome, enable audio input and in Google Search speak a few sentences of at least five words, and see how these are transcribed by the Google Audio API. Calculate precision and recall.

Exercise 2

Repeat Exercise 1 with the same words; however, also have loud background noise in the room (e.g., turn on a Web radio and/or open the window if you are in a noisy environment, or just ask someone else in the room to speak loudly). Measure precision and recall and compare with the previous run.

What do you conclude about this tool? Is it sufficiently robust also in noisy environments? Do you find it saves time compared to typing? How reliable would the result of the search be if you had not corrected the search terms?

Decryption

If one considers cryptography (techniques to make a message readable only by the intended recipient) within the scope of text mining, then one can go back in the history of humanity to about 1900 BCE, where non-standard hieroglyphs were used to prevent understanding by the non-intended recipients. In 1500 BCE, ancient Assyrians used cryptography to protect their trading secrets. Julius Caesar used cryptography in government communications, though the origin of cryptanalysis is due to William Frederick Friedman in 1917. The Enigma machine was then used during World War II by the Germans, and text mining techniques developed by the Polish mathematician Marian Rejewski broke it. In 1991, Phil Zimmermann released the first version of the Pretty Good Privacy (PGP) system, which was used daily at that time for protecting emails. Current applications of encryption/decryption algorithms are mostly for digital forensic investigations. Common encryption/decryption software is listed in Table 6.3.

Information Retrieval

As soon as utterances are available as plain text (regardless of whether they come from scanned documents via OCR, or from voice via speech recognition engines, or decrypted in some way), these are typically stored as files. With the growing number of files, a major task is in the identification

TABLE 6.3

Some Cryptographic and Forensic Software

Vendor	Product	License	Algorithms
Bouncy Castle	Bouncy Castle Crypto API (Java, C#)	Open source	X.509, S/MIME, CMS, OCSP, TSP, CMP, CRMF, OpenPGP, EAC, TLS, JCE
AccessData	Forensic Toolkit	Commercial	Credant, SafeBoot, Utimaco, EFS, PGP, Guardian Edge, S/MIME
Elcomsoft	Forensic Disk Decryptor	Commercial	BitLocker, PGP, TrueCrypt

of the important documents. This task is called *information retrieval*, and research in this field started recently at the beginning of the 1960s, with a collection of 1,400 documents and 225 queries/relevant judgments used to quantitatively benchmark the performance of manual and automatic systems. Since 1992, the field has obtained major support by the National Institute of Standards and Technology (NIST) and the Defense Advanced Research Projects Agency (DARPA) through the establishment of a public benchmarking conference (Text Retrieval Conference) traditionally held at NIST. In the more than 20 years of this scientific benchmarking, dozens of text collections and relevance judgments have been produced and are available for benchmarking information retrieval systems—for example, in the fields of Web crawling, blogs, chemical IR, genomics, law, question answering, relevance feedback, spoken document retrieval, terabyte data sets, million query data sets, and much more.

The selection of the input data is particularly important, since it affects the subsequent step of information extraction and analysis. Several aspects need to be considered under the general information retrieval task, such as quality/reliability of the data source (this also includes spam detection and author identification), fit for purpose of the specific data source, and legal and ethical considerations.

Information retrieval capabilities are provided off-the-shelf by a number of content management systems, and partially by the operating system of any computer. For example, Microsoft Windows search functionality allows finding files by matching filename, file attributes (such as creation date, size, modification date, etc.), and match to content. However, it allows matching only by precise matching, and for very large collections

TABLE 6.4

Selected Information Retrieval Engines

Vendor	Product	License	Language
University of Glasgow	Terrier	MPL	15 (UTF-8 encoding)
University of Massachusetts	Indri	BSD	(UTF-8 encoding)
Apache	SOLR, LUCENE	Apache License 2.0	32 (UTF-8 encoding)
University of Sheffield	Mimir	LGPL3.0	Most languages
Giorgio Vassiliadis	Puggle	LGPL	Many languages
ANGOSS	Text Analytics	Commercial	Many languages
Google	Google Search appliance	Commercial	Most languages
Thunderstone	Search Appliance SBE	Commercial	Most languages

it is not particularly fast. All document and content management systems currently provide embedded information retrieval functionality; even relational database management systems (e.g., ORACLE, MySQL) provide it from their core application. Table 6.4 reports some core information retrieval tools.

As soon as utterances are available in digital format, the core of text mining, namely, structuring the unstructured, or "finding the *meaning*" takes place. Hereafter, we report on the major concepts that are essential to understanding the process of information extraction and its role in text mining activities.

Regular Expressions

The core activity of text mining is the conversion of unstructured text into structure. This conversion practically consists in transforming a stream of bytes into concepts—in other words, identifying and extracting patterns. Several text mining technologies utilize regular expressions in order to specify patterns to be extracted. "Regular expressions" are computational representations of patterns aimed at extraction of information. For example, a pattern "black|white" would be useful to find anything that is either "black" or "white." Some patterns and their example applications are shown in Table 6.5.

TABLE 6.5

Examples of Regular Expressions

Pattern Name	Regular Expression	Example
ISBN numbers	(ISBN(:\s))?[0-9]+-[0-9]+-[0-9]+-[0-9]+-[0-9X]	ISBN: 978-1-8456-4131-3-3978-3-642-03654-5
Internet address of computers	((2[0-4]\d|25[0-5]|[01]?\d\d?)\.){3}(2[0-4]\d 25[0-5]|[01]?\d\d?)	1.2.3.4
Email address	^[_]*([a-z0-9]+(\.|_|_*)?)+@([a-z][a-z-z0-9\-]+(\.|\-*\.))+[a-z]{2,6}$	Book.orders@tandf.co.uk orders@taylorandfrancis.com
Detect blood pressure	\b(blood\b.+\bpressure)\b/	The measurement of blood pressure
Anti-hypertensive treatment intensification	/^\s*($CHANGING)\s+((this\|it)\s+)?to\s+[\d.]+\s+($UNITS)\s+)?(of\s+)?$BPMEDS/oi	We will be switching it to 30 of Isordil
Guilt feelings	(/forgive\ me|(am'm)\ sorry|god\ forgive|hate\ myself|i\ hate\ to\ leave|making\ you\ unhappy|causing\ (constant|a\ lot\ of|endless|much)?\ (unhappin ess|misery|pain)|always\ wrong/ ix)	Manually developed patterns on i2b2 2011 suicide notes. Pedersen (2011)*

*Pedersen, 2011, *Biomedical Informatics Insights* 5:185–193.

In spite of the importance of regular expressions, there are several different ways to achieve the same goal. There is not a single unique "regular expression language," and there are many regular expression software packages that implement features specific to the engine. Therefore, the regular expression that one uses to identify a specific pattern is also related to the engine that one is using to execute the pattern search. Table 6.6 shows some representative examples of free tools supporting development and testing of regular expressions on a variety of platforms.

Named Entities

The core of information extraction is the identification (also called *tagging* or *extraction* or *adornment*) of named entities and relationships between named entities. A named entity is a "definite noun phrase that refers to specific types of individuals, such as organizations, persons,

TABLE 6.6

Common Regular Expression Testing Software

Software	Source	Regular Expression Engine
"Expresso 3.0"	Ultrapico	.NET Framework Regular Expression Engine
RegExpEditor	Tbudde	Java and Scala
Regex Assistant	http://regex-assistant. sourceforge.net/	HTML application developed with PerlScript, Perl syntax regular expressions
TextCrawler	DigitalVolcano.co.uk	VBScript and Javascript ECMA-262 compliant
RegexTester	http://www.regextester.com/	Currently this site is able to test JavaScript, PCRE, and POSIX dialects

Source: JavaScript dialect is used in ECMAScript, JScript and VBScript programming languages. PCRE dialect is mainly used in Perl, PHP, Apache's .htaccess, grep and most software. POSIX is mainly used in PHP and UNIX programming languages. Despite the fact that there may be some differences, in most cases all regular expressions regardless of the dialect are compatible. (REGex Tester)

dates, and so on" (Bird, Klein, and Loper 2009). The task of identifying named entities is not simple, since it involves:

a. Defining the *token boundary* (e.g., where a word starts and ends; this is typically a "space"—however not always and not in every language).
b. Deciphering if the term is single or multi-token concept. (For example, "Merck KGaA" is a multi-token concept that represents the company whose name is Merck and whose legal status is Kommandite Gesellschaft auf Aktien; that is, a different company from Merck & Co. If one would assume single-term tokens, then one would mix up information from both companies!)
c. Disambiguating the term (e.g., cold might mean *having a cold*, namely, having an influenza, or something being cold).
d. Handling acronyms (e.g., COLD is also a valid abbreviation for Common Obstructive Lung Disease ..., see task c above).

There are several different techniques to address this task:

a. *Gazetteer*: A gazetteer consists of a list containing names of entities that are used as *seeds* for string matching. Different gazetteer implementations are more or less *smart* in modifying the matching text and/or the list gazetteer in order to be able to overcome various problems with typographical errors, singular/plural, time (present, past, conditional), passive versus active, and so forth.
b. *Ontology*: An ontology is a formalization of a conceptualization. Ontology-driven taggers offer in principle an advantage compared to plain gazetteers since they may use the semantics of the structure of the ontology to resolve ambiguities.
c. *Rules*: These systems are similar to gazetteers, however the lists contain not only single or multi-token terms, but also rules (also called *patterns*, or *linguistic/semantic regular expressions*, or *Smart queries*). The individual item elements are therefore sort of mini-programs manually casted to detect the entity (or a relationship). For example, the following regular expression could be useful for detecting the dose of a drug expressed as "10 mg" or "10 g."

$$[0-9]+<SPACE>^*(m)^*g$$

as soon as [0–9] be defined as <DIGIT> then one could transform that regular expression in a RULE or semantic pattern: <DIGIT>+(m|K)*g.

d. *Machine-learning*: A manually annotated corpus of named entities is provided to a computer system that is able to automatically generalize the linguistic patterns surrounding the entity and therefore guess new entities from the context. Typically, maximum entropy categorizers or support vector machines are used for this task.

e. *Hybrid systems*: The latest research shows that combining multiple judgments delivers better results; however, the problem in these combined systems is on how to judge. Majority voting is a common model; however, in the cases where the majority of the taggers do not detect the match, those specialized taggers that detect it would be ignored. Table 6.7 lists some named entity recognition software packages.

Relations

Several applications of text mining are appropriately solved simply by identifying and counting the occurrence of entities. However, there are cases where the *relation* between two entities is the task to be solved. For example, in the case where the task is to identify which company acquires which other company, then the relation would be "acquisition" and require two entities: "A acquired B." Obviously, the complexity lies in the variability of describing the action of acquiring (in this example). Further complexity is in handling inter-sentence relationships. For example "A has announced the acquisition of a start-up in the field X. The recently launched B, specialist in X, confirmed the announcement of A."

Intra-sentence relation extraction is methodologically well covered by the previously mentioned entity recognition approaches: named-entity and co-occurrence filtering followed by rule and/or machine-learning.

Inter-sentence relation extraction task is still a subject of intensive academic research. A general pipeline for relation extraction detection is shown in Figure 6.4. The software landscape specific for relation extraction is fairly narrow and dominated by academic or open-source projects. Table 6.8 lists some text mining technologies for relation extraction.

Tagging Techniques

In spite of the always increasing spectrum of applications, the core technique of text mining can be summarized in one word: *tagging*. Tagging is the action performed by software (when performed by humans, it is called

TABLE 6.7

Selected Named Entity Recognition Software Package

Vendor	Product	License	Languages	Domain
Sheffield University	GATE	GPL	Various	Dictionary based
Netherlands Bioinformatics Center	Peregrine (https://trac.nbic.nl/data-mining/)	GPL	Various	Dictionary based
SCAI	ProMiner	Commercial	English	Configurable
TEMIS	LUXID	Commercial	Various	Medical, Biological, Business, Trainable
Apache	OpenNLP TokenNameFinder	APL	Various	Trainable
InfoGlutton	YooName	Commercial	English	9 entities and 100 sub-categories, semi-supervised
U-Compare Stanford University	GENIA Tagger Stanford	GPL	English	Trainable
Averbis	Averbis extraction framework	Commercial	German, English	Medical
SAP	Netweaver HANA	Commercial		
Linguamatics	I2E	Commercial	English	Smart queries

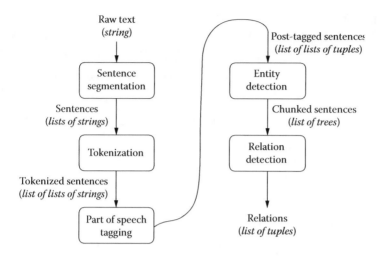

FIGURE 6.4

Simple pipeline architecture for information extraction system (Steven Bird, Ewan Klein, and Edward Loper, 2009, *Natural Language Processing with Python*, O'Reilly.)

annotation) through which a set of characters/words/sentences is assigned a meaning (tag). Once this operation is performed, subsequent steps in the text mining procedure could imply extracting the tagged information, or exporting it for qualitative or quantitative analytics purposes (e.g., visualization, statistics, etc.). Table 6.9 shows an example of a text passage, artificially built, and some of the tags that could appropriately be associated.

As shown in the table, a tag could be a simple "Entity," a relation between Entities, a sentence, and even a zone of a document. An entire document

TABLE 6.8

Selected Relation Extraction Platforms

Vendor	Product	License	Languages	Domain
Fondazione Bruno Kessel	JSRE	Apache	English	Trainable
NLTK Project	NLTK	Open source	English	Trainable
University of Sheffield	GATE	LGPLv2	English	Trainable
TEMIS	BER SC MER SC CI SC RF SC	Commercial	Various	Biological, medical, chemical, competitive intelligence Trainable

TABLE 6.9

Semantic Assignments

Example	The other day I went to the doctor since I had a problem with one of the drugs he prescribed me to help reach my BMI. Acomplia 500 mg made me feel dizzy after ingestion. He said to me that it is a known side effect; however since then the drug has been removed from the UK market, and since my BMI was almost normal, he recommended me discontinuing it.	
Single token term	TERM	Acomplia
Single token term	TERM	500
Multi-tokens term	ENTITY	500 mg
Two or more terms	RELATION	Potential
Sentence	CONTEXT	Acomplia 500 mg makes me feel dizzy after ingestion

Source: Modified from TEMIS Skill Cartridge™ Development documentation (2008).

could also be given one or more tags. Actually, the length of a text passage (be it few characters or an entire manuscript) is irrelevant to the fact that it can have one or more tags.

The use of those tags then is what one would call *analytics,* or *semantic enrichment,* and it allows the connection of knowledge derived from different parts of one or more documents, regardless of how this knowledge is expressed (as far as the tagging "worked"). For example, one could use those tags as descriptors for the document, and then train the software in order to automatically categorize the incoming documents based on those tags. This whole process can be made fully automatic and then associated with a user preference profile (containing Entities and/or a set of documents of interest to be used as reference) to ensure that only the documents of interest are delivered to the customer. This could be applied both to emails as well as news, and so on, and thus filter the incoming content only to that of interest.

Clustering

A classical application of text analytics is the automatic identification of clusters of similar *units*. Although it is debatable if this task belongs to the information extraction or information retrieval tasks, due to its widespread adoption, it is briefly described here. Computation of clusters is an Non-deterministic Polynomial time (NP)-complete problem and as such there are a variety of methods that one can apply; as such clustering is a classical application of data mining and therefore not something specific to text analytics.

Document Categorization

While clustering is a method utilized to automatically find a set of similar documents, categorization is used to identify (tag, categorize, filter) documents according to a well-defined profile. While this is a typical information retrieval task, text mining is often used to build components (categorizers) that enable going beyond the limitations of formally specifying a precise set of terms to be matched in the document (or in the metadata, such as author, publication date, etc.).

The most widely adopted approaches for document categorization are **machine learning** systems, namely, methods that can automatically *learn* from data. Unfortunately, the field of machine learning is so large that a detailed handling exceeds the scope of this chapter. Mohri, Rostamizadeh, and Talwalkar's book (2012) is recommended to get a good foundation in this field. Machine learning techniques are useful not only to categorize complete documents but also for categorizing sentences, as engines for named entity recognition, and also for relation extraction (e.g., Giuliano, Lavelli, and Romano 2006). In recent works by Gurulingappa, Rajput, Roberts, et al. (2012) and Toldo, Bhattacharya, and Gurulingappa (2012), the use of machine learning in text mining is demonstrated for the pharmacovigilance field. By using different sets of classifiers, the authors are able to automatically find appropriate documents, relevant sentences, and specific adverse drug events, thus spanning almost the entire application range of text mining. The "Machine Learning Open Source Software" (www.mloss.org) is a valuable resource of open-source tools dedicated to machine learning.

Several text mining environments have components that enable document categorization in various ways and therefore are not listed here. Among the academic software, a special mention is **MA**chine Learning for **L**anguag**E** Toolkit (available at mallet.cs.umass.edu) for the richness of algorithms and very high scientific achievements. Its lack of a graphical user interface makes it ideal for command line users and programmers, and as well for embedding in larger systems.

Word or Tag Clouds

A commonly used method to rapidly visualize the content of a document or of a group of documents is the so-called word or tag cloud. These visualizations utilize crude textual analysis techniques (such as removal of terms with little intrinsic content, and counts of frequencies) to represent the most frequent terms.

FIGURE 6.5
Word or tag clouds of 1 John (wordle.net versus tagxedo.com).

There are several different tools that produce these visualizations. A recent study using eye tracking data (Lohmann, Ziegler, and Tetzlaff 2009) confirms previous research findings on tag cloud perception and performance that showed that the layout of a cloud influences its perception; large tags in the middle attract more user attention, while tags in the upper left quadrant are better recalled and found more quickly; the user scans rather than reads; tag clouds provide suboptimal support when searching for specific terms. For example, Figure 6.5 represents the word cloud visualization created with two different tools of the same content (first chapter of the Gospel according to John). Which of the two is "better"? Most of the tools for computing tag clouds are available as free online services; however, standalone tools exist, both commercial and free. Table 6.10 lists some of them.

In spite of their widespread use, however, one should also be aware that "the biggest problem with word clouds is that they are often applied to situations where this kind of analysis is not appropriate" (Harris 2011)— thus one should use them with caution. This topic is closely related to the cluster labeling task described above, whereby one could utilize the

TABLE 6.10

Selected Tag Cloud Generators

Source	Business Mode, Availability
www.tagxedo.com	Free, Web only, Java plugin
www.wordle.net	Free, Web only, Java plugin
IBM Word Cloud	Free, local, Java
KNIME Tag Cloud node	Free, local, Java

weighted labels (semantic or semantic-less) generated by those intelligent tools as input for the visualization components of the tag cloud generators. In other words, one could replace the natural language processing process of the tag cloud generators using the more advanced techniques of cluster labeling and then apply the nice visualizations on those data.

APPLICATIONS

The applications of text mining are countless. Therefore, in the following sections, just a few selected examples will be discussed, with detailed references for more information.

Sentiment Analysis/Opinion Mining

Changes introduced by software developers to facilitate content creation and sharing, and new business models that allow personalized publishing at no cost, are the enabling factors of the Web 2.0 paradigm. The availability of unscreened consumer content raised the immediate interest of business and industrial analysts who use that data as an additional information source for forecasting (e.g., U.S. elections), early detection of device failure, new market directions, corporate image and brand equity assessment, and early detection of potential adverse drug events. The information that is sought in these cases is what customers like and dislike, their expectations, the risks that they identified, and so on; namely, what Feldman (2013) describes as "aspect-based sentiment analysis." Figure 6.6 summarizes domains covered by sentiment analysis and a few application examples. Sentiment analysis technologies have been gaining in momentum. Table 6.11 shows some of these sentiment analysis technology solutions.

Fraud Detection

Fraud detection is an increasingly attractive use of text mining since its results directly translate into business actions. The same method can be applied by governmental agencies on corporate emails to find potential signatures of fraud, for example, by internal compliance offices, in order to detect early signals of fraud and drive actions to prevent them. Insurance companies apply text mining on the adjuster's notes and referrals to

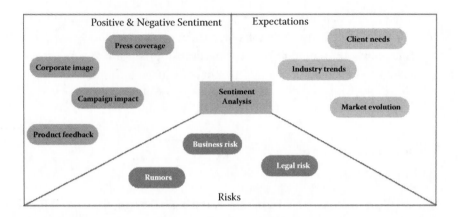

FIGURE 6.6
Domains covered by sentiment analysis and a few applications examples. (From TEMIS Sentiment Analysis Skill Cartridge™, 2008.)

determine a fraud case: unusual levels of detail are a highly suspicious candidate for fraud (http://bit.ly/ZFROYb). Granville (2011) reported a real-life example of text mining to detect fraudulent buyers, using "a tiny bit of web crawling and text analytics."

Plagiarism

Although the Internet is a great facilitator of plagiarism (e.g., copy/paste without reporting the source), it is also a valuable tool for detecting it (e.g., search in Google for the text…). Text mining techniques are a natural instrument to detect plagiarism (e.g., Oberreuter and Velasquez 2013), and several online services are available to verify the extent of plagiarism for any text. Plagiarism detection software is so widespread that even teachers utilize it to assess the originality of the contributions of their students.

Rumor Categorization

A rumor is an unverified and instrumentally relevant statement of information spread among people (DiFonzo and Bordia 2007). Such rumors could have major impacts on decision making as well as the stock market. Text mining techniques are well suited to identify this kind of information from social media, applying categorization techniques described previously (Qazvinian, Rosengen, Radev, et al. 2011).

TABLE 6.11

Some Technologies of Sentiment Analysis

Vendor	Product	Architecture	Language
Google Prediction API team	Sentiment Predictor	Google	English
TEMIS	Opinion Mining	UIMA	English, French
KNIME	KNIME Desktop	Java	English
OpenText	OpenText Content Analytics	UIMA	English, French, Spanish, German, and Portuguese
Clarabridge	Clarabridge Analyze		English
Alchemy Api	Sentiment Analysis	WebService	English, German
Repustate	Sentiment Analysis API	WebService	English, French, Spanish, German, and Arabic
OpenDover	OpenDover	WebService	English
Saplo	Text Analysis API	WebService	English, Swedish
Converseon	Convey API	WebService	English
Lexalytics	Salience Engine	Local installation	English, French, Spanish, German, and Portuguese
Chatterbox.co	Social Technology Engine	WebService	English, French, Spanish, German, Dutch and Portuguese
Bitext	Bitext API	WebService	English, Spanish, and Portuguese
IBM	Social Media Analytics	Local	English
Sysomos	Sentiment API	WebService	
Semantria	Semantria API	WebService	English, French, Spanish, German and Portuguese
Daedalus	STILUS Sentiment API	WebService	English, French, Spanish, and Italian
API cultur	Stmtlk 1.0.0	WebService	Spanish

Contradiction Detection

With the growing amount of digital content and the vast numbers of scientific papers, patents, and all sorts of documents, it is currently an impossible task for any human to systematically detect contradictions through the whole of published science. In industrial settings, on the fly contradiction detection could help in preventing violations to specific management decisions, and could be also useful for business development in the assessment of businesses to be acquired. Contradiction detection could therefore be used to ensure consistency across large document collections (such as those created to support development of new drugs) and within the legal system of a country or of all European laws. There are different levels of contradiction, such as antonym, negation, factual, structural, lexical, and world knowledge (de Marneffe, Rafferty, and Manning, 2008), and these have different levels of tractability with current text mining systems.

Text Mining in Legal Information Systems

The legal domain offers several scenarios where the current practice of manual reading is not scalable and thus prone to errors. The discipline of legal informatics now incorporates text mining. Use cases of text mining in legal informatics involve the automatic detection of overlaps between claims of different patents, as well as helping to identify case precedents in courts, and the previously cited digital forensics, just to name a few. The major difficulty in deploying text mining in the legal setting is the "human dimension" of established legal experts that have not yet adopted the digital methodologies.

TRENDS

Like voice technology, which is now a commodity (e.g., Siri agent in the iPhone), text mining is becoming a pervasive and powerful Swiss knife for all major human tasks involving knowledge and creativity. The examples in the previous sections and the extensive bibliography should be sufficient to show that text mining is now widely adopted. Although still an area of scientific research, it has certainly left the academic settings and is now industrialized and commoditized. The intelligence domain was certainly the "early adopter" of text mining and greatly contributed to the scientific growth in the field through the DARPA sponsored research activities.

NLP + Machine Learning + Distant Supervision

As we have seen, any text mining task requires the creation of corpus for benchmarking. Even larger corpora are required for training machine learning systems to build entity and relational categorizers. Unfortunately, annotation of corpora is a very costly task. The current trend in this field is to adopt distant supervision based upon crowdsourced resources (e.g., Mintz , Bills, Snow, et al. 2009).

Crowdsourcing for Creation of Annotated Corpora

Manual creation of annotated corpora is an essential task for technology assessment and development; however, it is very costly. Thanks to platforms such as the "Amazon mechanical turk," the creation of corpora is becoming a crowdsourced task, with lower costs and faster deployment rates than traditional approaches.

Cloud Computing for Application Hosting

For those cases where WebService tagging is not an option (for legal, confidentiality reasons, huge data volumes, or others), application hosting is still needed. While in the past this involved data centers, or outsourcing, with huge investments, the current trend by major businesses is to rely on cloud computing for application hosting and execution.

FURTHER READINGS

Books/Chapters/Proceedings

Bird, Steven, Ewan Klein, and Edward Loper (2009) *Natural Language Processing with Python*, O'Reilly. Sebastopol, CA.

Cunningham, Hamish, Diana Maynard, Kalina Bontcheva, et al. (2011) *Text Processing with Gate*, University of Sheffield. Sheffield, UK.

Goyvaerts, Jan and Steven Levithan (2012) *Regular Expressions Cookbook*, O'Reilly. Sebastopol, CA.

Lupu, Mihai, Katja Mayer, John Tait, and Anthony J. Trippe (2011) *Current Challenges in Patent Information Retrieval*, Springer. Heidelberg, Dordrecht, London, New York.

Moens, Marie-Francine (2006) *Information Extraction: Algorithms and Prospects in a Retrieval Context*, Springer. Dordrecht, The Netherlands.

Mohri, Mehryar, Afshin Rostamizadeh, and Ameet Talwalkar (2012) *Foundations of Machine Learning*, MIT Press. Cambridge, Massachussets, London, UK.

Tur, Gokhan and Renato De Mori (2011) *Spoken Language Understanding: Systems for Extracting Semantic Information from Speech*, Wiley. Chichester, West Sussex, UK.

Weiss, Sholom M., Nitin Indurkhya, and Tong Zhang (2010) *Fundamentals of Predictive Text Mining*, Springer. London, Dordrecht, Heidelberg, New York.

Wynne, Martin (2005) *Developing Linguistic Corpora: A Guide to Good Practice*, Oxbow Books. Oxford, UK.
Zanasi, Alessandro (2007) *Text Mining and Its Applications to Intelligence, CRM and Knowledge Management*, WIT Press. Southampton, MA.

Scientific Papers

Bach, Nguyen and Sameer Badaskar (2007) "A review of relation extraction" (Available at www.cs.cmu.edu/~nbach/papers/A-survey-on-Relation-Extraction.pdf).
de Marneffe, Marie-Catherine, Anna N. Rafferty, and Christopher D. Manning (2008) "Finding contradictions in text" *Proceedings of ACL-08: HLT*, pp. 1039–1047, Columbus, OH, June 2008.
DiFonzo, Nicholas and Prashant Bordia (2007) "Rumor, gossip and urban legends," *Diogenes* 54(1):19–35.
Feldman, Ronen (2013) "Techniques and applications for sentiment analysis," *Communications of the ACM*, 56(4):82–89.
Giuliano, Claudio, Alberto Lavelli, and Lorenza Romano (2006) "Exploiting shallow linguistic information for relation extraction from biomedical literature," In: *Proceedings of the 11th Conference of the European Chapter of the ACL* (EACL'06). Trento: The Association for Computer Linguistics; 401–408.
Graddol, David (2004) "The future of language," *Science* 303, 1329–1331.
Gurulingappa, H. et al. (2012) "Development of a benchmark corpus to support the automatic extraction of drug-related adverse effects from medical case reports," *Journal of J Biomed Inform.* 45:885–892.
Hobbs, Jerry (2002) "Information extraction from biomedical text," *J Biomed Inform.* 35:260–264.
Makhoul, John, Francis Kubala, Richard Schwartz, and Ralph Weischedel (1999) "Performance measures for information extraction" *Proceedings of DARPA Broadcast News Workshop*, 249–252.
Mather, Laura A. (2000) "A linear algebra measure of cluster quality," *J American Society for Information Science and Technology* 51(7):602–613.
Mintz, Mike, Steven Bills, Rion Snow, and Dan Jurafsky (2009) "Distant supervision for relation extraction without labeled data," In: *Proceedings of the Joint Conference of the 47th Annual Meeting of the ACL and the 4th International Joint Conference on Natural Language Processing of the AFNLP*: Vol. 2 (ACL '09), Vol. 2. Association for Computational Linguistics, Stroudsburg, PA, 1003–1011.
Montgomery, Scott (2004) "Of towers, walls, and fields: Perspectives on language in science," *Science* 303, 1333–1335.
Morell, Carlos, Jorge Vivaldi, and Núria Bel (2012) "Iula2Standoff: A tool for creating stand-off documents for the IULACT," *Proceedings of the Eighth International Conference on Language Resources and Evaluation* (LREC'12). Istanbul, Turkey: European Language Resources Association (ELRA), pp. 351–356.
Neamatullah I., Douglass M., Lehman L. H., et al. (2008) "Automated de-identification of free-text medical records," *BMC Med Inform Decis Making* 2008.
Oberreuter, Gabriel and Juan D. Velásquez (2013) "Text mining applied to plagiarism detection: The use of words for detecting deviations in the writing style," *Expert Systems with Applications*, Vol. 40, Issue 9, July 2013, pp. 3756–3763.

Pedersen, Ted (2011) "Rule-based and lightly supervised methods to predict emotions in suicide notes," *Biomed Inform Insights* 5:185–193.

Qazvinian, Vahed, Emily Rosengren, Dragomir R. Radev, and Qiaozhu Mei (2011) "Rumor has it: Identifying misinformation in microblogs," *Proceedings of the 2011 Conference on Empirical Methods in Natural Language Processing*, pp. 1589–1599, Edinburgh, Scotland, July 27–31, 2011.

Raaijmakers, Stephan and Wessel Kraaij (2008) "A shallow approach to subjectivity classification," *Proceedings of the Second International Conference on Weblogs and Social Media*, ICWSM 2008, Seattle, Washington, March 30–April 2, 2008, AAAI Press.

Rajput, Abdul Mateen (2012) "If it's on web it's yours!" *CEUR Workshop Proceedings* Vol 882.

Segura-Bedmar, Isabel, Mario Crespo, Cesar de Pablo-Sanchez, and Paloma Martinez (2009) "Resolving anaphoras for the extraction of drug-drug interactions in pharmacological documents," *BMC Bioinformatics* 2010; 11(Suppl 2):S1.

Toldo, Luca (2001a) "Letter to the editor: Measurement of cluster quality," *J American Society for Information Science and Technology* 52(7):602–602.

Toldo, Luca, Sanmitra Bhattacharya, and Harsha Gurulingappa (2012) "Automated identification of adverse events from case reports using machine learning," *Proceedings XXIV Conf of the European Federation for Medical informatics*. Workshop on Computational Methods in Pharmacovigilance Pisa, Italy.

Tomanek, Katrin, Philipp Daumke, Frank Enders et al. (2012) An interactive de-identification-system," *Proceedings of the 5th International Symposium on Semantic Mining in Biomedicine* (SMBM 2012). Edited by Ananiadou, S., Pyysalo, S., Rebholz-Schuhmann, D., Rinaldi, F., and Salakoski, T. Zurich, 2012.

Turchin, Alexander et al. (2006) "Using regular expressions to abstract blood pressure and treatment intensification information from the text of physician notes," *JAMIA* 13(6):691–695.

Web Sources

Granville, Vincent (2011) "Real life example of text mining to detect fraudulent buyers," www.analyticbridge.com/profiles/blogs/real-life-example-of-text-mining-to-detect-fraudulent-buyers; accessed April 11, 2013.

Harris, Jacob (2011) "Word clouds considered harmful," www.niemanlab.org/2011/10/word-clouds-considered-harmful/; accessed April 11, 2013.

7

Neural Network Fundamentals

Angelos Barmpoutis

CONTENTS

Learning Objectives

The learning objectives of this chapter are the following:

- The reader will understand the strengths and limitations of various types of artificial neural networks.
- Several representative neural network algorithms will be presented and discussed in detail.
- Practical applications of neural networks will be explored by the reader through a set of exercises at the end of the chapter.

INTRODUCTION

Artificial Neural Networks is a term that has been used in computer science, mathematics, and engineering to describe an artificial system that imitates the fundamental learning processes of biological neural networks. The process of learning is part of what is perceived as experience in living organisms and is based on their sensory input, which is a lifelong sequence of input signals generated by the surrounding environment including the organisms themselves. These signals are processed by a set of neural systems that produces the result of perception, which is one of the primary stages of learning. Living organisms more often than not learn by categorizing experiences based on their similarities/differences. For example, understanding what a day is would be very difficult and maybe unnecessary without experiencing a night, and vice versa.

Furthermore, living organisms learn by example, for instance, by imitating behaviors of other experienced members of their species. Learning what is considered to be good or bad behavior would be difficult without the assistance of a supervisor. In this case, the role of the supervisor is to teach what good or bad behavior is by specific, though limited, examples, and the trainee can extrapolate and apply this knowledge to arbitrary new cases as a result of the learning process.

In computational systems, every sensory input is expressed as a number, which is, without loss of generality, a real-valued number or a discretized version of it. Colors and sounds are two primitive types of sensory inputs commonly used in everyday computers, which are represented by numbers. In general, any sensor or process that generates a numerical value (such as a person's age, weight, educational level, monthly expenditures, profit, and others) can be considered sensory input to an artificial neural network. By imitating the ability of biological organisms to categorize experiences, several learning problems in artificial neural networks can be expressed in the form of a mathematical classification problem. Figure 7.1 shows a graphical representation of a supervised classification problem between two classes in two dimensions. Several input samples are given to the system from each of the two classes along with their labels. These are called *training samples* and will be used by the system to learn the underlying classification pattern. Once the learning/training process is completed, the neural network will be able to classify new unlabeled testing samples (depicted in Figure 7.1 by question-marked circles). The dashed line denotes a possible solution that separates the 2-dimensional space into two regions (shown with or without dots), which correspond to the two labels assigned by the trained system to any arbitrary testing sample.

The classification problem presented in Figure 7.1 can be generalized using non-discrete labels/values in order to represent more complex learning problems. In such case the value of the label could correspond to a third sensory input value that is given for the training samples, but is missing from the test samples, and hence will be predicted by the trained neural network. In problems where there are no given labels, the system should

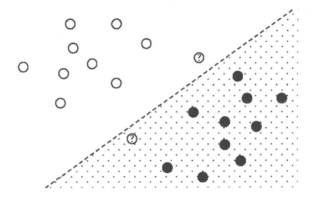

FIGURE 7.1
Illustration of a supervised classification problem. Given a training set of labeled samples (black and white circles) we need to find a function/classifier that assigns the desired value/label to any training or testing (shown with question mark) sample. The dashed line shows a possible solution.

decide how to classify the given sample patterns. This type of learning problem is known as *unsupervised learning*.

MATHEMATICS PRIMER

The majority of the artificial neural networks can be described as mathematical algorithms using a sequence of basic mathematical steps from linear algebra and probability theory (Nering 1976), and therefore a solid background on these areas is required for an in-depth understanding of the material presented in this chapter. This section offers a brief review of the main mathematical operations between vectors and matrices that are commonly used in artificial neural networks.

An n-dimensional vector is a collection of n scalars $a_1, a_2, \ldots a_n$ arranged linearly in the form of a column as follows:

$$a = \begin{bmatrix} a_1 \\ a_2 \\ \vdots \\ a_n \end{bmatrix}$$

Typically, the elements of a vector are real-valued scalars unless stated otherwise, and therefore a vector can be considered an element of the n-dimensional space of real numbers $\mathbb{R}^n$. Transposition is an operation that acts on vectors and re-arranges its elements in the form of a row: $a^T = [a_1 \quad a_2 \quad \cdots \quad a_n]$.

Similarly, an $n \times m$ matrix is a collection of $n \times m$ scalars arranged in n rows and m columns, and transposition re-arranges its elements in the form of m rows and n columns as follows:

$$A = \begin{bmatrix} a_{1,1} & a_{1,2} & \cdots & a_{1,m} \\ a_{2,1} & a_{2,2} & \cdots & a_{2,m} \\ \vdots & \vdots & \ddots & \vdots \\ a_{n,1} & a_{n,2} & \cdots & a_{n,m} \end{bmatrix} \quad A^T = \begin{bmatrix} a_{1,1} & a_{2,1} & \cdots & a_{n,1} \\ a_{1,2} & a_{2,2} & \cdots & a_{n,2} \\ \vdots & \vdots & \ddots & \vdots \\ a_{1,m} & a_{2,m} & \cdots & a_{n,m} \end{bmatrix}$$

The basic mathematical operations can be extended to the case of same-size matrices. Addition and subtraction of $n \times m$ matrices produces a same-size matrix computed by adding or subtracting the corresponding elements of the original matrices. Matrix multiplication is defined between two matrices A of size $n \times m$ and B of size $m \times k$ and its result is a matrix C of size $n \times k$ whose elements are given by $c_{i,j} = \sum_{l=1}^{m} a_{i,l} b_{l,j}$. In the special case of square matrices, i.e., $n \times n$, the inverse of a matrix is defined as the matrix A^{-1} that satisfies the following equation: $AA^{-1} = A^{-1}A = I$, where I is the $n \times n$ identity matrix, whose diagonal elements are equal to 1 and all non-diagonal elements are equal to zero.

Vectors can also be treated as matrices of size $n \times 1$. The *inner* or *dot* product between two same-size vectors a and b is denoted by $a \cdot b$ and is equal to the matrix multiplication $a^T b$, which is also equivalent to $b^T a$, and produces a matrix of size 1×1, i.e., a scalar. In the case of $a \cdot a$, this scalar corresponds to the squared magnitude of the vector, i.e., $a \cdot a = a^T a = \sum_{i=1}^{n} a_i^2 = \| a \|^2$.

In this section as well as the rest of this chapter scalars will be denoted by lower case italicized letters, vectors by lower case bold letters, and matrices by capital bold letters.

NEURAL NETWORK MODELS

Perceptron

Let us assume that a finite set of n-dimensional data samples x_i is given along with their desired binary labels $d_i \in \{0,1\}$. Perceptron (Rosenblatt 1958) is a simple and robust algorithm, which uses the equation of a hyper-plane $f(x) = w \cdot x$, a linear classifier, to split the n-dimensional space into two regions as follows:

$$y(x) = \begin{cases} 1 \text{ if } f(x) > 0 \\ 0 \text{ if } f(x) \leq 0 \end{cases} \qquad (7.1)$$

where w is the unknown n-dimensional weight vector that will be estimated from the given samples: $\{(x_1, d_1), (x_2, d_2), \cdots\}$. It should be noted that the boundary between the two regions is given by the equation of the hyper-plane $f(x) = w \cdot x = 0$, and the points that lie exactly on this plane are given label $y(x) = 0$. In the case of 1 dimension, the separator is basically a point expressed in the form $w_1 x_1 + w_2 = 0$, in the 2-dimensional case is a line given by $w_1 x_1 + w_2 x_2 + w_3 = 0$ (see dashed line in Figure 7.1), in the 3-dimensional case the classifier is a plane defined by $w_1 x_1 + w_2 x_2 + w_3 + w_4 = 0$, and in the case of higher dimensions it is a hyper-plane given by $w \cdot x = 0$, where the last element of every vector x is assumed to be equal to 1, without loss of generality. Therefore, the last element of the unknown vector w is always multiplied by 1 and in neural networks is commonly called *bias*.

The goal of the learning process is to minimize the discrepancy between the predicted and the desired labels given by $|y(x_i) - d_i|$ for all the samples in the training set. This learning problem can be seen as an energy minimization problem, which can be solved using gradient-based optimization techniques (Snyman 2005), such as gradient descent. The energy function is given as a function of the unknown vector $E(w) = (y(x_i) - d_i)^2$, and its gradient with respect to w can be approximated by $\frac{\partial E}{\partial w} = (y(x_i) - d_i) x_i$. The unknown vector w can be estimated by using the following simple gradient-descent update rule given by $w_{new} = w_{old} - a\frac{\partial E}{\partial w}$, where a is a small positive constant known as *learning rate*, $0 < a \leq 1$.

The aforementioned update rule is repeatedly applied using all the available training data samples, and the overall learning algorithm is summarized into the following steps:

Step 1. Set an initial value to the unknown vector w (usually initialized as the zero vector).
Step 2. Apply the rule $w_{new} = w - a(y(x_i) - d_i) x_i$ for all training samples (x_i, d_i).
Step 3. Repeat Step 2 until a convergence or termination criterion is satisfied.

It can be proven that if the samples in the training dataset are linearly separable, then the training of the perceptron converges, i.e., the estimated vector *w* does not change after a certain number of iterations (Haykin 2008). However, if the dataset is not linearly separable, a termination criterion should be employed, such as a maximum number of iterations allowed. The perceptron has two key advantages: (1) it has a very simple linear form, which leads to light implementations, and (2) it guarantees convergence if there is a linear solution to the given problem. The main drawback is that it fails in any non-linearly separable problems, even a simple one.

Perceptron as well as other types of artificial neural networks can be represented graphically using structures inspired from biological neurons. Figure 7.2 shows the main parts of a single neuron and their corresponding role in the perceptron model. Overall, perceptron is the artificial equivalent of a single neuron with *n*-inputs and one output (neural response). Several perceptrons can be employed in order to implement a set of neurons that receive the same *n*-dimensional stimuli and produce *m* independent outputs.

There are several variations of the perceptron model that differ mainly in the employed activation function. In the above discussion the activation function was defined as a step function (Eq. 7.1). Such step function performs hard classification, since it assigns a 0 or 1 label to every input vector *x*. Other commonly used step functions assign values –1 and +1 to the elements of the two classes. Soft classification can be performed by activation functions that generate real-valued responses within a specific interval. The neural response in this case can be interpreted as being linearly related

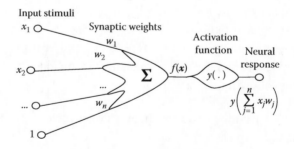

FIGURE 7.2

Graphical representation of the perceptron neuron. The input stimuli are weighted by the synaptic weights and then are summed together to trigger an activation function that generates the response of the neuron.

to the probability of a sample belonging to class A or B. One of the most widely used activation function is the *logistic function* defined by

$$y(t) = \frac{1}{1 + e^{-\beta t}} \tag{7.2}$$

where β is a positive-valued constant that controls the slope of the function. The logistic function produces responses in the interval $(0,1)$ and is also called *sigmoid* due to the shape of its plot. In neural networks the logistic function is used as $y(f(x))$, where $f(x) = w \cdot x$. In the case of $f(x) = 0$ the sigmoid function takes value $y = 0.5$, while in the cases of $f(x) > 0$ or $f(x) < 0$ its value is $y > 0.5$ or $y < 0.5$, respectively. It should be noted that the responses $y = 0$ or $y = 1$ belong to the limit of the sigmoid function and cannot be practically obtained. One of the advantages of the sigmoid function is that it is continuous and its derivative is defined in its entire domain, which is a useful property for gradient-based optimization.

In the next section a more complex neural network model is presented that uses multiple perceptron neurons arranged in different layers and is able to solve non-linear problems.

Multi-Layer Perceptron

The process of learning in living organisms is a result of multiple neurons that interact with each other through numerous connections in a complex neural network. In artificial neural networks the perceptron can be employed as the fundamental element in a large network of interconnected neurons (Minsky and Papert 1969). The overall network will play the role of an autonomous neural system that processes a number of input stimuli and produces responses in one or more output neurons. The internal structure of such neural network is organized into hierarchical layers as shown in Figure 7.3. The first layer of a multi-layer perceptron (also known as *input layer*) consists of neurons that directly process the input stimuli. The responses generated by the neurons of the first layer are used as input to the neurons of the second layer; the output of the second layer is fed to the third layer, etc. The neurons of the last layer (output layer) produce the output responses of the overall network. Multi-layer perceptrons can be designed in various architectures of different complexities depending on the number of input nodes, the number of hidden layers, the number of neurons in each layer, and the number of output neurons.

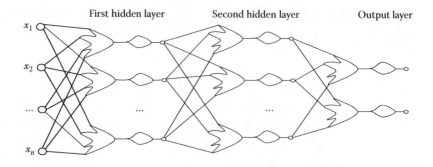

FIGURE 7.3

Graphical representation of a multilayer perceptron with two hidden layers and two output neurons.

A multi-layer perceptron can be trained from a given set of data samples $\{(x_1,d_1),\ (x_2,d_2),\ \cdots\}$ using an extension of the energy-based iterative method that was discussed above, in the "Perceptron" section. The behavior of each neuron is controlled by its vector of synaptic weights w, hence the goal of the learning process is to estimate the value of the weights of each neuron. The number of elements in the weight vector w_j^l of the jth neuron in the lth layer is equal to the number of its input nodes. Typically, each neuron of the first hidden layer has as many weights as the number of input stimuli; each neuron of the second hidden layer has as many weights as the number of neurons in the first hidden layer, etc. Therefore, the total number of unknowns in a multi-layer perceptron depends on its internal architecture.

The training of the multi-layer perceptron can be performed by minimizing the error between the desired responses and the actual responses of the output neurons. For simplicity we will assume that in our multi-layer perceptron there is only one output neuron, and that there are L layers of fully connected neurons. The squared error of the neural network for a given training sample (x_i,d_i) is $E=(y^L(x_i)-d_i)^2$, where $y^L(x_i)$ is the response of the activation function of the output neuron located in the Lth layer. In order to compute the value of $y^L(x_i)$, one needs to compute the responses of the activation functions of the neurons in the previous layer $y_1^{L-1}(x_i)$, $y_2^{L-1}(x_i)$, ... , which also require the values of $y_1^{L-2}(x_i)$, $y_2^{L-2}(x_i)$, ... etc. Therefore, starting from the first layer, all neural responses $y_1^1(x_i), y_2^1(x_i), \ldots$, must be computed and fed to the neurons of the next layer in order to compute the responses of the neurons of all the consequent layers in the multi-layer perceptron. This sequence of computations is called *forward computation*, and its goal is to compute the overall error of the neural network for a given data sample.

Once the forward computation step is completed, the unknown synaptic weights can be updated using gradient-based minimization similar to the one used in the single perceptron case (see "Perceptron" section). The update rule for the unknown weight vector w_j^l of the jth neuron in the lth layer is given by: $w_{new\,j}^l = w_j^l - a\delta_j^l(x_i)y^{l-1}(x_i)$, where a is the learning rate and $y^l(x_i)$ is a vector that consists of the output responses of the neurons in the lth layer $y^l(x_i)=[y_1^l(x_i)\ y_2^l(x_i)\ \cdots]^T$ and $y^0(x_i)=x_i$. The scalar function $\delta_j^l(x_i)$ corresponds to the local gradient of the neuron in the layer and is defined as follows:

$$\delta_j^l(x_i)=\begin{cases} \left(y_j^L(x_i)-d_i\right)y_j'^L(x_i) & \text{if } l=L \\ y_j'^l(x_i)\sum_m \delta_m^{l+1}(x_i)w_{m,j}^{l+1}(x_i) & \text{otherwise} \end{cases}$$

where $y_j'^l(x_i)$ is the derivative of the activation function (with respect to t in Eq. 7.2), which usually has a sigmoid shape, such as the logistic function that was mentioned earlier. For the calculation of the value of $\delta_j^l(x_i)$, the values of the next layer are required $\delta_k^{l+1}(x_i)$, $k = 1,2, ...$, therefore one needs to start computing the gradient values of the output layer $\delta_j^L(x_i)$, then the values of the previous layer $\delta_j^{L-1}(x_i)$, and continue until the first hidden layer $\delta_j^1(x_i)$. Similarly, all the synaptic weight vectors are updated in a backward fashion.

The aforementioned forward and backward computations are performed repeatedly using all the available training data samples and the overall multi-layer perceptron learning algorithm is summarized into the following steps:

Step 1. Set an initial value to the unknown vectors w_j^l.
Step 2. For all training samples (x_i,d_i) do:
  Step 2.1 Perform the forward computation step in order to compute the responses of all neurons in the multi-layer perceptron: $y_1^1(x_i), y_2^1(x_i), \dots, y_1^2(x_i), y_2^2(x_i), \dots y_1^L(x_i)$.
  Step 2.2 Perform the backward computation step in order to compute the local gradients and update the unknown synaptic vectors: $w_1^L, w_1^{L-1}, w_2^{L-1}, \dots, w_1^1, w_2^1, \cdots$
Step 3. Repeat Step 2 until a convergence or termination criterion is satisfied.

There are various stopping criteria that can be employed in Step 3 of the learning algorithm, such as defining a minimum allowed value for the absolute change of the average squared error computed using all training data samples. However, depending on the dataset, the algorithm may converge very slowly, due to small absolute changes in the error that may cause a premature termination if the stopping threshold is not small enough. The convergence speed may also be affected by the initialization of the unknown synaptic weight vectors. Although any arbitrary random initialization may be used, the training algorithm converges faster if the synaptic weights are chosen in such a way so that the average input of each activation function is close to zero, or the average output response of each neuron is about *0.5*.

One of the key advantages of multi-layer perceptrons is their ability to solve non-linear problems. Depending on the complexity of the classification problem, a proper number of neurons as well as number of hidden layers should be employed, so the total number of degrees of freedom in the neural network is large enough to accommodate the complexity of the problem. It has been shown that a neural network with a single hidden layer can solve any non-linear classification problem if the number of the hidden neurons is large enough. However, it may be more practical to use more than one layer with smaller number of neurons in each layer instead of a very large number of neurons in a single layer. The simplicity of the forward-backward propagation algorithm is also another advantage of multi-layer perceptrons, as it leads to efficient software implementations.

The slow convergence rate is the main drawback, not necessarily of the multi-layer perceptron model, but of the forward-backward propagation learning algorithm. It should be noted that once the neural network is trained it performs in constant computational complexity, i.e., it produces neural responses for arbitrary new stimuli vectors in constant speed, proportional to the speed of the CPU being used. Another issue related to the convergence is that the training algorithm may be trapped in local minima if the learning rate or the computed gradients are very small, which is a common issue in many gradient-based optimization methods. On the other hand, large learning rates may cause instability due to consecutive oscillations in the gradient vectors.

Several variations of the forward-backward propagation algorithm have been proposed in order to optimize the convergence of the algorithm and solve the aforementioned problems. The convergence and stability of the training algorithm can be significantly improved by adding to the rule for updating the vector w_j^l the term $\beta w_{old\ j}^l$, where $w_{old\ j}^l$ is the previous (older) value of the vector w_j^l, and $0 \le \beta < 1$. Furthermore, an adaptive learning rate a can be used instead of a constant value in order to advance the speed of the learning, by observing the behavior of the gradients using second-order partial derivatives (known as the *Hessian* matrix). Typically, the adaptive learning rate is larger in the first stages of learning and becomes smaller as the algorithm converges, which is similar to the learning curve observed in living organisms.

Other variations include steps for pruning of the neural network after the end of its training. So far in this section multi-layer perceptrons were assumed to consist of fully connected neural layers, i.e., the output response of each hidden neuron is fed as input to every neuron of the next layer (Figure 7.3). However, it is quite possible that in certain problems fewer connections may be necessary. In this case, the training algorithm assigns very small values to some of the possibly unnecessary neural connections. After the end of the training process, the significance of each neural connection with respect to the overall output response of the neural network is estimated, and neural connections can be pruned if their presence does not affect significantly the output of the network. Unnecessary network connections may also lead to misbehavior of the neural network in various testing stimuli that differ significantly from the training samples. Avoiding such over-fitting problems is another advantage of network pruning, besides the complexity reduction of the trained network.

Function Approximation Using Neural Networks

The neural network models that were discussed in the "Perceptron" and "Multi-Layer Perceptron" sections can be trained to solve linear or non-linear hard classification problems. For example, every financial institution develops their own rules for deciding whether to approve an application for a credit card or a loan based on various parameters that describe the economic level of the applicant. This underlying set of rules can be learned by a neural network given a set of training samples that consist of various parameters, such as age, annual income, debt, credit score, and others, as well as the corresponding desired response, i.e., the decision of the financial institution in the form of *1* for approval and *0* for denial. A multi-layer perceptron can learn from the given examples and then be able to respond to new applications, using its own experience. This learning problem is a typical example of a hard classification problem with two classes (YES or NO response).

However, there are several learning problems that require soft classification. In these problems the neural network should produce a real-valued response in the interval [0...1], instead of a discrete binary {0,1} response. An example of this category that is related to the aforementioned financial institution decision problem is described below. When a financial institution approves a credit card or loan application there is a set of rules that determine the approved interest rate for the particular applicant based on the applicant's financial potential. In this problem the training set is similar to the one defined earlier for the application approval problem, with the only difference in the desired responses, which are now real numbers such as 0.04 (4%), 0.3 (30%), etc. The underlying function that determines the interest rate for a particular applicant can be learned by a multi-layer perceptron with one hidden layer and one output neuron. The activation function of all hidden neurons will be the logistic function, and the output neuron will have no activation function.

The total response of the neural network is given by $y_1^2(x) = \sum_j w_{1,j}^2 y_j^1(x)$. The values $y_j^1(x)$ generated by the hidden neurons are restricted by the sigmoid function to the interval (0,1). On the contrary, the values $y_1^2(x)$ of the output neuron are not restricted by any function and depend on the weights $w_{1,j}^2$. The learning of the unknown function can be performed by using the forward-backward propagation method, properly modified to account for the absence of activation function in the output neuron. This type of neural network can approximate any real-valued function, and its approximation error depends on the number of hidden neurons. The approximation error can become arbitrarily small by choosing a large enough number of hidden neurons, according to the universal approximation theory (Funahashi 1989; Hornik, Stinchcombe, and White 1990).

Radial Basis Networks

The perceptron-based models, single- or multi-layer, use the function of a hyper-plane $f(x) = w \cdot x$ to divide the input samples into two classes that correspond to the two sides of the hyper-plane. Even in the case of multi-layer perceptrons, a non-linear classification problem is divided into several smaller linear classification problems that are solved individually by the hidden neurons. This is why heavy non-linearly separable problems require a very large number of hidden neurons in order to approximate small parts of the problem by using linear classifiers. However, a dataset may be non-linearly separable in the domain of the input feature vectors x, but it could be linearly separable in a different domain defined by a set of mapping functions $\varphi(x) = [\varphi_1(x) \quad \varphi_2(x) \quad \cdots \quad \varphi_m(x)]^T$. If $\varphi_i(x)$ defines a non-linear mapping, and the dimensionality m of the new space is significantly larger than the dimensionality n of the original space, then the original non-linear problem is more likely to be linearly separable in the new domain (Cover 1965).

There are many different choices for the functions $\varphi_n(x)$ depending on the nature of the given problem. Radial basis functions are the most commonly used functions because they can define a mapping that uniformly covers the input space and can be applied to various generic problems. The Gaussian kernel is one example of a radial basis function: $\varphi_i(x) = e^{-\frac{\|x-c_i\|^2}{2\sigma^2}}$, where c_1, c_2, ... c_m are n-dimensional centers of the radial functions, and σ is the standard deviation. Note that the Gaussian kernels do not have any scaling factor, because they do not play the role of a probability function, and can be arbitrarily scaled by the synaptic weights of the neural network. Without any additional scaling the Gaussian kernels produce output values in the interval (0,1]. The shape of these kernels is a lobe in the n-dimensional input domain and is centered at the location c_i. The function φ_i gets its maximum value, which corresponds to a strong neural response, for stimuli vectors x similar to its center c_i, and the similarity is measured with their Euclidean distance $\|x - c_i\|$. The neural responses produced by the kernel decay with the distance from its center, i.e., stimuli vectors that are very different from the vector c_i do not activate that particular radial basis neuron associated with φ_n.

Figure 7.4 shows the network diagram of a radial basis neural network with n input nodes, m hidden radial basis neurons, and one output neuron. The network can be easily extended to support multiple output nodes by adding more neurons to the output layer. It should be noted that the complexity of a radial basis neural network is proportional to the number of radial basis functions as well as the number of output neurons. Equivalently, the total number of unknowns is equal to $m \times$*output neurons*. In the case of a single output neuron, there is only one unknown vector w that consists of m synaptic weights w_1, w_2, ... w_m.

The training of a radial basis neural network can be performed by using the method for training a single perceptron ("Perceptron" section) and replacing the input vectors x_i with the vector $\varphi(x_i)$. The update rule is given by $w_{new} = w - a(y(x_i) - d_i)\varphi(x_i)$ and is applied iteratively using all

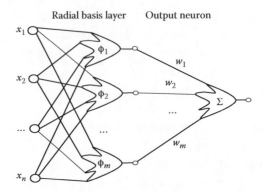

FIGURE 7.4
Graph representation of a radial basis neural network.

the given training samples $\{(x_1, d_1), (x_2, d_2), \cdots\}$ as it was discussed in the "Perceptron" section. Optionally, the output neurons may have an activation function such as the one employed by the single perceptron model. In general, the radial basis neural networks can be seen as single perceptrons that process m-dimensional stimuli vectors (x), and their learning process employs data sets of training samples in the form $\{(\varphi(x_1), d_1), (\varphi(x_2), d_2), \cdots\}$. The same type of m-dimensional mapped stimuli vectors can also be used as the input in a multi-layer perceptron. In this case, each of the neurons in the first hidden layer will have m synaptic weights in their unknown vector w_j^1. The training of such network can be performed using the forward-backward propagation algorithm that was discussed in the "Multi-Layer Perceptron" section by replacing the input vectors x_i with the vector $\varphi(x_i)$.

There are several other choices for the radial basis function besides the Gaussian kernel, such as multi-quadratic functions in the form $\varphi_i(x) = \sqrt{\|x - c_i\|^2 + a^2}$, or their inverse form (inverse multi-quadratics), where a is a positive constant. The common characteristic of all radial basis functions is the term $\|x - c_i\|$, which makes the basis function $\varphi_i(x)$ symmetric with respect to the center c_i. Another property of the radial basis functions is that c_i is the center of a hill or a valley and corresponds to the global maximum or the global minimum, respectively.

The centers of the radial basis functions can be chosen in different ways depending on the application. For example, the centers can be manually determined based on prior knowledge about the problem. Another commonly used technique is to use the training data samples as the centers of the radial basis functions, $c_i = x_i$. This implies that the number of the radial basis functions is equal to the number of data samples in the training dataset, which means that the number of unknown synaptic weights in the neural network shown in Figure 7.4 becomes equal to the number of linear equations $w \cdot \varphi(x_i) = d_i$. In this case the training problem can be expressed as a linear system $\Phi w = d$, where Φ is a matrix of size $m \times m$ whose (i,j) element is given by $\varphi_i(x_j)$, and d is an m-dimensional vector that consists of the desired responses d_i. The solution can be computed by matrix inversion $w = \Phi^{-1} d$, assuming that the matrix Φ is non-singular, which is true for the aforementioned radial basis functions if the training dataset contains distinct points (Haykin 2008).

Radial basis functions can be employed to learn an unknown function out of given training samples by interpolating the values of the desired responses between the given points. For example, consider the case of m same-type sensors located at m distinct locations in a geographic region (e.g., thermometers, traffic sensors, average housing costs, average annual income, or others). A radial basis function could be used to guess what the value of the sensor would be in a new arbitrary location within the same geographical region by properly interpolating the given values of the m sensors. In general, it is possible to approximate a function with unknown analytic form using a set of its sample values. The distribution of the samples may be non-uniform. The accuracy of the learned function is improved when there are enough samples to capture the shape of the underlying unknown function. For instance, smoothly varying areas of a function require a small number of samples, while regions with large gradients or discontinuities require a large set of given data samples.

One of the disadvantages of the use of radial basis functions for interpolation is that their complexity may become unnecessarily high when very large training datasets are given. Typically, the complexity of the network increases linearly with the number of given samples, while the accuracy increases asymptotically and therefore it does not change significantly after a certain number of samples. This problem can be solved by not using all the input samples as the centers of the radial basis functions, but instead by selecting a small number of centers using an automated selection process before the training of the neural network. One simple method for selecting K centers out of m given samples is the *K-means* algorithm, which consists of two main steps that are executed iteratively (Seber 1984). The algorithm is initialized by randomly selecting K centers out of the *m* given samples. Then, iteratively execute the following two alternating steps until convergence:

> **Step 1**. Assign each sample in the dataset to the class with the closest center.
>
> **Step 2**. Update the center of each class by computing the mean of its members.

K-means is a popular algorithm for unsupervised clustering of a dataset into K clusters. There are many variations with different proposed ways of initialization as well as methods for automatically determining the number of clusters. If K-means is used in conjunction with radial basis neural networks, the complexity of the network becomes K, which is typically significantly smaller than the total number of training samples.

Lattice Neural Networks

Another type of artificial neural network capable of solving non-linear problems is the so-called Lattice Neural Network. The main difference from the previously discussed types of neural networks is the fact that the fundamental components of lattice neural networks are the dendrites and not the neurons. The role of a dendrite is to form a set of lower and/ or upper bounds in each dimension of the input stimuli, which creates a bounding box in the input domain. Several dendrites can operate together and form a neuron. Figure 7.5 shows an example of a non-linear classification problem. The samples of the class A (black circles) can be separated from the samples of the class B (white circles) by using three bounding boxes. Each box can be implemented as a dendrite in a lattice neural network. Boundaries of arbitrarily high complexity can be approximated by a large enough number of bounding boxes, which is the key advantage of lattice neural networks.

A bounding box in *n*-dimensions is defined by $w_i^0 < x_i < w_i^1$, $i = 1,\ldots,n$, where w_i^0 and w_i^1 correspond to the lower and higher bounds along the ith dimension of the *n*-dimensional vector *x*. The bounding inequalities can be equivalently written as $0 < x_i - w_i^0$ and $0 < -(x_i - w_i^1)$. According to these two inequalities, a stimuli vector *x* lies inside the bounding box if the quantity $(-1)^l(x_i - w_i^l)$ is positive for all $i = 1,\ldots,n$ and $l = 0, 1$. If, at least, one of these values drops below zero, then the vector *x* lies outside the bounding box. Therefore, in order to perform this test, it is enough to find the minimum value of $(-1)^l(x_i - w_i^l)$ for all i, l and feed it to the step

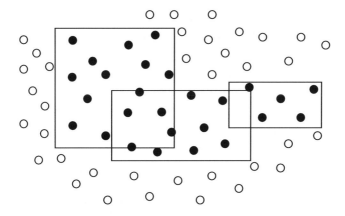

FIGURE 7.5
A non-linear classification problem solved using a lattice neural network with three dendrites.

function defined in Equation 7.1. Using the *minimum* operator, which is denoted by ∧, the bounding box test can be expressed in the following form:

$$f(x) = \wedge_{i=1}^{n} \wedge_{l=0}^{1} (-1)^l \left(x_i - w_i^l \right) \tag{7.3}$$

This equation is the fundamental computation performed by a dendrite in a lattice neural network and replaces the function $f(x) = w \cdot x$ that was employed by the perceptron. If the value of Equation 7.3 is negative, then the activation function in Equation 7.1 produces a zero response, which means that x lies outside of the bounding box.

If there are multiple dendrites in a neuron that correspond to multiple bounding boxes, it suffices for a sample x to belong to at least one box. Therefore, the maximum dendritic response should be calculated by $\vee_j f_j(x)$, where $\vee$ denotes the *maximum* operator for all j, and $f_j(x)$ is the response of the jth dendrite given by Equation 7.3.

Given a sample dataset $\{(x_1, d_1), (x_2, d_2), \cdots\}$, the training of a lattice-based neuron can be performed using the following three steps:

Step 1. Find the smallest possible box that contains all the samples with $d_i = 0$, and assign the appropriate weight values to the first dendrite.

Step 2. If there are misclassified points with $d_i = 1$, pick arbitrarily a misclassified point and go to Step 3.

Step 3. Find the biggest box that contains the selected misclassified point, but it does not contain any point with $d_i = 0$. Create a new dendrite and assign the appropriate weight values to it and go to Step 2.

The above training algorithm converges very quickly, and the total number of iterations is less than the total number of training samples. Unlike the previous types of networks, there is no predefined number of elements in the network (dendrites), and the neuron is populated with new dendrites during the learning process. The number of generated dendrites depends on the complexity of the boundary between the two classes in the dataset. The weights w_i^0 and w_i^1 of a dendrite may also take values $-\infty$ or $+\infty$, respectively, which correspond to an open box on its left or right side of the ith dimension. Depending on the dataset, a dendrite may leave one or more dimensions without any bounding limits. Finally, boundaries that separate more than two classes can be formed if more lattice-based neurons are employed.

Several applications of lattice neural networks have been proposed, due to their high capability of resolving some difficult non-linear problems. Lattice neural networks have been employed in applications for face and object localization (Grana and Raducanu 2001), auto-associative memories (Ritter and Iancu 2004), color images retrieval and restoration (Yun, Ling, and Yimin 2004), etc. Furthermore, various models of fuzzy lattice neural networks were studied in Kaburlasos and Petridis's work (2000) with applications in the area of text classification and classification of structured data domains.

The key limitation of the lattice neural networks is the fact that a large amount of training samples is required in order to achieve a decent accuracy of the approximated function near the boundary between the two classes. However, if the number of samples is not an issue, the recovered boundary can be infinitesimally approached. The main reason for this limitation is the fixed orientation of the bounding boxes, which causes pixilated boundaries as a result of merging multiple boxes (see Figure 7.5). These problems can be solved by allowing the dendrites to vary the orientation of their lattice. Each dendrite may operate on a different lattice and define a bounding box with particular scale, location, and orientation. The cost of these additional degrees of freedom is the increased computational complexity of the training algorithm, which in this case requires an additional step for estimating the optimal orientation of the lattice (Barmpoutis and Ritter 2006, 2007).

DISCUSSION AND CONCLUSIONS

The models that were reviewed in this chapter use connectivity structures inspired by findings regarding the functions and connections of biological neurons. All of the aforementioned models of artificial neural networks have several common characteristics. First of all, the main computation is performed by a fundamental unit that plays the role of a brick element in a neural network. Furthermore, these networks are structured internally using a hierarchical connectivity pattern. Several brick elements are employed within the same artificial neural network in order to collectively perform more complex computations. The complexity of a neural network depends on the total number of these brick elements and the number of connections between them. The connectivity structure can be depicted as a directed graph (Figures 7.2 through 7.4) in which every component of the network has a number of distinct input and output channels. Due to this directed flow of information the internal (hidden) components of an artificial neural network are typically structured in layers according to their distance from the input nodes that sense the original unprocessed stimuli. The neurons that process the raw input signals belong to the first hidden layer, and their output is fed to the neurons of the second hidden layer, etc.

The examples of networks presented throughout the chapter were feed forward neural networks, since they did not have any backward connections. By adding backward connections to a network graph (data flow loops), the neurons can process older stimuli simultaneously with the current input data. This is useful for learning specific types of temporal patterns of input stimuli or for predicting the expected future value of the input data based on their history. In this case the past few previous instances of the input signal can be used as part of a larger input signal by stacking the last k input vectors together, which produces a $k \times n$ vector $[x^T \quad x_{-1}^T \quad x_{-2}^T \quad \cdots \quad x_{-(k-1)}^T]^T$ where x_{-k} is the instance of the input vector k discrete time intervals ago. This technique works also without necessarily introducing backward connections in the network. The components of the produced $k \times n$-dimensional input vector are treated as independent sensors, which has the advantage of not adding any further processing steps to the aforementioned training algorithms. The learning of time-based patterns works better when the signals are natively discrete states of a variable instead of a discretized version of an originally continuous signal.

For example, consider the following set of rules: "if it was raining for the past 3 days, turn the irrigation system off," "if, however, the temperature today is above a specific threshold, turn the irrigation system back on," "if it was not raining for the past 2 days, turn the irrigation system on." In this case, some of the input signals are given in binary form (it was raining: Yes = 1/No = 0) and some others as real numbers (temperature), and can be used by one of the aforementioned supervised learning algorithms in order to train a neural network to automatically control an irrigation system. However, processing of speech signals require algorithms that are aware of the temporal relationship between the data samples, and time-agnostic neural network training algorithms may fail in learning complex speech patterns. In this case, other types of machine learning algorithms can be used that may not be inspired by biological systems.

In practice, artificial neural networks are algorithms that convert input stimuli to output signals. These are generic signal processing algorithms, which can be used as encoders/decoders of an input signal. The output signal usually contains higher-level information compared to the raw input signal. For example, the input signal may contain the pixel information from a digital camera located on a highway, and the output of the neural network may indicate whether there is a vehicle present in the exit lane or not. The neural network can be trained to understand what "presence of a vehicle" means based on a set of given examples. Neural networks have been successfully applied to many real-life problems. However, as any system, they have limitations. Using neural networks to predict the economic growth of a company based on its history may be inefficient because such prediction may be affected by many input parameters, and some of them may have unexpected behavior, such as natural disasters, global financial crisis, military conflicts, and others.

Finally, although artificial neural networks imitate the structure and behavior of biological neural networks, they cannot produce new knowledge or resemble the sophistication of human intelligence, and their "intelligence" is limited to the ability of learning patterns from experience, i.e., from given training datasets. Like any computer algorithm, artificial neural networks are nothing else but a finite sequence of mathematical steps, which is executed by a computer system in a command-by-command fashion, in order to help the users, intelligent human beings, effectively solve complex real-life problems, such as those in the fields of business or economics.

Exercises

1. Consider the following training dataset: $x_1 = [0 \quad 0]^T$, $x_2 = [0 \quad 1]^T$, $x_3 = [1 \quad 0]^T$, $x_4 = [1 \quad 1]^T$ with the corresponding desired responses: $d_1 = 0$, $d_2 = 1$, $d_3 = 1$, $d_4 = 0$. Design four neural networks based on the given training dataset by calculating manually the corresponding unknown weights for the following models: (a) perceptron, (b) multi-layer perceptron, (c) radial basis neural network, and (d) lattice neural network. Do not estimate the unknown weights by following the iterative training methods discussed in this chapter, but by manually choosing the geometric boundaries between the two classes in the 2-dimensional space (i.e., lines, circles, or boxes depending on the type of neural network).

2. Follow the steps of the iterative methods discussed in this chapter in order to train four different types of neural networks: (a) perceptron, (b) multi-layer perceptron, (c) radial basis neural network, and (d) lattice neural network, using the dataset given in Exercise 1.

3. Assume that you are the person who takes the decisions for credit card applications in a small financial institution. Define your own rules for accepting an application based on the applicant's age, educational background, and credit score. Create two particular examples of accepted applications and two examples of rejected applications based on the rules you defined. Train a neural network using these examples as the input in one of the methods for supervised training that were discussed in this chapter. Create more examples of accepted and rejected cases (different from the training examples) and use them to test the trained neural network. In how many test cases was the response of the neural network the same as the desired response? Repeat the same experiment using four training examples of accepted and four examples of rejected applications.

4. Repeat the experiments in Exercise 3 in order to train and test a neural network that computes the interest rate that will be offered to a credit card applicant based on the applicant's age, annual income, debt, and credit score. Evaluate the trained neural network by computing the average absolute difference between the desired response and the one given by the network. The test cases should be different from the training examples.

5. Implement three versions of a multi-layer perceptron using different numbers of hidden layers and different numbers of hidden neurons. Train these three different networks using the dataset you created in Exercise 4. Which of the three neural networks gives better results and why?

ANSWERS

1. The given data set is non-linearly separable. (a) Since there is no line that separates the two classes, a single perceptron cannot successfully solve the problem. (b) A multi-layer perceptron with two neurons in a hidden layer and one output neuron can solve the problem. The two hidden neurons can implement two line boundaries, one separating x_1 from the rest of the points, and another one separating x_4 from the rest of the points. In both cases, the isolated points x_1 and x_4 should lie on the same side (positive or negative) of the boundary line. Then the output neuron can properly separate the responses of the hidden neurons by defining a line that isolates the point (0,0) from the points (1,0) and (0,1). There are other possible configurations of a multi-layer perceptron that solve the same problem. (c) A radial basis neural network that solves this problem is defined by two positive Gaussians centered at (0,1) and (1,0), and two negative Gaussians centered at (0,0) and (1,1). (d) Finally, a lattice neural network with two dendrites, corresponding to two boxes can solve the problem, that is, one box that isolates (0,1) from the rest of the points and another one that isolates (1,0) from the rest of the points.
2. The algorithms in this exercise can be implemented in any computer programming language.
3. In this problem the educational level can be parameterized using an integer value in the range 1–4, denoting that the applicant has earned a high-school, college, post-graduate, or doctorate diploma, respectively. The credit score can be an integer in the range 0–1000 describing the financial credibility of a person. An example of a simple set of rules for this problem is: Rule 1: "If the applicant is more than 26 years old, or has a college degree, or has credit score more than 600, then the application is approved." Rule 2: "If the applicant's credit score is less than 350 then the application is rejected." Rule 3:

"Rule 2 has higher priority than Rule 1." Sample data from this set of rules are: $x_1 = [30 \quad 2 \quad 400]^T$, $d_1 = 1$, $x_2 = [18 \quad 1 \quad 450]^T$, $d_2 = 0$, $x_3 = [40 \quad 3 \quad 300]^T$, $d_3 = 0$ $x_4 = [60 \quad 2 \quad 800]^T$, $d_4 = 1$ (the order of the elements in the vector x is: age, education, credit score). Depending on the complexity of the rules you have defined, a large enough training data set should be given in order that the neural network learns properly the desired behavior. A set of two examples from class 0 and two from class 1 may not be enough for the successful training of the network. Better results can be achieved by increasing the number of given examples and also by finding examples that better represent your underlying rules. Multi-layer perceptrons, radial basis neural networks, or lattice neural networks may be used.

4. The solution to this problem is closely related to the solution given for Exercise 3. In this case the given data samples are 4-dimensional. Furthermore, the desired response is a real number (interest rate); hence the output neuron should not have any activation function. Multi-layer perceptrons or radial basis neural networks may be used in your experiments. Lattice neural networks, as they were presented in this chapter, work only with binary desired responses, and cannot be used to approximate an unknown real-valued function.

5. The neural networks in this exercise can be implemented in any computer programming language. Depending on the problem as well as the given training data set, one type of network may behave better than the others. To quantitatively evaluate the effectiveness of various solutions you can compare their average absolute error from the desired response.

REFERENCES

Barmpoutis, A. and Ritter, G. X. (2006) "Orthonormal basis lattice neural networks," In *Proceedings of IEEE International Conference on Fuzzy Systems*, pp. 331–336.

Barmpoutis, A. and Ritter, G. X. (2007) "Orthonormal basis lattice neural networks," In *Computational Intelligence Based on Lattice Theory*, V. Kaburlasos and G. X. Ritter (ed.), pp. 43–56.

Cover, T. M. (1965) "Geometrical and statistical properties of systems of linear inequalities with applications in pattern recognition," *IEEE Transactions on Electronic Computers*, vol. EC-14, pp. 326–334.

Funahashi, K. (1989) "On the approximate realization of continuous mappings by neural networks," *Neural Networks*, vol. 2, pp. 183–192.

Grana, M. and Raducanu, B. (2001) "Some applications of morphological neural networks," In *Proceedings of the International Joint Conference on Neural Networks,* vol. 4, pp. 2518–2523.

Haykin, S. (2008) *Neural Networks and Learning Machines*, Prentice Hall, Upper Saddle River, NJ.

Hornik, K., Stinchcombe, M., and White, H. (1990) "Universal approximation of an unknown mapping and its derivatives using multilayer feedforward networks," *Neural Networks*, vol. 3, pp. 551–560.

Kaburlasos, V. and Petridis, V. (2000) "Fuzzy Lattice Neurocomputing (FLN) models," *Neural Networks*, vol. 13, no. 10, pp. 1145–1170.

Minsky, M. L. and Papert, S. A. (1969) *Perceptrons*, MIT Press, Cambridge, MA.

Nering, E. D. (1976) *Linear Algebra and Matrix Theory*, Wiley, New York.

Ritter, G. X. and Iancu, L. (2004) "A morphological auto-associative memory based on dendritic computing," In *Proceedings of IEEE International Joint Conference on Neural Network*, vol. 2, pp. 915–920.

Rosenblatt, F. (1958) "The perceptron: A probabilistic model for information storage and organization in the brain," *Psychological Review*, vol. 65, pp. 386–408.

Seber, G. A. F. (1984) *Multivariate Observations*, Wiley, New York.

Snyman, J. (2005) *Practical Mathematical Optimization: An Introduction to Basic Optimization Theory and Classical and New Gradient-Based Algorithms*, Springer, New York.

Yun, Z., Ling, Z., and Yimin, Y. (2004) "Using multi-layer morphological neural network for color images retrieval," In *Proceedings of the 5th World Congress on Intelligent Control and Automation*, vol. 5, pp. 4117–4119.

8

Measuring Success in Social Media: An Information Strategy in a Data Obese World

Jeremy P. Floyd

CONTENTS

Learning Objectives

In this chapter, we cover:

- The purpose of your engagement.
- The method of measurement.
- The tools to analyze the results considering the purpose-driven goals.

A helpful Digital Marketing & Measurement spreadsheet is provided. Along the way, we will be populating the sheet through a series of four exercises.

INTRODUCTION

Every day hundreds of gigabytes of tracking data are generated. Under perfect circumstances, every interaction, link, like, and mention are trackable; but knowing what to track and how to report it are critical to "knowing" results. Moore's law's impact on data means that the world's data is doubling every 72 hours now, and that means that there is more tracking of more useless metrics than ever.[*] While data is ever increasing, resources to compile and analyze the results are not.

If you are already contributing to social media then you understand the importance of tracking, and if you are just thinking about it, then pay attention. Building content and a following from Facebook to YouTube requires an extraordinary investment of time. Tracking the results is critical to the overall success of digital marketing, but successful tracking begins before the first character is typed. Proper planning and setup on the front end will produce better results and better tracking of the results.

GOAL-BASED REPORTING

To avoid analytics overload, we have to know where we are going, how, and why. As Jim Sterne says, there are only three "purposes" to use digital media: "increasing revenue, lowering costs, or improving customer satisfaction."[†] Measurement of social media efforts is only instructive when viewed in the context of the purpose and goals of the activities.

Strategy is the bridge from our current state to the future state, as shown in Figure 8.1. Imagine standing on top of one side of a river valley looking to the other side. How could you possibly travel to the other side? You might decide to climb down into the valley, ferry across the river, and ascend the other side. Alternatively, you might construct a bridge to get over the river. Ultimately, the strategy to navigate over the river depends on the reason for crossing it first. If, for example, you were crossing over the water this one time as part of a much larger journey, then crafting a

---

[*] White Paper. IBM Global Technology Services. "The Toxic Terabyte: How Data-Dumping Threatens Business Efficiency." July 2006. 2.

[†] Sterne, Jim. *Social Media Metrics: How to Measure and Optimize Your Marketing Investment.* Hoboken, NJ: John Wiley, 2010. 5.

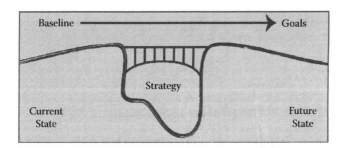

FIGURE 8.1
Current to future state.

bridge would be a waste of time and resources. On the other hand, if this path were part of the daily commute, then building a bridge would eventually save time and resources. The difference in the "purpose" of getting from point A to point B one time versus regularly ultimately dictates the strategy of the route.

By analogy, when we construct a social media strategy our decision first is determined by the business purpose and second by the digital purpose that we are trying to achieve. According to the purpose, the goals determine specifically where we want to be, and the strategy is the bridge from our current state to the future state.

Typically, however, our overall digital activities are lumped into one bucket—to make more money. Organizations attempt a number of social tactics to this end, and to justify the expense and time investment, someone in an organization requests a report that "ties all of this social media" to increased revenues. Unfortunately, that particular report doesn't exist. The report that ties all of "your" social media endeavors back to the results that you have received must be built by "you."

Let's start with an exercise where you will define the metrics that you are going to track based on your business and digital purpose.

Exercise 1: Create an Objective—The First Page Strategy

In this exercise, we will create a copy of the Digital Marketing & Measurement spreadsheet, which is available as a Google Spreadsheet at *bit.ly/jfloyd-sm-spreadsheet*. Click on File > Make a copy... to create an editable version for your use.

First, describe the project; define the overall business purpose (as shown in Figure 8.2). You might consider some variation of increase income,

	A	B	C
1		**Social Media Planning**	
2	Desciption of Project:		
3	Business Purpose:		
4	Digital Purpose:		
5	Current Assessment:		
6		**Objective #1**	**Objective #2**
7	Description of objective		
8			
9	Strategy		
10			
11	Measurable Outcome		
12			
13	Completion Date		
14			
15	Revenue		
16			
17	Who is accountable?		
18			
19	Who is the champion?		
20	**Tactics & Audience**		
21			
22	Tactic #1		
23	- Audience(s)		
24	- Accountability		
25			
26	Tactic #2		
27	- Audience(s)		
28	- Accountability		
29			
30	Tactic #3		
31	- Audience(s)		
32	- Accountability		
33			
34	Tactic #4		
35	- Audience(s)		
36	- Accountability		
37			

FIGURE 8.2

Planning document available at bit.ly/jfloyd-sm-spreadsheet.

decrease expense, or improve customer satisfaction. Then you will move into the preliminary purpose of the social media engagement.

A. What is the digital purpose that supports your business purpose? Here are a few examples:

Increase Revenue and Cut Expenses

Generate Leads	Either through engagement or through driving traffic to your Website signup forms to lead collection forms, the digital objective may be to generate leads.
Generate Sales	Retailers of all shapes and sizes are using social media to announce new products, announce special promotions, and increase sales with customers.
Establish Expertise	By providing expert content, links, and engagement, you establish confidence and trust that you are the subject matter expert.
Focus Group	Listening to your customers using social channels can save money on focus groups and improve product or service development.

Increase Customer Satisfaction	
Customer Service	Like Comcast, Salesforce, Best Buy, and Zappos social media has proven as an effective tool to respond quickly to customer comments.
Product Enhancement	Social channels allow companies to learn how their customers use their products and more importantly how to use their products.
Awareness and Engagement	By either increasing the awareness of a company's brand or engaging customers directly, a great purpose of social media is direct engagement.

B. **Objective**—Now that you know the purpose, you have answered the "why." Now, where do you want to go? For example, an objective would be to grow your email list by 500 names in the next 30 days.

C. **Strategy**—How are you going to move from your current location to your objective? In this section list specific, measurable, achievable, relevant, time bound goals.

D. **Measurable Outcome**—Sometimes called Key Performance Indicators (KPIs), identify the metrics that are most critical to the success of the objective. KPIs will be discussed in more depth later in this chapter.

E. **Completion Date**—While the objective may be ongoing, the measurable outcome must be tied to a specific date.

F. **Impact on Revenue**—Will this objective increase income? Reduce expenses? Improve the customer experience?

G. **Accountability and Champion**—Who is responsible for the implementation? Usually the accountability and the champion are the same. It is important, however, that this person rallies the cause in the face of opposition.

H. **Tactics**—The tactics portion of the spreadsheet breaks the objective into the single pieces that will eventually lead to the completion of the objective. For example, you might create a refer-a-friend Facebook contest to build a larger email database.

I. **Costs**—What is the cost of the services and products that you are planning to use? How much time will it take to execute the plan?

In the final part of this exercise, let's fill in the Goals tab of the spreadsheet (as shown in Figure 8.3). The Tactical Goals are a snapshot of relevant measurements at the time of this writing. Feel free to modify the sources and measurements.

	A	B	C	D	E
1	Tactical Goals	Current State	Monthly % Increase	6 Month Goal	12 Month Goal
2	**Website**				
3	Referred Traffic	3000	5.00%	4,020	5,388
4	Leads (from social)	23	4.00%	29	37
5	Sales (from social)	34	6.00%	48	68
6					
7	**Twitter**				
8	Tweets	345	10.00%	611	1,083
9	Followers	458	10.00%	811	1,437
10	Mentions	120	10.00%	213	377
11	Content Shares (bit.ly)	35	10.00%	62	110
12	Retweets	64	10.00%	113	201
13					
14	**Blog**				
15	Unique Blog Visitors	967	10.00%	1,713	3,035
16	RSS Subscribers	83	10.00%	147	260
17	Email RSS Subscribers	68	10.00%	120	213
18	Visitors from Social Media	367	10.00%	650	1,152
19					
20	**Facebook Pages**				
21	Posts	22	8.00%	35	55
22	Likes	120	8.00%	190	302
23	Reach	1345	8.00%	2,134	3,387
24	PTAT	345	8.00%	547	869
25	Check-ins	2	8.00%	3	5
26	Comments	34	8.00%	54	86
27	Shares	23	8.00%	36	58
28					
29	**Google+**				
30	Number of Circles You're In	324	4.00%	410	519
31	# Posts	13	4.00%	16	21
32	G+1's	45	4.00%	57	72
33	Shares	2	4.00%	3	3

FIGURE 8.3
Goals tab of spreadsheet.

Here we are establishing the starting point or the current state. Considering the tactics identified in the first exercise, identify all the digital channels that you are going to benchmark. Collect the data from the sources and enter the previous month's measurements. If you are planning to begin using a source but have no previous data, enter zeros in the Current State column.

START WITH WEBSITE TRACKING

Before diving into the analytics of the different networks, we are going to evaluate effective measurement of goals on the central Website. Regardless of all the wonderful social media tools, the Website or in

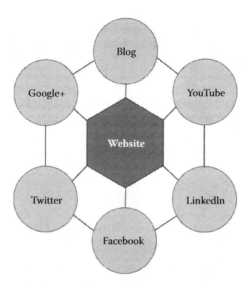

FIGURE 8.4
Hub and spoke graphic in the digital landscape.

some cases blogs are the central point of all online activity. As Figure 8.4 indicates, the site becomes the hub of all online activity. The hub and spoke analogy is nothing new, but it is important when considering this section.

Regardless of the campaign or digital activity, the Website is typically a key destination in the digital landscape. For example, if you are using Twitter or StumbleUpon to share a link to your blog, the goal is to drive the maximum number of visitors to view the blog post. If you are lucky the visitor will take time to read other posts and may even subscribe to your blog through email.

To determine the effectiveness of the overall digital activity, we will first ensure that measurement of the central Website is in place. Stepping back and planning the configuration of Web analytics is critical to the overall measurement of digital success.

Google Analytics

Google Analytics is one of many Website analytics tools available to measure traffic of your Website and/or blog. Mint (haveamint.com), KISSmetrics (kissmetrics.com), and Mixpanel (mixpanel.com) are all alternatives that digital marketers use. Google Analytics, however, is free, widely used (thus has a large community), easy to set up, and is continuously updated by Google. For broad analysis and reporting of your Website traffic, try several of the tools to see which works best for you. In this section, we cover the basics of Google Analytics.

Defining Goals—Based on your defined goals, Google Analytics will allow you to track key goal conversions such as URL Destination, Visit Duration, Page/Visit, or an Event, which is a combination of the others. For example, if you have a shopping cart that requires a login or registration on `login.html ->registration.html` then with an order confirmation, `confirm.html`, and finally a thank you page, `thanks.html`, you can see exactly where you are losing customers in the funnel. These goals should match the goals that you defined in Exercise 1.

Dashboards—Taking the time to create customized dashboards will reduce the overall time that it takes to find the key information. You can create custom widgets that display information in the following formats: Metric (number), Pie Chart, Timeline, Tabular form, Map, or Bar Chart. Most of the widgets will allow you to display "metrics" and "dimensions," which is like saying the number of women (metric) that are employed in different industries (dimension). In your car, your speed, engine temperature, and fuel gauge are critical measures that are always available. Your Analytics dashboard should likewise include the most critical success information.

Token Tracking—Google Analytics provides a wonderful tool for tracking social media results: Regardless of source or tracking tools, a best practice is using Google's Token Tracking to each inbound link.* By adding the following snippet to the end of the link, you will be able to accurately track the referral.

```
http://www.testsource.com/?utm_medium = social&utm_source
= twitter
```

In this example the medium is "social" and the network is "Twitter." Then when the results are viewed in Google Analytics, the results can be segmented by the five variables. This URL tagging provides you the opportunity to measure and segment success of the campaigns.

---

* For more information on Google's Token tracking code visit Google Analytics URL Builder at bit. ly/token-tracking.

The potential tracking variables are listed below in order from most general to most specific:

utm _ medium—Define the originating medium.

utm _ source—Define the originating network source: Twitter, Facebook, Pinterest, etc.

utm _ campaign—If the link is part of a larger campaign, add the campaign name or ID here.

utm _ content—This variable allows you to specifically define where the link is being used on the page or on the Web. For example, you may define one content tag in your Facebook information section and a different content source used in one of the Facebook tabs.

utm _ term—You may define the specific keyword that corresponds to the link. This is specifically valuable when using pay per click advertising.

In this example (see Figure 8.5), Kristi Hines demonstrates how token tracking allows focused reporting of inbound links.[*]

If you need help building the URLs, Google has a tool available at http://bit.ly/token-url-builder.

Link Shorteners

From tinyurl.com to Hootsuite's ow.ly, there are plenty of options of link shorteners. The basic service of a link shortener is to save space when using limited character counts in social media. Bit.ly, however, offers a number of helpful features. Bit.ly offers tracking and analytics of the links that it shortens. It tracks both short- and long-term usage.

You can access the analytics of any bit.ly link by adding a plus sign to the very end of the URL. For example, visiting http://bit.ly/ZElCE6+ will show the number of clicks, number of global shares to the same URL (using bit.ly data), and access to a QR code to that link.

By default, bit.ly assigns a randomized URL string. For example, in the URL http://bit.ly/ZElCE6, the letter and number combination after the hash mark are random, but as part of the free plan you can create a custom alias that makes it easier for your visitors to remember. Best practice is to

---

[*] Hines, Kristi. "How To Use UTM Parameters In Google Analytics 5." "Learn More About Your Traffic: How to Use UTM Parameters in Google Analytics 5." *KISSMetrics*, January 2012. Web. 30 April 2013. http://kikolani.com/.

FIGURE 8.5
Google analytics Campaigns sorted by UTM variables.

use aliases anytime that the users are not just clicking on the shortened URL (i.e., presentations, print, etc.). As a side note, you can use your own URL instead of "bit.ly" in the pro settings.

Considering Token Tracking, each UTM variable URL can be given a distinct link. Clearly, the token links get long and clearly communicate to the user that they are being tracked. Using a link shortener makes that less obvious.

Real-Time Analytics

Google Analytics provides excellent information about visitors over time. With social media tracking, real-time or in-the-moment analytics are instructive to how followers are behaving.

Tools like Woopra and Clicky offer robust, real-time Web analytics. These tracking software applications provide a great view into what is happening on the site right now. This is especially important when running a campaign and traffic spikes or lulls might be offset with social media.

Woopra—This application allows you to see real-time visitors by location, referral source, and top page. In addition, you can tag visitors to see recurring visits. Woopra also offers an onsite chat application, but primarily it is reporting software.

Clicky—Another real-time application that tracks visitors, location, referral source, and content. Custom alerts allow you to know in real time when Website visitors are performing desired actions.

Google Analytics—In 2012, Google Analytics began testing real-time visitor reporting. This feature is not nearly as robust as the applications that are specifically dedicated to this function, but it is available.

Visitor Visualization

Another approach to analyzing visitor behavior is visualizing their behavior on the Website.

Crazy Egg—This application is one of most affordable heat map and eye tracking applications. Look at heat maps of your pages and determine where specifically on the page they are clicking. Determine from this data whether your information and site is usable. Crazy Egg also offers a Scroll Map, which displays how far visitors of the site scrolled. This is especially valuable when determining whether information is posted below the fold.

ClickTale—In addition to the heat map, scroll map, and overlay offered in Crazy Egg, ClickTale allows the owner of the site to view videos (including mouse movements) of users on the Website. While it is premium software, ClickTale's features, including mouse maps, allow you to make informed decisions about how visitors are using your site.

Exercise 2: Use Bit.ly and the UTM Source to Create Trackable Links

In this exercise, you will create a series of shortened links using the UTM Codes.

First, build a basic spreadsheet that contains a base URL and your variables (there is an example sheet on the spreadsheet used in Exercise 1). This exercise will work best if you use a Website where you already have Google Analytics installed. Enter the variables that you would like to track, and then enter the base URL to a page that you would like to track.

Provide a few unique variables per URL (i.e., Facebook, Twitter, Google+, email marketing, etc.).

If you don't already have a Bit.ly account, go to http://bit.ly and create an account by authenticating your Twitter account.

1. Once you are logged in to the service, click on the top right of your screen where it says, "Paste link here..."
2. Paste the Campaign URL and press ENTER.
3. Once your shortened URL is displayed, paste the shortened URL back in your spreadsheet along with the date.

Then share the shortened links in the appropriate mediums for 7 days. Finally, at the end of the 7-day period, generate a report from Google Analytics detailing the results of the activity on the campaign. As part of the report, compare the Google Analytics visits with the Bit.ly clicks (by using the bit.ly/*example*+) link.

FOCUS ON MEASUREMENT

Now that we have a grasp on reporting the results to the Website destinations, let's look at the measurement of each social network. Clicks, retweets, shares, likes, follows, comments, links, sales, and friends can all be measured. So which numbers are really important? It depends, right? The purpose of the digital engagement is the benchmark to contrast the results. Let's look at a few of the most important numbers that we want to track. Social networks and tools will change. Here today, gone tomorrow has been the nature of the business. Regardless of the particular network, let's first look at the key measures of each network

Engagement—In the social space, talking or shouting does not work. Engagement is the measure of interaction among your networks. Depending on the service or type of interaction, engagement will be different on each network. Table 8.1 shows a few popular networks and types of engagement measures.

Direct Goal Completions—If your objectives include a particular call to action, like leads, subscribers, or signups, then you will measure the goal completions through your network's behavior. For example,

TABLE 8.1

Popular Social Networks and Engagement Measures

	Blog	Facebook	Instagram	LinkedIn	Pinterest	Twitter	YouTube
Likes/Favorites—"Liking" is one of the lowest investments in engagement. It is easy to click a "like" button. It is also carries the least value.		•	•	•	•	•	•
Mentions—Publishing someone's name or site in an update or post.	•	•	•	•	•	•	
Comments—Direct published interactions with posts. Comments are one of the most important measures of engagement.	•	•	•	•	•		

if the call to action was to subscribe to an email list, then your measurement will include the number of new subscribers.

Reach and Impressions—How many people saw your post? YouTube provides direct data on how many times each video is viewed. Facebook Insights provides information on the total number of impressions that each post has received, which is the "reach" multiplied by the number of times the post. Tools like TweetReach try to decipher what the potential impressions of a tweet might be. The problem is that reach and impressions only calculate the total number of people whose feed the update appeared in, not the number of people who saw it.

Referrals—How much traffic did the network refer to a Website or blog? As covered in the previous section, this is ultimately one of the greatest measurements of digital marketing success.

Connections—Listed last is one of the most popular measurements: connections. Followers, friends, and/or connections are highly gamed results and really do not correlate directly to influence or effectiveness.

Common Terms

Each network defines terms slightly differently. Table 8.2 shows how each network uses terms for the general categories.

Here are a few of the most important metrics from each of the most popular social networks, as shown in Table 8.2. A network's popularity is in constant flux, so always look to the key measures to see how each network defines that measurement.

Facebook

Everyone wants more likes, but likes alone provide very little information. Using Facebook Insights, you can measure the results and response of your Facebook activity:

1. **Number of posts** (and the corresponding response).
2. **Number of people** actively engaging through comments and likes.
3. **PTAT (People Talking About This)**—This number includes the number of people talking about a particular topic.
4. **Likes**—clicking the Likes tab at the top of the page will reveal the demographic breakdown of your community.

Measuring Success in Social Media • 219

TABLE 8.2

Comparison of Terms for Each Social Network

	Blog	Facebook	Google+	Instagram	LinkedIn	Pinterest	Twitter	YouTube
Connections	Subscribers	Friends/Followers	Circle	Follower	Connection	Follower	Follower	Subscriber
Like	Like	Like	+1	Like	Like	Like	Favorite	Like
Share	Link	Share	Reshare	—	Share link	Repin	Retweet	—
Comment	Comment	Comment	Comment	Comment	Comment	Comment	Mention	Comment
Reach	Visitors	Reach	—	—	—	—	Followers	Views
Mentions	Inbound Links	Page Mention	Mention	Mention	—	—	Mention	—
Post	Post	Status	Share	Photo	Update	Pin	Tweet/Post	Video

Source: Comparison of terms for each social network. For a comprehensive list of definitions visit Simply Measured at http://bit.ly/metrics-defined.

5. **Reach**—This allows you see your page views and unique visitor views (those who searched for you as opposed to clicking on the Facebook ad).
6. **Impressions**—Edgerank is Facebook's algorithm to determine what posts are published in followers' timelines.

Twitter

1. **Followers and Following**—While Follower and Following counts were once thought to be the key indicator of influence, connections are now just one in a sea of many factors used to determine Twitter influence. Following a number of spam accounts, following a number of dormant accounts, following more than you follow are all thought to affect your overall influence.
2. **Tweets**—The number of tweets per account is worth monitoring. Specifically, the number of tweets per day/week/month should be consistent. Using a tool like TweetStats will provide a snapshot of number of tweets by hour, day of the week, and months. For example, if you are a restaurant monitoring the customer comments and your angry customer has only tweeted complaints but they only have 78 tweets, that would be instructive how to engage the customer.
3. **Mentions and Retweets**—The most important measure on Twitter is the amplification of the Twitter account. How many times is the Twitter account retweeted, mentioned, and favorited?

HTML Email

1. **List size**—Total number of subscribers that are being emailed on a regular basis. Some organizations will create very segmented lists.
2. **Opens and Clicks**—For each campaign determine the number of people that opened and clicked on the email.
3. **Unsubscribes**—One of the most important measures is how many people unsubscribe from the email list. If this number fluctuates, it is critical to determine the cause of the unsubscribes and take corrective action.

Key Performance Indicators (KPIs)

As noted from the beginning of this chapter, reporting all the numbers provides confusing information that spurs no action. Determining the numbers that are critical and actionable is the goal of putting all the data into meaningful, useful format.

As mentioned, a car dashboard has a few key numbers that it reports: speed, amount of fuel, temperature of the car, among others. Why isn't the oxygen sensor info on the dashboard? It is important, right? It did not make the cut. Of the 6–8 values reported to the driver, the oxygen levels were not critical to the daily operation of the vehicle. It is important, just not "stop the car right now" important. As you think about your KPIs, what are "stop the car" or "rev the engine" numbers?

Each organization's reporting will be determined by the purpose and goals discussed earlier. These "indicators" are critical numbers that are reported daily on dashboards and shared with the management and executive team. As Jim Sterne says, if the number that you are tracking "changes suddenly and unexpectedly does not inspire someone to send an e-mail, pick up the phone, or take a quick walk to find help, then it is not a KPI worth reporting."*

Depending on your goals, you should establish the most important numbers that impact your business success. Some of the most common calculations include:

> Cost per impression
> Cost per click
> Cost per mention
> Cost per conversion/sale
> Reach
> Engagement
> Customer retention
> Revenue per customer
> Lifetime value of a customer
> Cost per subscriber
> Cost per lead
> Conversion rate

---

* Sterne, Jim. *Social Media Metrics: How to Measure and Optimize Your Marketing Investment.* Hoboken, NJ: John Wiley, 2010. 167.

Exercise 3: Monthly Reporting

After you have established and executed at least one month of your strategy, go back to the Digital Marketing & Measurement document and open the Monthly Reporting Tab. The baseline data that you entered into the Goals tab in Exercise 1 should be auto-populating into the Starting, 6 Month Goal, and 12 Month Goal columns. Using the reporting methods from Exercise 1, gather all the data from the previous month for the networks that you are tracking.

AGGREGATION MEASUREMENT TOOLS

After going through the process of populating the spreadsheet in Exercise 3, let's take a look at some of the tools that will simplify the data collection. Like grade school when the teacher made you do long-form division by hand, and then the following week allowed you to use a calculator, here are a few tools that make life a little easier.

Adobe Social—Adobe provides a comprehensive, enterprise reporting and social media engagement tool. This service and software solution promises simplified reporting and tracking across all networks.

Hootsuite (hootsuite.com)—Hootsuite started as a management tool for multiple social media accounts across Twitter, Facebook, LinkedIn, and Google+ Pages. Hootsuite offers the ability to create Enhanced Analytics Reports that integrate social media with Google Analytics. Through each network's API, the Enhanced Analytics Reports pull all the data into a single report. Each custom report requires credits, which will increase the overall monthly cost, but the reports are a major timesaver.

Raven Tools (raventools.com)—Raven Tools initially offered robust tools and reporting, but now the service offers a variety of reporting and management tools including Social Media, SEO, paid search advertising, and competitor analysis.

Sprout (sproutsocial.com)—Sprout Social offers a single dashboard social media management and reporting system. The user interface is designed differently than Hootsuite, but there are a number of similarities between the two platforms. While the initial sticker price seems higher than Hootsuite, by the time that reports are added the platforms are similarly priced.

Salesforce Social (www.salesforcemarketingcloud.com)—Originally Radian6 came to market as an enterprise social media monitoring and listening tool. In 2011, Salesforce.com acquired Radian6, and in 2012 the company also acquired the social media agency Buddy Media. Bringing all the enterprise expertise under one roof provides an excellent social media tool.

Exercise 4: Build Your Own Dashboard

The last tab on the spreadsheet is entitled BUILD YOUR OWN DASHBOARD. Go back to the Planning tab and determine the most important metrics based on your goals. What are your KPIs? What 6–8 numbers does everyone in your organization need to be tracking? Building your own calculations will help you determine which automated tools will best serve your needs.

INFLUENCE

Remember the advertising phrase "When E.F. Hutton talks, people listen"? Today social media influencers are talking and companies are listening ... and acting. Influencers are a powerful force. While measuring and reporting influence is still in its infancy, understanding and measuring your stakeholder's influence should be on every company's radar.

Mark Schaefer, author of *Return on Influence*, leveraged his social media following to build a large annual conference in Knoxville, Tennessee called Social Slam (http://soslam.com). Seth Godin has spent years building a powerful following on his blog. Now, he self-publishes bestsellers without the promotion and press of a major publisher. Influencers use their networks to create or demolish amazing feats.

Companies like Klout, Kred, and Peer Index are making a business of analyzing online "influence." Using algorithms that measure engagement, reach, referrals, and connections, these companies use algorithms to determine whether users of social media truly have an impact on or influence some part of their network. These services, still in their infancy, are working to improve their algorithms to truly be predictive to each person or brand's overall influence—not just how many followers they have.

Unlike E.F. Hutton, having influence is not just about people listening to you, it is a measure of trusting the influencer, which may affect their knowledge and opinions and may sometimes drive them to action. Tapping into influencers is a powerful social media strategy. Tools like Friend or Follow (FriendorFollow.com), ManageFlitter (ManageFlitter.com), and Hootsuite allow you to identify and sort followers by Klout score.

CONCLUSION

After completing the four exercises, you should have a completed Digital Marketing & Measurement spreadsheet. While the spreadsheet is rudimentary, it should provide you with the insight to the goal-based metrics that truly matter to your digital campaigns. Do the things that you are measuring increase revenue, reduce expenses, build your brand, increase awareness, or serve your customers? If not, you may want to remove them.

While the tools and reporting will continue to change, the focus on business purpose first will always be relevant to social media. You will not always be able to track every dollar made back to every tweet sent. Sometimes customers carry your published information in their brain with a "passive awareness" of your service or product. Then some other stimulus causes them to act. This overall increase in revenue, subscribers, or leads is known as lift. While marketers and programmers work hard to make everything trackable, there will always be some number of actions that won't be trackable. Being armed with the best goal-based data will prepare you to explain what "lift" actually means.

9

The Legal and Privacy Implications of Data Mining

Elana Zeide

CONTENTS

Learning Objectives

- Understand the history of privacy rights and regulation in America.
- Understand the constitutional, legal, and privacy implications of governmental use of data mining.
- Understand the legal and privacy implications of private sector use of data mining.
- Identify what types of data collection, analysis, and dissemination prompts legal and privacy concerns.
- Understand the practical, ethical, and legal difficulties governments and corporations face in attempting to provide legal and privacy protection in the context of data mining.

INTRODUCTION

This book details many ways in which the analysis of large collections of data can benefit both businesses and consumers. However, privacy and civil liberties advocates caution that the use of data must be carefully regulated in order to prevent companies, and the government, from misusing personal data.

Some people claim that privacy is dead. In truth, it has only been a legally articulated concept for little more than a century. It did not become an issue until the late 19th century when the development of instantaneous photography and the growth of widely dispersed gossip-mongering newspapers suddenly permitted the rapid capture and transmission of information. Until then, these moments were lost to history, because no one noticed or because they were not recorded. As described in the article by Samuel D. Warren and Louis D. Brandeis (1890) which set the foundations for current concepts of a right to privacy, this new technology:

> [I]nvaded the sacred precincts of private and domestic life; and numerous mechanical devices threaten to make good the prediction that "what is whispered in the closet shall be proclaimed from the house-tops. " (Warren and Brandeis, 1890)

With a little updating of the archaic phrasing, a similar statement could be made today. We are at a similar moment where rapid technological advances now give us the opportunity to uncover, analyze, and share information that could not have been captured before. As this book illustrates, Big Data can provide useful information in a variety of contexts. However, privacy advocates and the public-at-large worry about ways in which such data may be misused or abused.

Older means of protecting individual privacy are no longer effective at addressing the concerns raised by data mining and analysis. They were developed when privacy existed to protect individuals from the government's intrusion on private physical space, or undisclosed intrusion into private communication by, for example, wiretapping a telephone. These do not protect against new concerns raised by today's ability to collect, analyze, and disseminate data, and the commodification of information itself. They also employ concepts that are less clear in the digital context.

For example, what does it mean for an individual to make private information "public" and no longer be entitled to privacy protection? Do we consider information regarding someone's search engine entries and shopping habits "personal" if they do not contain unique information that would identify a person by name? How can we balance the utility of government monitoring of data to protect national security with our desire to keep information independent of scrutiny?

WHY DATA MINING RAISES NEW CONCERNS

The government and private companies have always collected information to use to their advantage. The threat of data mining is the extraction of implicit knowledge, revealing "patterns or relationships among data items or records that were not previously identified (and are not themselves data items) but that are revealed in the data itself" (Taipale, 2003).

The following are some of the new concerns raised by data mining:

Scope of Private Information: What information should the government or companies have a right to collect? To share? To sell? What should be considered personally identifiable information? How long should data be stored?

Anonymity: What identifying personal information should be attached to data collected? What about identifying information that may not be present in one set of data but becomes obvious using various collections or after analysis?

Transparency: What information are people entitled to about the scope of data being collected about them? The content of the data? What analysis is conducted on the data? The conclusions reached by such analysis? When and to whom is the data shared or sold?

Accountability: What obligation do companies create when they have a privacy policy? Should online privacy policies be considered contracts that would make Web sites responsible for violations of their stated policies, or simply notifications regarding the company's procedures, which do not make any binding promises to users?

Accuracy: What control should people have over the information that has been collected about them? Should they be able to correct inaccurate data or conclusions reached by analyzing objectively correct data? What procedures for reviewing accuracy or petitioning corrections should be put in place?

Security: What measures must the government or companies take to ensure data security? What technological aspects do they have to put in place? What types of training programs or oversight?

Liability: Who should be liable if information is not secure, misused, or improperly disclosed? How should we determine who is responsible and what harm has been done by the privacy violation?

Remedies: What remedy, if any, should people be entitled to if their private data is misused?

Enforcement: How should privacy standards be enforced? By industry self-regulation; the creation of new privacy torts; federal and state piecemeal government regulation, or a unified federal government framework?

While privacy law is too varied and changing to set forth a comprehensive set of privacy regulations that govern data mining here, this chapter will address some of the major ways that data collection is being monitored and regulated. While it cannot be a substitute for legal advice about specific situations, this summary will provide a sense of the types of issues that data collectors and analysts must take into account.

AN OVERVIEW OF PRIVACY LAW

Protection from Government Intrusion

Limitations on the government's data mining are relevant to commercial uses for several reasons. Privacy concerns first developed in the context of protecting citizens from unreasonable government searches and seizures and these fundamental norms continue to inform what will be viewed as acceptable in the commercial sphere. Additionally, increased data sharing between the public and private sectors means that private companies may need to contend with limitations on public data collection and use.

In the federal system, the concept of privacy has developed in the context of law enforcement, with the Fourth Amendment of the United States Constitution protecting Americans from searches and seizures that go beyond a "reasonable expectation of privacy." Traditional means of protecting the individual's privacy from government intrusion are difficult to apply in today's digital age where "technologies that provide for easy access and analysis of aggregated data challenge the concept of privacy protection afforded to individuals through the inherent inefficiency of government agencies analyzing paper, rather than aggregated, computer records" (Taipale, 2004).

The body of law that is most relevant to private sector data mining is often called *Information Privacy Law* in the United States, although much of the rest of the world uses the term *Data Protection Law* (Solove and Schwartz, 2013). This includes traditional tort protection against intrusion into private affairs and the publication of private information. These long-standing sources of privacy have been supplemented more recently by the implementation of statutory regimes, which speak more directly to privacy interests in the context of electronic data storage and communication. In the United States, privacy protection has developed in patchwork fashion, in contrast to Europe, where privacy law is uniform and centralized.

Privacy and the Federal Constitution

While there is no explicit federal constitutional right to privacy, several constitutional amendments touch upon concerns and expectations of privacy.* These place limits on government's ability to intrude into citizens' private space affairs, but are difficult to apply to provide privacy protection in the context of data mining.

The Fourth Amendment

In the U.S. Federal System, the concept of privacy has developed in the context of law enforcement, with the Fourth Amendment of the United States Constitution protecting Americans from searches and seizures that go beyond a "reasonable expectation of privacy."† Generally, if a person has a reasonable expectation of privacy, then law enforcement officers cannot intrude within this zone without a warrant supported by probable cause. However, the distinction between public and private can be difficult to make in the digital context.

Digital Searches and Seizures

Experts note that it is difficult to apply Fourth Amendment protection in the context of data collection and mining. Recent rulings by the United States Supreme Court suggest that when "information maintained by third parties is exposed to others, it is not private, and therefore not protected by the Fourth Amendment" (Solove, 2002). Privacy scholars have also theorized that the government's collection and computerized analysis of data should not even be considered a "search," which would also remove

---

* Several states provide for a right to privacy against government intrusion explicitly in their Constitutions. These include Alaska, Arizona, California, Florida, Hawaii, Illinois, Louisiana, Montana, South Carolina, and Washington State.
† The Fourth Amendment of the United States Constitution states: "The right of the people to be secure in their persons, houses, papers, and effects, against unreasonable searches and seizures, shall not be violated, and no warrants shall issue, but upon probable cause, supported by oath or affirmation, and particularly describing the place to be searched, and the persons or things to be seized."

it from Fourth Amendment (Kerr, 2011). For these reasons, privacy advocates increasingly recommend legislation to regulate privacy.

Legislation Restricting Government Surveillance

Three major laws that create the framework for the government interception of communications:

- Title III: Requires probable cause, a high legal standard to meet, from a judge for real-time interception of the content of voice and data communications.
- Electronic Communications Privacy Act (ECPA): Governs government access to stored email and other electronic communications and real-time interception of "numbers dialed or otherwise transmitted on the telephone line to which such device is attached." It states that the government can use such devices as long as they have a court order, which does not require a showing of probable cause, and the court must authorize the surveillance if a government attorney certifies that the information likely to be collected is relevant to an ongoing criminal investigation.
- Foreign Intelligence Surveillance Act (FISA): Authorizes the government to carry out electronic surveillance domestically upon obtaining a judicial order based upon probable cause that the target is a foreign power or an agent of a foreign power.
- The U.S. Department of Justice has also argued that it does not need a warrant to review an individual's electronic messages that are older than 180 days. This has been disputed by at least one federal Court of Appeals, in *United States v. Skinner*, and legislation is currently pending which explicitly addresses the need for warrants in the context of email communication (Jaycox, 2013).

In 2012, the U.S. Supreme Court addressed the issue of privacy and GPS tracking activities of law enforcement authorities in the case of Antoine Jones, who was tracked for a period of four weeks through use of a GPS monitor secretly installed on his automobile as part of a drug case. In *United States v. Jones*, the court unanimously concluded that the use of the GPS monitor without a warrant violated the defendant's constitutional rights, although they presented different rationales in support. Legislation to codify this ruling is currently pending before Congress (Jaycox, 2013).

NATIONAL SECURITY

Further, these traditional privacy rights may be superseded if the governments or private companies have a national security justification for data collection, analysis, and sharing.

After the attacks on 9/11, the government accelerated its collection and analysis of data in an attempt to preempt future attacks, and enacted legislation to support electronic surveillance. For example, Uniting and Strengthening America by Providing Appropriate Tools Required to Intercept and Obstruct Terrorism Act of 2001, better known as the USA/PATRIOT Act, amended legislation protection of informational privacy to permit greater government surveillance. Section 215 of the Act allows the Federal Bureau of Investigation to require third parties, such as doctors, libraries, and Internet service providers, to turn over records on their clients or customers. It permits secret searches. It also provided an exception to general Fourth Amendment search restrictions as long as the search was created to collect "foreign intelligence information." Civil liberties advocates considered the Act an invasion of citizen privacy and authorization for the government to spy on its own citizens in secret without accountability (American Civil Liberties Union, 2010).

In response to objections raised by privacy and civil liberties advocates, the government has attempted to increase the transparency and oversight of its data surveillance. The Federal Agency Data Mining Reporting Act of 2007 requires the Department of Homeland Security to provide Congress a detailed description of each DHS activity that meets the Act's definition of "data mining," including the methodology and technology used, the sources of the data being analyzed, the legal authority for the activity, a discussion of the activity's efficacy in achieving its purpose, and an analysis of the activity's impact on privacy and the policies and procedures in place to protect the privacy and due process rights of individuals.

The Right to Financial Privacy Act (RFPA) limits the government's ability to obtain financial information held by banks and federal regulatory authorities about individual borrowers without the customer's consent, a search warrant, subpoena, or a formal written request in connection with "a legitimate law enforcement inquiry" (with a copy provided to the consumer to allow for an opportunity to object). Financial records or information not logically associated with an identifiable person, however, may be freely disclosed.

The laws lag far behind technological advances, however. For example, numerous law enforcement agencies now make use of a device that can be attached to an iPhone and can scan a person's face from up to five feet away or scan their iris from up to six inches away, and use that information to conduct identity checks (Steel and Angwin, 2011).

GOVERNMENT AND PRIVATE SECTOR DATA COLLECTION OVERLAP/SHARED USES

This legislation and the resulting concerns are not relevant only to the public sector. The public and private sectors often share information. For example, the private sector obtains demographic information from the government (Solove, 2004). In turn, federal law enforcement agencies acquire data that is collected in the private sector for purposes of national security. For example, the FBI may collect data from the travel, telecommunications, financial, and services industries to attempt to track terrorist activity.

> The FBI buys files of information about individuals from ChoicePoint, Inc., a major data aggregation company that "cull[s], sort[s] and packag[es] data on individuals from scores of sources, including credit bureaus, marketers and regulatory agencies," and "FBI agents can also go to a dedicated Web intranet site for help in conducting their own searches." (Tien, 2004)

Some commentators feel the distinction between public and private sector data collection is insignificant in the current era. For example, agencies like the Department of Education and the Income Revenue Service request and collect information from companies like Facebook and Twitter (Bell, 2013).

Such collaboration appears to be the way of the future. The Cyber Intelligence Sharing and Protection Act (CISPA) is making its way through Congress. The law would permit the federal government and technology and manufacturing companies to share information to help the government prevent cyber-attacks. While aimed at allowing private companies and the federal government to share information in order to protect and defend against attacks against computer systems and networks, broad provisions permit companies to identify, obtain, and share your emails and text messages with the government.

Civil liberties groups have adamantly opposed the legislation because it provides a vague "cybersecurity" exemption to all existing federal and state privacy laws. Privacy advocates believe the Bill does not provide sufficient limitation on searches or judicial oversight on data mining (Steele, 2012). For example, under CISPA, companies can mine and share information if they need to guard against "improper" information modification and ensure "timely" access to information, purposes that are not necessarily tied to national security and the prevention of cyber-attacks. Further, companies do not have to notify users of the sharing of information and will not be held liable for improper data mining as long as they acted "in good faith."

Once handed over, the government may use this information for investigating crimes that are unrelated to the underlying security threat and, more broadly, for "national security" purposes, which is broadly defined to include "threats to the United States, its people, property, or interests" and "any other matter bearing on United States national or homeland security." The Executive Branch has openly admitted its hesitancy about these provisions (Albanesius, 2012).

Some private companies have taken it upon themselves to increase the transparency of government surveillance. Microsoft and Google, for example, release reports on law enforcement requests for user data to increase transparency (Galperin, 2013).

PROTECTION FROM PRIVATE INTRUSION

Common Law/Tort Protection of Privacy

Data collectors should be aware of the common law framework that has developed to protect traditional notions of privacy rights. These were first conceptualized in the Warren and Brandeis article* and percolated

---

* "The common law secures to each individual the right of determining, ordinarily, to what extent his thoughts, sentiments, and emotions shall be communicated to others. Under our system of government, he can never be compelled to express them (except when upon the witness-stand); and even if he has chosen to give them expression, he generally retains the power to fix the limits of the publicity which shall be given them" (Warren and Brandeis 1890).

through the state court systems to come up with four basic claims that can be brought to seek remedies for privacy violations. They are:

1. Unreasonable intrusion, or intentional interference with a plaintiff's interest in solitude or seclusion (either in his or her person or private affairs), known as "Intrusion upon seclusion."
2. Public disclosure of private facts.
3. Publicity that places the plaintiff in a false light.
4. Appropriation of a character's name or likeness, often referred to as the "right of publicity" (Prosser 1960).

Some variation of these claims is recognized at common law in most, but not all, states. Some have been codified into statutes. The proof required to establish a claim varies widely from one state to another (Solove and Schwartz, 2013). While these categories remain influential today, they are difficult to apply in the context of data mining.

One difficulty is that privacy torts are often structured around whether information is private or "public"—that is, if it has been disclosed to any third party. In this framework, a person would have no protection for privacy violations once he has voluntarily disclosed private information to at least one party. For example, in *Dwyer v. American Express*, the court found that American Express cardholders could not bring a cause of action for intrusion upon seclusion after the company sold their information to marketers because the cardholders had voluntarily disclosed their information to American Express.

A successful tort claim also requires demonstrating a quantifiable harm. Traditionally, harm might be assessed by proving, say, damage to a business venture as a result of unconsented-to disclosure of private information. Today, it is difficult for claimants to demonstrate specific harm that has occurred as the result of a data mining privacy violation. In *Dwyer v. American Express*, the court also found that the cardholders' individual names had no value aside from their value as a commodity to be sold.

Defining the value of information and any harm caused by its unauthorized disclosure may become an easier task as courts become more aware of the economic value of data. In *Fraley v. Facebook*, the court found that the plaintiffs had established that their "personalized endorsement" of products and services to their friends on Facebook had "a concrete, provable value."

The changing valuation of privacy in the courts demonstrates a way in which the tort system may be a good choice to regulate information law and privacy. These types of private remedies provide a flexible system to define what we consider appropriate regarding data mining without having to go through the lengthy process of passing formal new regulations. The common law system allows the law to adapt to new technologies as cases make their way through the court system.

For example, privacy expert Daniel Solove proposes four types of activities that serve as useful torts. These include Information Collection (such as surveillance and interrogation), Information Processing (which includes aggregation/insecurity/secondary use/exclusion), Information Dissemination (breach of confidentiality, disclosure, exposure, distortion), and Invasion (intrusion and decisional interference) (Solove, 2006).

PRINCIPLES GOVERNING FEDERAL DATA MINING REGULATION

Against the backdrop of common law tort protection, the federal government has enacted statutes and regulations to deal with concerns regarding information made available by new technology. Most of the restrictions on intrusion involved transparency of law enforcement investigations conducted with recording devices like wiretaps. Generally, these prohibited public and private intrusion into private communications without consent or a warrant: first of the mail, then of telephone, data, and radio transmissions. Some of these have been applied in the next context of digital information and data mining, with mixed results, as will be discussed next.

More recent federal and state regulations have been developed to provide protection for large collections of data. These regulate data collection, analysis, and dissemination in both the public and private sector. These rules are frequently enforced by the Federal Trade Commission (FTC) or its state equivalents. Common triggers for FTC enforcement are inadequate data security, breaking privacy use policies, and failing to disclose data collection or doing so deceptively. Special areas of protection are also carved out for particular types of information, such as medical and credit history records, and for particular classes of people, such as students and children (Solove and Schwartz, 2013).

The American piecemeal approach is in stark contrast to international privacy regulation, which is significantly more unified and standardized. In comparison with the centralized privacy protection in the European Union, for example, the American system may cause more confusion for companies and consumers to navigate a proliferation of very diverse and sometimes inconsistent privacy regulations from government agencies, the federal and state governments.

A month after Europe proposed to update its data protections, the Obama administration called on Congress to enact a "consumer privacy bill of rights" that would apply to industries not already covered by sectoral privacy laws, including data brokers and e-commerce sites which collect details on an individual's likes, leisure pursuits, shopping habits, financial status, and health statistics. The White House's blueprint for legislation, for example, would give Americans the right to some control over how their personal data is used as well as the right to see and correct records that companies hold about them (The White House, 2012).

Fair Information Practice Principles (FIPPs)

Much of the modern regulatory framework attempts to address issues that are included in the FTC's Fair Information Practice Principles (FIPPs). They were first promulgated in 1974 as part of the Privacy Act (PPA), but have been consistently updated as new technologies create new concerns. These non-binding rules provide guidance as to the information practices companies should use to ensure adequate privacy protection for adults. Even though these suggestions are not enforceable in and of themselves, their core principles underly binding rules set forth in other legislation and regulations (FTC, FIPPs, 2010).

The five core fair privacy practices described in FIPPs include:

1. Notice

The FTC Guidelines state that "[c]onsumers should be given notice of an entity's information practices before any personal information is collected from them" (FTC, FIPPs, 2010). It recommends this notice contain:

- Identification of the entity collecting the data.
- Identification of the uses to which the data will be put.
- Identification of any potential recipients of the data.

- The nature of the data collected and the means by which it is collected if not obvious (passively, by means of electronic monitoring, or actively, by asking the consumer to provide the information).
- Whether the provision of the requested data is voluntary or required, and the consequences of a refusal to provide the requested information.
- The steps taken by the data collector to ensure the confidentiality, integrity, and quality of the data (FTC, FIPPs, 2010).

FIPPs also advises that:

In the Internet context, notice can be accomplished easily by the posting of an information practice disclosure describing an entity's information practices on a company's site on the Web. To be effective, such a disclosure should be clear and conspicuous, posted in a prominent location, and readily accessible from both the site's home page and any Web page where information is collected from the consumer. It should also be unavoidable and understandable so that it gives consumers meaningful and effective notice of what will happen to the personal information they are asked to divulge (FTC, FIPPs, 2010).

2. Choice/Consent

The FTC advises that consumers should be given choices related to secondary uses of information, meaning uses "beyond those necessary to complete the contemplated transaction" (FTC, FIPPs, 2010). These can be either internal uses, such as placing the consumer on a mailing list, or external, such as transferring the information to a third party. The Guidelines note that opt-in and opt-out choices may be used to certify this consent.

3. Access/Participation

The Guidelines propose that individuals should be able to view the data an entity has collected about him and contest that data's accuracy and completeness. Data collectors should have the "mechanism by which the data collector can verify the information, and the means by which corrections and/or consumer objections can be added to the data file and sent to all data recipients" (FTC, FIPPs, 2010). The Guidelines note that this access "must encompass timely and inexpensive access to data, a simple means for contesting inaccurate or incomplete data, a mechanism by which the data collector can verify the information, and the means by which corrections and/or consumer objections can be added to the data file and sent to all data recipients" in order to provide meaningful protection.

4. Integrity/Security

Data collectors should assure data integrity by taking "reasonable steps, such as using only reputable sources of data and cross-referencing data against multiple sources, providing consumer access to data, and destroying untimely data or converting it to anonymous form" (FTC, FIPPs, 2010). This involves putting technical protective mechanisms into place, such as limiting access through use of passwords and storing data on secure servers, and managerial measures, including limiting who can access the data within a company.

5. Enforcement/Redress

The Guidelines clearly state that these principles are "suggestive rather than prescriptive," and the FTC has no power to enforce them aside from violations of these principles which violate other federal statutes and regulations (FTC, FIPPs, 2010). The FTC also notes alternative enforcement mechanisms which may be put into place in the future, including industry self-regulation, legislation to create private rights of action for consumers harmed by unfair information practices, and government enforcement of unfair practices by imposing civil or criminal penalties for violations.

Mobile Application Privacy Procedures

The FTC has recommended similar practices regarding mobile app privacy. The report recommends that app developers establish and maintain privacy policies that are conveniently accessible to users (FTC, Mobile Privacy Disclosures, 2013). It also suggests that all apps use specific disclosures regarding collection of sensitive information, including geolocation tracking, and put mechanisms into place to obtain express user consent for such collection.

These guidelines follow the California Online Privacy Protection Act, which requires all software apps developers who make their apps available in California to post their privacy policies conspicuously within each app. The policies must identify what personally identifiable information will be collected by the app and what uses will be made of the collected information. Failure to comply can result in a fine of $2,500 for each download of a non-compliant app (Delta and Matsura, 2013). For example, California has filed a suit against Delta Air Lines, Inc. alleging failure to comply with the apps privacy notice requirement (Johnson, 2013).

Do Not Track Campaign

The FTC has also advocated the development of a "Do Not Track" system which would permit users to control the monitoring of their online activities (FTC, Protecting Consumer Privacy in an Era of Rapid Change, 2012). It suggests integration of the Do Not Track system into all Web browsers, incorporation of privacy protection measures into all future software and online products, and real-time notification of data collection to Internet users. The FTC guidelines also suggested that mobile platforms should consider making a Do Not Track mechanism to all smartphone users (FTC, Mobile Privacy Disclosures, 2013). However, several leading Web site operators believe that elimination of online tracking is not a technically feasible option (Duncan, 2012). Industry participants have, however, accepted the FTC's call for implementation of a Do Not Track capability embedded in Internet browser systems, to provide users with more control over online tracking activities.

REGULATION OF PRIVATE SECTOR INFORMATION

The next section describes various ways in which these principles play out. However, traditional governmental regulation and consumer private actions have been difficult to apply in the context of Big Data (Tene and Polonetsky, 2012). The examples below illustrate this and highlight areas in which data miners should beware of continuing conflicts.

Notice of Data and Consent to Data Collection

As indicated in the FIPP Guidelines, providing adequate notice to users regarding the collection and use of personal information is a crucial component of today's privacy protection. Privacy policies have become a standard method of providing such disclosure. While no specific practices and procedures are mandated by the Federal Trade Commission, companies must post an accurate description of their policies and comply with these policies in order to avoid potential penalties.

In federal cases like *Dyer v. Northwest Airlines Corp* and *In re Jet Blue Airways Corp. Privacy Litigation*, privacy policies have been found by several courts to not create binding contracts. They instead consider the policies as mere notification of a company's practices. Accordingly, an individual cannot claim the company has broken a promise if a company changes or violates their terms.

However, the FTC considers violation of a company's own privacy policies to be a deceptive practice under the Federal Trade Commission Act (FTCA), a broad statute that was developed to regulate general business practices as opposed to information and privacy practices in particular (Solove and Schwartz, 2013). For example, *In re Google, Inc.*, Google agreed to pay a $22.5 million dollar fine based on charges that it placed a tracking cookie on the computers of Safari users in violation of its privacy policies. Similarly, Facebook settled with the FTC after the Commission alleged that retroactive changes in the Web site's privacy policies were deceptive because they failed to provide proper notice and unfair by retroactively changing the policies without consumer consent.

While the FTC guidelines also call for companies to obtain explicit consent to collect and use personal data, it has been difficult for private plaintiffs or the FTC to prevail when making consent arguments against data collection and use. Like the traditional common law torts protecting privacy, most statutes and regulations consider information public once someone has consented to any disclosure to a third party. They also provide little guidance as how to determine the harm caused (or value lost) by the unauthorized collection, disclosure, or sale of private data.

For example, plaintiffs and the FTC have unsuccessfully attempted to bring suits claiming that the commercial use of tracking mechanisms like cookies was unlawful under older privacy protection statutes like the ECPA mentioned above. Courts, however, have found that notice of the use of cookies was sufficient authorization to provide consent to the tracking and make it permissible under such statutes. On the other hand, it is clear that companies cannot ask for consent and then collect information without receiving it. In *In re Google, Inc.*, Google Buzz was found to have violated the FTCA by suggesting users could join Buzz and then enrolling some in the program without their consent.

Companies may also be held liable for a third party's privacy violations. After consumers contended that Apple's collection of geolocation information from iPhones violated their privacy, the company stated that users could opt-out of the collection of GPS data. However, Google and other service providers operating mobile advertising networks have allegedly implemented user tracking systems that circumvent the limitations imposed by the Apple equipment and privacy setting to monitor users' locations and online activities. In *In re iPhone Application Litigation*, a court concluded that Apple's promise to protect consumer privacy includes data it provides to others.

Another problem is unexpected sources of data collection or inadvertently collected data. The lawsuits surrounding Google's Street View feature illustrate these difficulties (The Editorial Board of *The New York Times*, Googling You, 2013).

Finally, some experts debate whether mere notice to consumers is an effective protection of their rights. Research conducted by Aleecia McDonald, a privacy researcher and Fellow at the Center for Internet and Society at Stanford Law School, indicates a significant knowledge gap between users' understanding of digital behavior and the actual privacy protection in place. "They think they are protected by laws that don't exist," she said. "Many people don't realize that third parties can track them across the Internet and are invisible to them. Others don't realize that ad content is influenced by what they write in emails" (Sultan, 2012).

Special Protections

Other federal statutes focus on protection of the privacy of specific categories of personal information or information collected from certain users.

Financial Information

For example, federal law imposes privacy requirements for certain forms of financial information. The Fair Credit Recording Act (FCRA) regulates the use of data associated with personal credit. The FCRA limits the disclosure of information regarding an individual's credit standing, credit capacity, or general credit reputation.

However, "financial information" may be defined more broadly. Another federal law governing privacy of personal financial information is Gramm–Leach–Bliley (GLB), which limits the disclosure of non-public financial information pertaining to consumers. It requires that a defined set of "financial institutions" disclose privacy statements and restricts as such their ability to disclose non-public personal information about consumers to non-affiliated third parties. The Act applies to personally identifiable information a consumer provides to the financial institution, information created as a result of a transaction with the consumer, or services provided to the consumer, and information otherwise obtained by the financial institution. Consumers are to be provided with an opportunity to "opt-out" of such disclosures to unaffiliated third parties. Data collectors should note that this Act applies very broadly. Its expansive definition of a "financial institution" in the statute is very broad, and applies to a wide range of entities involved in e-commerce.

Medical Information

The privacy of medical and health information is protected by the Health Insurance Portability and Accountability Act (HIPAA). HIPAA applies to personally identifiable information collected from an individual, which has been created or received by a health plan, health care provider, employer, or health care clearinghouse, and which relates to the physical or mental condition of an individual, the provision of health care to an individual, or future payment for the provision of health care to an individual.

Data mining may render some of these protections inadequate. For example, commenters note that insurance companies are increasingly active in accessing electronic data regarding individuals, their activities, and their medical records. Insurance companies mine these electronic records in an effort to identify the risks associated with providing insurance coverage for various people (Brooks, 2013). In *IMS Health, Inc. v. Sorrell*, a recent United States Supreme Court case regarding a Vermont privacy law which attempted to bar disclosure of prescription data for marketing purposes, privacy advocates argued that the "de-identification" techniques adopted by data-mining firms do not protect patient privacy. However, the Court found that these concerns did not outweigh the restriction on the companies' First Amendment right to freedom of speech.

Student Information

The federal government provides explicit protection for information contained the educational records of students under the age of eighteen. The Federal Educational Rights and Privacy Act of 1974 (FERPA) gives parents of minor students the right to inspect, correct, amend, and control the disclosure of information contained in education records. However, as educational institutions have incorporated electronic communication, blogs, and boards into their curriculum, the line between what is in a student's records and what are assignments-in-progress grows increasingly unclear.

Information Collected from Children

The federal government also provides extra protection for children's privacy. The Children's Online Privacy Protection Act (COPPA) defined children as individuals under the age of 13. COPPA makes it unlawful for a commercial Web site or online service directed to children, or any operator that has actual knowledge that it is collecting personal information from a child, to collect personal information from a child in a manner that violates FTC regulations.

Data Analysis and Personal Identification

Are privacy concerns eliminated when identifying information has been stripped from data? What should we consider personal information? How can we adapt this definition as technological capabilities advance?

Regulations and privacy policies often attempt to mitigate privacy concerns by not collecting (or stripping data of) Personally Identifiable Information (PII). There is no standard definition of PII, but, for example, the Privacy Act defines it as records that specifically identify an individual based upon name, identifying number, or other personal identification feature (e.g., photograph, fingerprint, and voice print). However, the scope of this protection does not extend to large collections or combinations of information that may essentially identify a specific person without identifying a "unique" feature. For example, consumer purchase records or search term entries that profile a particular user with a high degree of particularity would not fall under the statute if, say, they are not recorded in connection with the individual's name (Delta and Matsura, 2013).

Similarly, companies collecting data maintain they only collect "anonymous" information. What makes information "anonymous," however? Is anonymization even possible anymore?

Dataium LLC, for example, collects information from the browsing habits of car shoppers. It can tie this information to an individual's name, but maintains that the information is still "anonymous" because it does not give dealers click-by-click details of people's Web surfing history but rather an analysis of their interests (Valentino-Devries and Singer-Vine, 2012). Other companies consider information "anonymous" if it does not identify unique features about an individual, even though the collection of information could easily identify a particular individual. For example, *The New York Times* was able to locate an individual from the released and anonymized search records by cross-referencing them with phonebook listings (Barbaro and Zeller, 2006).

The FTC has attempted to deal with this difficulty by attempting to regulate "data that is reasonably linkable to a specific consumer, computer, or device," but data analysis techniques may make this definition useless. Computer scientists have repeatedly shown that even anonymized data can typically be re-identified and associated with specific individuals (Velasquez, 2013). Experts argue this makes any protection we feel from "anonymization" moot (Ohm, 2010).

New developments in facial recognition technology highlight these issues. For years, individuals have posted public or semi-public images of themselves on social networking Web sites like Facebook. In some cases they might not have identified or "tagged" themselves in a particular photograph—maybe they did not like how they looked or did not want to bring attention to a picture taken with an old boyfriend.

Most users consented without any inkling that Facebook would soon provide users access to face recognition software to identify individuals in photographs. This development may have more far-reaching implications than simply permitting people to see a picture where a user is not at his best. For example, researchers have used face recognition software to compare the images of individuals with publicly accessible information available through Facebook. The software and the social media site content enabled the researchers to identify individuals correctly approximately 30 percent of the time. The researchers were also able to use information publicly accessible on the Internet to guess the first five digits of an individual's Social Security number approximately 27 percent of the time (Sengupta, 2013).

Data Dissemination

Consumers and the government are now examining the scope of consumer control over personal information voluntarily surrendered online. The FTC is now targeting data brokerage firms in particular for improper harvesting and use of personal information (Wyatt, 2013). The FTC sent letters to ten data broker companies warning that their practices could violate the Fair

Credit Reporting Act (FCRA) because they were willing to sell consumer information without abiding by FCRA requirements that require they reasonably verify the identities of their customers and make sure that these customers have a legitimate purpose for receiving the information (FTC, FTC Warns Data Broker Operations of Possible Privacy Violations, 2013).

Data Security

Companies must be diligent about their data security practices. State and federal liability may be imposed for lax security or poor training, potentially resulting in significant fines. Companies are required to put both technological and operational mechanisms in place to ensure data security. They must ensure that their hardware is adequately maintained and their software up to date. Perhaps less obviously, they must also provide systems to reduce human error. These calls for stringent controls of who within a company may access sensitive data, how employees handling such data are trained and monitored, and what audit systems are in place to ensure compliance with internal security structures.

International Approaches

The American system involves a patchwork of federal and state privacy laws that separately govern the use of personal details in spheres like patient billing, motor vehicle records, education, and video rental records. The European Union, on the other hand, has one blanket data protection directive that lays out principles for how information about its citizens may be collected and used, no matter the industry.

The rights that Europe enforces are also more far-reaching than their American counterparts. For example, the European Commission proposed modifications to the data protection rules which would implement a "right to be forgotten" for individuals and a right to data portability (The Editorial Board of *The New York Times*, Europe Moves Ahead on Privacy, 2013).

CONCLUSION

This chapter has discussed some of the legal and privacy concerns raised by data mining and current attempts to address these concerns. It illustrates the difficulty in creating protections that balance the need for protection from government intrusion with national security concerns. It also shows the various ways in which data mining may trigger public concern or government enforcement. Information privacy law is difficult to pin down, however. Not only do the rules and regulations come from a variety of sources, but they are constantly struggling to keep up with quickly evolving information technology and the resulting evolution in what we think should be considered private. As we develop the positive potential of data mining, consumers, companies, and the government must also be alert to protect such powerful and valuable technology from being misused.

Questions

1. Warren and Brandeis were prompted to consider privacy protection by new technologies used to capture and spread information. What does this say about the contemporary rise of concern about privacy rights?
2. What are the five core Fair Privacy Practices (FIPPs) as defined by the FTC? Can the FTC take action against you if you violate one of these principles?
3. Consent is a cornerstone of data mining regulation. However, some behavioral economists have suggested that we do not value privacy as much as we think we do because studies consistently show that people's behavior is inconsistent with how much they claim to value privacy. Does this change the way you think protection should be approached?
4. How do you think personal identifiable information should be defined? What protections should be put into place to ensure this information remains private? Should it remain private? Technogically, is it possible to keep it private?

REFERENCES

American Civil Liberties Union (ACLU), Surveillance Under the USA Patriot Act, December 10, 2010. Retreived at http://www.aclu.org/national-security/surveillance-under-usa-patriot-act. Albanesius, C. White House Threatens to Veto CISPA. *PCMag.* April 25, 2012. Retrieved at http://www.pcmag.com/article2/0,2817,2403549,00.asp.
Barbaro, Michael and Zeller Jr., Tom. A Face Is Exposed for AOL Searcher No. 4417749. *The New York Times.* September 8, 2006.

Bell, Kay. The IRS May Be Following You on Twitter. *MSN Money*. April 11, 2013. Retrieved at http://money.msn.com/tax-tips/post.aspx?post=98079651-79d1-4b64-976a-932d9a222dd8.

Brooks, David. What You'll Do Next. *The New York Times*. April 15, 2013.

Delta, G. and Matsuura, J. (2013) *Privacy and the World Wide Web, Law of the Internet*. New York: Aspen Publishers.

Duncan, G. Why Do Not Track May Not Protect Anybody's Privacy. *Digital Trends*. June 9, 2012. Retrieved at http://www.digitaltrends.com/mobile/why-do-not-track-may-not-protect-anybodys-privacy/.

The Federal Trade Commission (2010) Fair Information Practice Principles. Retrieved from http://www.ftc.gov/reports/privacy3/fairinfo.shtm.

The Federal Trade Commission (2012) Protecting Consumer Privacy in an Era of Rapid Change: Recommendation for Businesses and Policy Makers. Retrieved at http://www.ftc.gov/os/2012/03/120326privacyreport.pdf.

The Federal Trade Commission (2013) FTC Warns Data Broker Operations of Possible Privacy Violations. May 7, 2013. Retrieved from http://www.ftc.gov/opa/2013/05/databroker.shtm.

The Federal Trade Commission (2013) Mobile Privacy Disclosures: Building Trust Through Transparency. Retrieved at http://www.ftc.gov/os/2013/02/130201mobileprivacyreport.pdf.

Galperin, E. Victory for Transparency: Microsoft Releases Report on Law Enforcement Requests for User Data. *Electronic Frontier Foundation*. March 21, 2013. Retrieved at https://www.eff.org/deeplinks/2013/03/victory-transparency-microsoft-releases-report-law-enforcement-requests-user-data.

Jaycox, M. Congress Will Battle Over Internet Privacy in 2013. *Electronic Frontier Foundation*. January 31, 2013. Retrieved at https://www.eff.org/deeplinks/2013/01/congress-will-battle-over-internet-privacy-2013.

Johnson, K. California AC Sues Delta Air Lines For Lack of Mobile App Privacy Policy. *BNA* December 10, 2013. Retrieved at http://www.bna.com/california-ag-sues-n17179871357/.

Kerr, Orin S. (2011) Searches and Seizures in a Digital World. Harvard Law Review. Vol. 119:531–585.

Ohm, Paul. (2010) Broken Promises of Privacy: Responding to the Surprising Failure of Anonymization. *UCLA Law Review*. Vol. 57: 1701–1777.

Prosser, W. (1960) Privacy. *California Law Review* Vol. 48: 383–423.

Sengupta, S. Letting Our Guard Down with Web Privacy. *The New York Times*. March 30, 2013.

Solove, D. (2002) Digital Dossiers and the Dissipation of Fourth Amendment Privacy. *Southern California Law Review* Vol. 75: 1083–1169.

Solove, D. (2004) *The Digital Person*. New York: New York University Press.

Solove, D. (2006) A Taxonomy of Privacy. New york: *University of Pennsylvania Law Review* Vol. 154: 477–560.

Solove, D. and Schwartz, P. (2013) *Privacy Law Fundamentals*. Portsmouth: International Association of Privacy Professionals.

Steel, E. and Angwin, J. Device Raises Fear of Facial Profiling. *The Wall Street Journal*. August 8, 2011.

Steele, P. Voices of Opposition Against CISPA. *Electronic Frontier Foundation*. April 19, 2012. Retrieved at https://www.eff.org/deeplinks/2012/04/Voices-Against-CISPA.

Sultan, A. Digital Data Mining Spurs Efforts to Curb Use without Permission. *St. Louis Post-Dispatch*. September 23, 2012.

Taipale, K. A. (2003) Data Mining and Domestic Security: Connecting the Dots to Make Sense of Data, *Columbia Science and Technology Law Review* Vol. 5: 34–116.

Tene, O. and. Polonetsky, J. (2012). Big Data for All: Privacy and User Control in the Age of Analytics. *Northwestern Journal of Technology and Intellectual Property* Vol. 11: 239–274.

The Editorial Board of *The New York Times*. Europe Moves Ahead on Privacy, Editorial. *The New York Times*. February 3, 2013.

The Editorial Board of *The New York Times*. Googling You. *The New York Times*. March 16, 2013. Retrieved at http://www.nytimes.com/2013/03/17/opinion/sunday/google-street-view.html.

The White House. (2012) Consumer Data Privacy in a Networked World: A Framework for Protecting Privacy and Promoting Innovation in the Global Digital Economy. Retrieved at http://www.whitehouse.gov/sites/default/files/privacy-final.pdf.

Tien, L. (2004) Privacy, Technology and Data Mining. *Ohio Northern University Law Review* Vol. 30: 389–418.

Valentino-Devries, J. and Singer-Vine, J. They Know What You're Shopping For. *Wall Street Journal*. December 7, 2012.

Velasquez, J. D. (2013) Web Mining and Privacy Concerns: Some Important Legal Issues to Be Consider before Applying any Data and Information Extraction Technique in Web-Based Environments. *Expert Systems with Applications* Vol 40: 5228–5239.

Warren, S. and Brandeis, L. (1890) The Right to Privacy. *Harvard Law Review* Vol. 4: 193–220.

Wyatt, E. F.T.C. Warns Data Firms on Selling Information. *The New York Times*. May 7, 2013.

10

Epilogue: Parting Thoughts about Business Analytics

Jay Liebowitz

CONTENTS

From the previous chapters, it is readily apparent that business analytics is an emerging and fast-growing field. Universities and colleges are developing programs in this area, and companies are developing relationships with universities (such as IBM and Ohio State University forming the IBM Client Center for Advanced Analytics as part of the College of Business at Ohio State) in order to meet the future needs for analytics talent. Combined with the onslaught of "Big Data," the field of analytics is a promising area for most sectors, such as healthcare, finance, emergency management, marketing, cybersecurity, and others.

Certainly, we can educate individuals for a "data scientist" or "business analyst" role, but there are several caveats that we need to be aware of. First, the sheer number of people needed to fill this vacuum is quite a demanding load and challenge. If the McKinsey report is accurate in predicting the need for up to 200,000 new analysts and re-trained managers in the United States alone, we have to think of new ways to provide this supply of talent, as universities and colleges can't do it alone. Companies, professional societies, and foundations may need to be proactive in offering training and education courses in these areas to refine the talent of those in related fields. This is certainly being done, as evidenced by the KDNuggets Website (www.kdnuggets.com). Perhaps MOOCs (Massive Open Online Courses) in the analytics area may be a remedy for this challenge. Other creative ways may be to look at the STEM (Science, Technology, Engineering, and Math) areas in high schools and introduce analytics during secondary education, so high school students will be more aware of the field for possible majoring or minoring in college.

A second caveat is that analytics is a number-intensive field that brings in applied mathematics, statistics, machine learning, and other computer-intensive techniques. However, a good analyst needs to have a set of other skills in order to portray and communicate the underlying meaning of the analytics results to managers and senior executives. Couching the terms in a way that the business leader can understand is ultimately an important part of being successful in analytics. If the meaning behind the analytics results can't be conveyed in a comprehensible way, then sub-optimization will occur. Certainly, the use of performance and executive dashboards for visualizing the KPIs (Key Performance Indicators) of an organization will help in this regard, but the data or business analyst must be well versed in the context of the organization for management to best value the results.

A final caveat is that there is the phenomenon of DRIP—Data Rich, Information Poor. This means that an organization may have plenty of data, but producing valuable information from that data is often where organizations lack the expertise. A variation of DRIP may be "Data Rich, Insight Poor." Using intuition and insights is also a key part of being successful in the field of analytics, and business in general. Developing interesting patterns from large datasets can be valuable, but insights put in proper context must also be applied in order to maximize the value of the analytics results obtained. Certainly, we are advocates of data-based decision making, but intuition-based decision making (the "gut feel") should also be applied to make sense of the results. Going back to my Preface in this book, the MIT Conference in December 2012 shed a similar theme in "Big Data Is Great—But So Is Intuition."

BUSINESS ANALYTICS AND DECISION MAKING

The hope is that business analytics informs decision making. There have been various studies in the past that seem to validate this statement. In August 2011, a Bloomberg Businessweek Research Services study sponsored by SAS showed that most firms say business analytics boosts the decision making process.

Business analytics have been effective in decision making for three of four enterprises. According to the survey results, companies that gain the most value from business analytics typically have a top-down embrace of analytics by senior leaders, put the right analytic talent in place, improve data management and governance, deploy the right analytic tools, and operationalize the results (http://www.sas.com/news/preleases/bloombergBAsurvey.html).

In Neal Leavitt's article, "Bringing Big Analytics to the Masses," in the January 2013 issue of *IEEE Computer,* he mentions that a 2012 study by IBM and *The Economist* found that firms that apply analytics outperform their peers that don't. Tom Davenport's work on analytics shows that business analytics make for smarter decisions (http://www.computerweekly.com/feature/Business-analytics-make-for-smarter-decisions). In addition, a sample of 310 companies from different industries from the United States, Europe, Canada, Brazil, and China showed that a statistically significant relationship exists between analytical capabilities and performance.[*]

To gain further insight in this area, Liebowitz conducted a convenience sample survey of senior managers in 78 organizations in January 2013 to better understand the possible linkage of business analytics to decision making. About 47% of the organizations surveyed had more than 1,000 employees. Screen shots from the survey results are shown on the next few pages. The main conclusions are:

- Key Performance Indicators (KPIs) are the analytics used most (42.3%) for informing decision making.
- Managers typically receive analytics on a monthly basis (36.4%).
- A quarterly basis (30.8%) is the frequency that analytics are often applied to help in decision making.
- 80.5% said that analytics that are received usually provide more insights than one's gut feeling.
- A combination of risks are measured by analytics, including Information Technology risks, Marketing/Sales risks, and others.
- Analytics have affected one's decision making on key issues 3–5 times a year (33.3%).
- About 51% said they do *not* have a dedicated Analytics unit.
- Statistical skills (47.3%) and communications skills (41.9%) are often lacking in today's analysts.

---

[*] Peter Trkman et al., "The Impact of Business Analytics on Supply Chain Performance," *Decision Support Systems Journal*, Elsevier, 2010.

Q1   Chart Type ▾   Display Options ▾   Export ▾

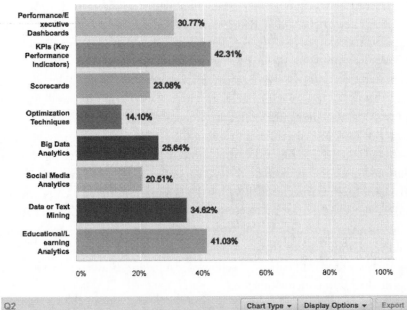

Which analytics do you use for informing your decision making?

Answered: 78   Skipped: 0

Category	Percentage
Performance/Executive Dashboards	30.77%
KPIs (Key Performance Indicators)	42.31%
Scorecards	23.08%
Optimization Techniques	14.10%
Big Data Analytics	25.64%
Social Media Analytics	20.51%
Data or Text Mining	34.62%
Educational/Learning Analytics	41.03%

Q2   Chart Type ▾   Display Options ▾   Export ▾

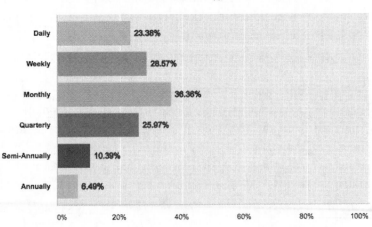

What frequency do you receive analytics?

Answered: 77   Skipped: 1

Category	Percentage
Daily	23.38%
Weekly	28.57%
Monthly	36.36%
Quarterly	25.97%
Semi-Annually	10.39%
Annually	6.49%

Q3   Chart Type ▼   Display Options ▼   Export ▼

What frequency do you apply the analytics received to help in your decision making?

Answered: 78   Skipped: 0

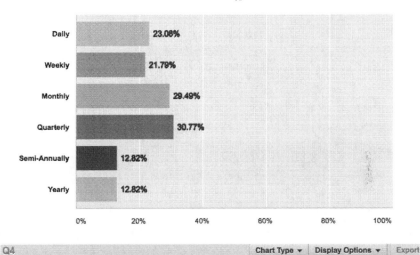

Q4   Chart Type ▼   Display Options ▼   Export

Have the analytics you receive usually provide new insights than what your gut tells you?

Answered: 77   Skipped: 1

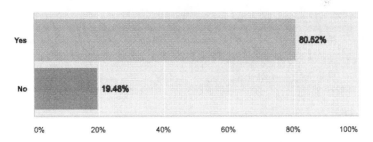

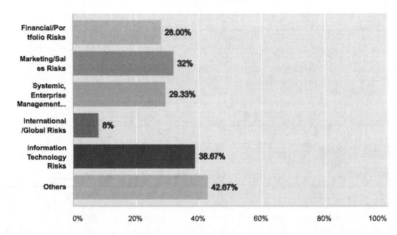

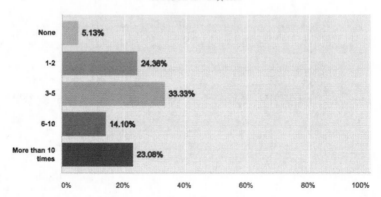

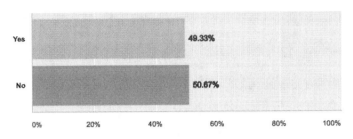

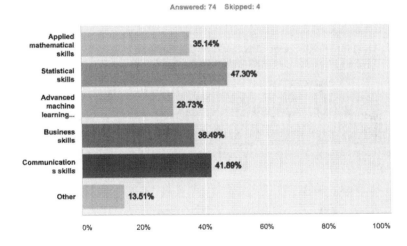

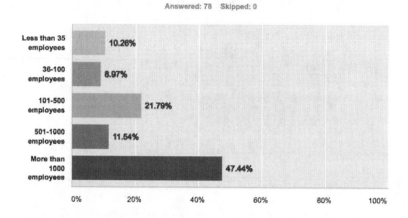

How large is your organization worldwide?

Answered: 78 Skipped: 0

- Less than 35 employees — 10.26%
- 36-100 employees — 8.97%
- 101-500 employees — 21.79%
- 501-1000 employees — 11.54%
- More than 1000 employees — 47.44%

Q7: In What Ways Would You Like to See Your Analytics Improved? Most ranked responses:

1. Greater visualization
2. Deepen an analytics culture among executives
3. Links to business plans and KPIs
4. Cleaner, integrated data
5. Easier access; more real-time data
6. Better processes producing more timely data
7. Big data support

THE YEARS AHEAD

On attending the National Institute of Standards and Technology (NIST) Conference on Big Data, Cloud Computing, and Analytics in January 2013, it is evident that Big Data and cloud computing are some of the driving factors propelling the need for advanced analytics. For example, in the U.S. Department of Veteran Affairs (VA), their Blue Button system (http://www.va.gov/bluebutton/), which allows veterans to download their healthcare data from the VA's electronic health records, could easily expand to thousands of terabytes as genetic data is included. Census, Amazon, Google, Merck, NIST, NASA, NIH/NCI (National Institutes of Health/National Cancer Institute), and many other organizations are deluged with data and are trying to make sense of what is there. Security and privacy issues are also prevalent, as discussed in Chapter 9.

Analytics can play a role in helping to provide useful information from the 3V's of Big Data (volume, velocity, and variety). However, the real challenge is how to extract "big knowledge" from this "Big Data." Certainly, various intelligent systems and knowledge discovery techniques can be applied to massage the data to uncover possible hidden relationships and patterns that could benefit the organization. However, the integration and synthesis of the Big Data are also a challenge. Developing a Big Data framework and taxonomy for the given organization are important elements in order for analytics to be properly applied to give value to the organization. And here again, to produce "knowledge," insights and intuition may play a role.

According to the McKinsey Global Institute report on Big Data (http://www.mckinsey.com/insights/mgi/research/technology_and_innovation/big_data_the_next_frontier_for_innovation), some of the key areas for future work include (1) policies related to privacy, security, intellectual property, and even liability will need to be addressed in a Big Data world; (2) organizations need not only to put the right talent and technology in place but also structure workflows and incentives to optimize the use of Big Data; and (3) access to data is critical—companies will increasingly need to integrate information from multiple data sources, often from third parties, and the incentives have to be in place to enable this. Darrell West's September 2012 Brookings report, "Big Data for Education: Data Mining, Data Analytics, and Web Dashboard" emphasizes a key point as related to education (http://www.brookings.edu/research/papers/2012/09/04-education-technology-west): Schools must understand the value of a data-driven approach to education—having performance systems will contribute to informed decision making.

One final thought to consider, and mention again, is that tomorrow's analysts must be able to converse in the "business language" that resonates with their management and senior executives. Having analytical and technical skills combined with business and communications skills will be a vital necessity for business analytics to have the impact that it should.

The times ahead are very exciting, and we hope this book will be just one small step toward getting to the right place!

Index